THE
HAMLYN
DICTIONARY
of
BUSINESS TERMS

Leo Liebster and Colin Horner

HAMLYN

F

First published 1980 by
The Hamlyn Publishing Group Limited

This edition, revised and expanded by Peter Collin
Publishing Ltd, published 1989 by
The Hamlyn Publishing Group Limited
Michelin House, 81 Fulham Road London SW3 6RB

ISBN 0 600 56537 8

Typeset by J&L Composition, Filey, England

Printed and bound in Great Britain by
William Collins and Sons

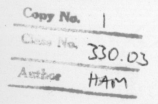

INTRODUCTION

The Hamlyn Dictionary of Business Terms provides comprehensive coverage not only of the ordinary language of commerce, accountancy and banking but also of the newest additions to the vocabulary of the rapidly changing and increasingly complex worlds of business and economics. It gives clear definitions and, where necessary, detailed explanations of the meanings of the specialized terms in a manner comprehensible to the ordinary reader, who is guided from one related topic to another by an extensive system of cross-referencing

The *Dictionary* will prove invaluable to those beginning a career in banking or insurance, to teachers and students of economics and allied subjects, and to businessmen in general who need easy access to a wide range of commercial terms.

A

A1 In perfect condition. Derived from the classification system used in Lloyds Register of British and Foreign Shipping, in which the letter indicates the condition of the hull, and the number and condition of the equipment, cables, etc., the combination A1 signifying perfect condition.

a.a. (Of a ship) 'always afloat', i.e. remaining afloat throughout the period of charter. The term is frequently included in a marine charter agreement to cover the possibility of damage to the hull.

AAA Letters indicating that a share or bond or bank is very reliable.

abandonment 1 (In marine insurance) the surrender of a vessel which is in a dangerous, unseaworthy condition and beyond recovery by the insured party to the underwriters in order to claim a total loss on the insurance policy. 2 The removal of a fixed asset from operational service because of wear and tear, obsolescence, etc.

ABC method A method of stock control in which each item is designated by the letter A, B or C depending upon its value relative to the total expenditure of production materials. A goods are low-volume, high-cost items and C goods are the numerous low-cost items. Also called **split inventory method**.

above par Denoting a share that has a market price above its face value. See also **at par; below par**.

above-the-line 1 Relating to that part of a government budget which deals with expenditure and revenue provided by and met principally from taxation. 2 The elements of revenue and expenditure contained in an income statement. Compare **below-the-line payments and receipts**. 3 Exceptional items deducted from or added to the accounts of a company before the pretax profit is calculated.

above-the-line advertising Advertising for which a commission is paid to an advertising agency, as for radio and TV commercials, posters on hoardings, etc. Compare **below-the-line advertising**.

absentee A person who, without good cause, fails to attend his place of employment.

absenteeism Regular absence from work for no good reason.

absolute bill of sale see **bill of sale, absolute**

absolute monopoly The exclusive control of the output of a commodity or service, for which no substitute is available, vested in a single product or supplier.

absorption 1 The process or result of relating actual or budgeted

absorption costing

expenditure to the output of goods or services. 2 The merging of two or more business organizations within the company structure of one of the organizations.

absorption costing The charging of all variable and fixed costs to operations, processes or output. Thus, stocks and output are valued on a total cost basis. Compare **marginal costing**.

abstinence The forgoing by consumers of expenditure on current consumption, or the forgoing by industry of the employment of resources to provide for current consumption, thus making resources available for capital accumulation and the increased future flow of consumer goods.

abstinence theory of interest The economic theory which regards interest received from investment as a payment for saving, i.e., abstaining from current consumption.

abstract of title A written outline of the evidence of ownership of property, usually beginning with the establishment of the original property right and summarizing all the relevant documents relating to the property.

accelerated depreciation A system of depreciating assets which reduces the value of the assets at a high rate in the early years in order to encourage companies, as a result of tax advantages, to invest in new equipment.

acceleration principle The link between a change in output and a change in capital investment. It is assumed that a change in the rate of change in output (in other words, an acceleration or deceleration in the rate of output) produces a proportionately larger change in the output of capital equipment. The implications of the acceleration principle play a crucial part in macroeconomic theories of investment.

acceptable quality level The highest proportion of defective goods or materials that is regularly acceptable under a quality control sampling plan.

acceptance 1 The act of agreeing to enter into a contractual relationship with another party following an offer from that party. Acceptance may be given orally or in writing, depending on the nature of the contract. Compare **offer**. 2 The signifying of assent to the terms of a bill of exchange by the drawee, done by adding the word 'accepted' and the drawee's signature to the bill. 3 A bill of exchange that has been accepted by the drawee. 4 The action of accepting an offer for a shareholding as part of a takeover bid.

acceptance credit A credit facility extended by an accepting house to a company. The accepting house will issue a bill of exchange on behalf of a foreign importer, which will be taken up as payment by a domestic exporter to that country. The bill of exchange may then be treated perfectly normally. Acceptance credit can also be arranged for domestic companies as a form of overdraft. The bank allows the company to issue bills of exchange which the bank then accepts for a fee.

acceptance for honour see **acceptance supra protest**

acceptance sampling Testing a small sample of a batch to see if the whole batch is good enough to be accepted.

acceptance supra protest The assumption of liability to pay a dishonoured and protected bill of exchange by one not party to the bill in order to save the reputation of the drawer or endorser of the bill. The liability of the acceptor supra protest extends to the holder of the bill and all parties subsequent to the person for whose honour the bill has been accepted. Also called **acceptance for honour**. See also **protest**.

accepting house A financial institution which undertakes the acceptance of bills of exchange, thus giving the bills greater security and marketability. Other banking, trade-financing and share-issuing activities are also performed by such an institution.

acceptor The person who assumes liability to pay a bill of exchange upon its maturity by the procedure of acceptance. The acceptor may be the person on whom the bill is drawn, or a guarantor, such as an accepting house.

access To call up data which is stored in a computer.

access time Time taken for a computer to display data from a data base on a screen.

accommodation bill A bill of exchange in which one person acts as drawer, acceptor or endorser in order to benefit another who is provided with temporary financial aid through the discountings of the bill. No consideration is given to the accommodating party for the bill, and generally he does not expect to pay on the bill. Also called **fictitious bill; windmill**.

accord and satisfaction An agreement between two parties in which one releases the other from his obligations under a previous contract. It was formulated as early as 1602 in the case between Pinnel and Cole.

account 1 To record financial transactions. 2 A statement showing amounts due from one party to another. 3 (On the Stock Exchange) the period between one settlement date and the next. 4 A customer or client. 5 An area of business assigned to an advertising agency by a customer. 6 (In a shop) an arrangement by which a customer can buy goods and pay for them at a later date (usually at the end of a calendar month). 7 See **bank account**.

accountant A person who keeps accounts. There are various types of qualified accountant in Britain including chartered accountants, certified accountants and management accountants. Each has a different function and needs different qualifications. Accountants act as financial

account books
advisers in many ways; their main role is that of auditing the accounts of companies.

account books see **books of account**

account days The days on which Stock Exchange bargains are settled, every day in the case of gilt-edge securities and approximately once every two weeks for other transactions. See also **Stock Exchange settlement**.

account end The end of an accounting period.

account executive 1 A member of a sales staff who is responsible for dealing with a particular customer. 2 One who is responsible for the supervision of an account within an advertising agency.

accounting The theory and practice of setting up and maintaining records of business transactions in monetary terms. See also **financial accounting; management accounting**.

accounting period The period of time covered by business, financial and management accounts. Financial accounts are generally prepared once or twice in twelve calendar months, but the interval for management accounts must be much shorter in order to ensure adequate management control.

accounting ratios The expression of various financial relationships in the performance of a business over a specified period or at a specific point of time. Many different ratios are in use to compare performance within one business over a period of time or to compare one business with another.

Accounting Standards Committee A committee set up by the British accounting profession in the mid-1970s to examine the means by which accounting treatments could be standardized.

account payee A phrase sometimes added to the general crossing of a cheque, indicating that the cheque is to be paid into the account of the payee named.

account period The time period during which Stock Exchange transactions are recorded prior to settlement in the settlement period (known as the **account day**).

accounts A statement of a company's financial affairs at the end of the financial year. It is divided into the profit and loss account and the balance sheet.

account sales An interim or final statement of sales rendered by an agent to his principal or by a consignee to a consignor, showing the amount realized on the sale of goods, expenses deducted, commission and the amount due or remitted.

accounts code The alpha or numeric code given to various classifications of expenditure and to various ledger accounts, facilitating the accurate allocation of expenditure to ledger accounts without the necessity for descriptions.

accounts payable 1 The personal accounts of the creditors of a business or the total of the balances on such accounts. 2 That section of a business which deals with the paying of debts.

accounts receivable 1 The personal accounts of the debtors of a business or the total of the balances of such accounts. 2 That part of a business dealing with debtors, such as credit-control, cash collection, etc.

account stated A statement of the agreed balance of money due by one party to another.

accredited (Of an agent) appointed by a company to act on its behalf.

accrual 1 A business expense incurred during an accounting period which remains unpaid at the end of the period, not being due until some later date. 2 The liability that thus arises. Also called **accrued charge**.

accrue To happen as a natural result or to arise in due course. A right accrues when it vests in a person gradually, as when a fund increases with additions which take place naturally.

accrued charge see **accrual**

accumulated profit Profit which is not paid as dividend but is carried into the accounts of the following year.

acid-test ratio The ratio of current liabilities to current assets excluding stocks. It is considered to be a more accurate indicator of a company's health than the current ratio. See also **liquidity ratios – financial**.

acquittance A written discharge of a contractual undertaking or liability given by the potential recipient.

across-the-board Having an effect on, or applying to, everything and everyone.

ACT see **advance corporation tax**

action limit A statistical measurement employed in quality control, being the level of acceptable deviation which may be reached in tested samples before remedial action is necessary to maintain the process in control. See also **quality control chart**.

active bond A bond bearing a fixed rate of interest which is payable in full from the date of issue. Compare **deferred bond; passive bond**.

active market A market in which there is a lot of buying and selling.

active partner A part-owner in a business partnership who is actively involved in the normal working operations of the business. Also called **general partner**. Compare **sleeping partner**.

active trade balance A favourable balance of trade, where the value of a country's exports exceeds the value of its imports. Compare **passive trade balance**. See also **balance of payments**.

activity chart A diagram showing fluctuations in, or changes in type of, work performed, against a time-scale.

activity ratio 1 The ratio between the budgeted and actual activity of a person, machine, department, etc. for a given period. 2 The ratio between the standard house equivalent of work produced and the budgeted standard hours for the same period. Both ratios are generally expressed as a percentage of the budgeted figures.

activity sampling A work study technique in which a large number of observations are made over a period of time, generally at random intervals. The observations record the activity of machines, workers, etc., and analysis of the results indicates the extent of time during which a particular activity occurs.

act of bankruptcy see **bankruptcy, act of**

act of God A sudden or violent act of nature which is neither caused by, nor can be prevented by, nor can be prevented by, human intervention and cannot reasonably be expected to have been foreseen. Contracts are frequently not enforceable where failure to perform is due to an act of God.

actual total loss Goods which have become, or may be presumed to be, a total loss, especially in marine insurance.

actuarial tables Lists showing how long people of certain ages are likely to live, used to calculate life insurance premiums.

actuary A person whose function is the assessment of insurance risks and premiums. Most are employed by insurance companies to advise on benefits likely to be claimed in a particular year, draw up mortality tables, calculate premiums, etc. Some are employed by the government and by pension funds.

ad See **advertisement**

adaptive control Statistical techniques employed to make adjustments in operating conditions to take account of variation in external factors.

adaptive system A business model, commonly in a computer program, which responds to variations in input by variations in output.

adding machine A manually or electrically operated machine which performs a series of additions or subtractions and indicates the results visually.

add-listing machine An adding machine which produces a printed record (generally on a paper roll) of calculations performed by the machine. Most machines also multiply and divide.

address commission The commission paid to a charterer's agent for arranging the loading of a vessel, the amount being generally calculated as a proportion of the freight value.

addressing machine A type of duplicating machine which reproduces a number of separate imprints once or twice instead of the same imprint many times. Although it was originally designed for addressing envelopes its use has been extended to labelling, payroll preparation, heading statements, etc.

adjudication order A court order which declares a person bankrupt and arranges for the disposition of his resources through a trustee acting on behalf of the creditors. The order may be granted on a creditor's petition after a public examination of the debts by the court, or on application by the debtor before the public examination.

adjuster A person who calculates losses on behalf of an insurance company.

adjustment (In marine insurance) the determining of the exact indemnity to which an insured party is entitled under his insurance policy after making all allowances and deductions.

adman A person who works in advertising.

ad measurement The measurement made to determine the tonnage of a vessel.

administered price (In the United States) a price fixed by a manufacturer which cannot be varied by the retailer.

administration 1 The business function concerned with the installation and operation of procedures and the progress of activity against plan. 2 The management of an estate by an executor or of a trust by a trustee. 3 The executive officers of an organization.

administration expense The costs of operating the administrative function of a business, a category covering overheads which do not fall under the headings of selling, research and distribution.

administration order (In bankruptcy proceedings) a court order for the disposition of a debtor's property where the total indebtedness is small.

administrator The person appointed by a court of law to attend to the estate of a deceased where no will has been left, or where no executors have been named in a will. The claimants who wish to act as administrator (normally relatives or creditors) must apply to, and obtain from, the court legal authority to act. See also **letter of administration**. Compare **executor**.

adoption The purchasing of a new product by consumers and businesses.

ADR see **American Depositary Receipts**

ad referendum 'To be considered further', as, for example, a contract which is signed but is still subject to further consideration on minor points.

ad valorem An ad valorem tax, duty, levy, etc. is calculated on total value rather than by weight, quantity or content. VAT is the best-known ad valorem tax.

advance 1 A sum of money lent in the form of a bank overdraft or simply a loan. 2 A part-payment for goods or services before the formal commencement or completion of the terms of a contract. 3 A part-payment to the supplier of goods upon receipt of the invoice or bill of lading, possibly before receipt of the goods. 4 To lend money, especially to lend money which is due at a later date.

advance corporation tax An element of a company's total corporation tax charge which is paid in advance of the main tax payment. The size and timing of the advance payment are related to the dividends declared by the company.

advance freight Goods for which carriage charges have been paid in advance, thereby permitting the recipient of the goods to obtain their release from the carriers.

advance note A draft for wages given to a ship's crew on signing articles but payable after the sailing date, thereby enabling the crew to make provision for their dependants during the voyage.

advancing market A market in which demand for a good greatly exceeds its supply. In this case the price would be expected to rise.

adventure A commercial undertaking of a speculative nature, often associated with overseas trading.

advertisement A printed notice which shows that something is for sale, or that a service is offered, or that a job is vacant, or that something will take place, etc. See also **classified advertisement, display advertisement**.

advertising The communication of information, usually in order to encourage, create or increase the demand for goods or services. Thus, publication of the merits of a product constitutes advertising but increasing demand by price cuts does not.

advertising agency A business concerned with advertising a client on the marketing of goods and services produced or provided by the client and implementing the client's advertising requirements through communications media.

advertising budget Amount of money allocated in a company's forecast of expenditure for spending on advertising.

advertising campaign An organized plan for promoting a product or service, carried out through various types of media, such as newspaper advertisements, TV commercials and special promotions in department stores.

advertising media Those agencies, means or systems through which advertising information is communicated, such as the press, television, etc.

advertising rates The scale of charges for different units of advertising, such as space in newspapers and magazines or time on radio and television. The charges are set out in a **rate card**.

advertising space Space in a newspaper or magazine which is set aside for advertisements.

Advertising Standards Authority An agency set up to monitor advertisements and see that they conform to the standards laid down by the advertising industry.

advice 1 A written communication on a business matter. 2 A written notification of the arrival or despatch of goods. 3 A legal opinion.

advice note A document containing the information that a stated transaction has taken place, or is about to take place. Most commonly, it is a note to a customer from a supplier indicating that the stated quantity and description of goods have been dispatched. Compare **delivery note; invoice**.

advise 1 To tell someone what has happened, such as that a shipment has been despatched. 2 To suggest to someone what action should be taken.

affidavit A sworn statement made before a commissioner of oaths. It is sometimes needed by a company when a deed of transfer is signed by power of attorney.

affiliated Connected with or owned by another company.

affluent society The type of society in which most members of the population are becoming richer.

after date Relating to a bill of exchange that is payable at a specified time after the date on which it has been prepared.

after-hours buying, selling or dealing Dealing in shares on the Stock Exchange after the exchange has officially closed for the day.

after-sales service 1 That part of a business's activities devoted to providing continued satisfaction to the customer after the sale of goods has been effected. This may include provision of parts, repairs, technical assistance, etc. 2 The items of assistance so provided.

after sight Relating to a bill of exchange that is payable at a certain fixed date after the date of its formal acceptance.

age admitted A phrase endorsed by an insurance company on a life insurance policy when the age of the insured is ascertained and confirmed.

age analysis 1 The analysis of stocks by the amount of cover provided, e.g. in terms of weeks of usage, by each item of stock. Also called **ageing of stocks**. 2 The analysis of debts according to the length of time during which they have been outstanding. Such analysis facilitates cash flow control. Also called **ageing of debtors** or **ageing of creditors**.

agency 1 An office or business which arranges things for other businesses, such as an advertising agency or an employment agency. 2 An office or the position of representing another company in a certain area.

agency broker A dealer on the London Stock Exchange who buys or sells shares for clients.

agenda A list of items scheduled to be brought before a meeting. Its sequence is a follows: the reading of the minutes of the previous meeting; discussion of any matters arising from that meeting; discussion of matters on the agenda; and the discussion of any other matters not listed in the agenda.

agent A person with express or implied authority to act on behalf of another, the principal, in making contracts with third parties. Such contracts are binding on the principal provided that they are made in the course of the principal's business and fall within the terms of the authority granted to the agent.

aggregated rebate scheme A discount scheme in which progressively higher discounts are given as purchases rise. The Monopolies Commission condemns such schemes on the ground that they 'impede competition from independent producers, because of their strong economic incentives to buyers to confine their purchases to members of the group [who give aggregated rebates]'.

agio The charge made for changing the money of one country with currency of another.

agio theory of interest see **abstinence theory of interest**

AGM see **annual general meeting**

agribusiness Farming and manufacturing products used by farmers, such as farm equipment, seen as a sector of a country's industry.

air consignment note a document prepared on behalf of the shipper of goods by airfreight, which acts as evidence of the contract of carriage. Also called **air way bill**.

air freight A method of shipping goods in bulk by air.

air time Time taken by a radio or TV advertisement.

ALGOL A computer-programming language that is especially suitable for scientific and mathematical applications. Its name is an acronym for *algo*rithmic *l*anguage.

all expenses paid With all costs paid by a company, not by the individual who incurs them.

all-in Which includes everything, such as an **all-in price**, which includes unit cost, insurance, packing and freight.

all-inclusive income statement A financial statement of performance for an accounting period, showing the effect of all transactions, except in share capital, on owners' equity.

allocation The allotment of whole items of cost to departments, processes, machines or individuals. Compare **apportionment**.

allocation period A time period which forms the basis for the collection, processing and reporting of accounting data.

allonge A slip of paper, used as an extension to, and attached to, a bill of exchange, to provide room for further endorsements to be added to the bill. Bills of exchange now change hands less freely and consequently allonges are no longer common.

allotment The second stage in the offer of company shares to the public. After the public has applied for the shares, they are allotted to them by the company. If the share issue has been oversubscribed, various criteria may be used for the allotment, such as by ballot, to small investors or to employees. Applicants who are allotted shares are advised in **allotment letters**.

allotment, return of A return sent to the Registrar of Companies showing details of allotment of shares.

allowable expense An expense prescribed by the Inland Revenue and permitted as a reduction of income or profit for taxation purposes.

allowance 1 A deduction from the price charged for a quantity of goods, in respect of faulty goods, shortages, etc. 2 A deduction for tax purposes. See also **personal allowance**.

allowed cost Any budgeted cost to be incurred in the production of a specified output.

allowed time The average time required for the performance of a task, taking into account differences in skill, effort, and conditions, and including allowances for fatigue and delays. It is frequently used as a basis for remuneration, a bonus being based upon time allowed less time taken.

all-risks policy An insurance policy which covers risks of any kind, with no exclusions.

alphanumeric filing A filing system based upon both numbers and letters. Thus, customers' accounts may be maintained by reference to the initial letter of the name and a sequential numbering system.

alpha shares Shares in the 70 leading companies on the London Stock Exchange.

alternate demand The situation which exists when two products are at least partial substitutes for each other, so that a movement in the price of one will affect the demand and supply and the price of the other.

alternate director A director who acts in the absence of another, named director. Such an appointment must have the express authority of the shareholders.

alternative cost A cost associated with a different set of circumstances. Thus, an existing cost may be compared with an alternative cost in order to evaluate a proposed change. For instance, the projected rents of two separate locations are alternative costs in considering a possible move.

amalgamation The combining of all or some of the assets and liabilities of two or more businesses into a single organization. This may be accomplished by the formation of a single new business or by the absorption by one business of the other.

amends, tender of The offer to pay a sum of money in satisfaction for the committing of an alleged wrong.

American Depositary Receipts Certificates which can be bought and sold by US citizens, conferring ownership of shares in British companies, without actually registering such ownership.

amortization 1 The gradual extinction of a debt or liability by means of periodic repayment or redemption, usually through the operation of a sinking fund. 2 The process of writing off intangible assets by charging the cost against revenue over the period during which benefit is derived. 3 Redemption of bonds or shares out of a fund specially set aside for that purpose. 4 The transfer of property in perpetuity to a charity or corporation.

analog computer A computer which works on the basis of electrical impulses representing numbers.

analysis book 1 An account book which records income or expenditure and the categories into which they fall. 2 Any book in which figures can be categorized.

anchorage A fee charged at certain ports and harbours for the right to anchor.

annual accounts The financial statements of a business, generally comprising the profit and loss account, balance sheet, directors' report and auditors' report. Also called **final accounts**.

annual allowance see **capital allowances**

annual charges Certain yearly business expenses (not neccessarily paid yearly) paid net of tax to the recipient, out of taxable profits or gains. The tax is collected from the party paying the charges and not from the recipient.

annual depreciation The reduction in book value of an asset at a certain percentage rate per annum.

annual general meeting A meeting of the members of a business organization held once every calendar year to consider the general state of the organization, including its financial position. Limited companies have a legal requirement to hold such a meeting within 15 months of the previous meeting. Matters discussed at such meetings include the financial accounts of the company, together with directors' and auditors' reports, the appointment of directors and auditors, and the declaration of dividends.

annual interest One of the most common charges falling into the category of annual charges.

annualized Shown on an annual basis.

annualized percentage rate The actual rate of interest on a credit transaction, shown as the rate per annum, which must by law be displayed on all credit transaction documents, such as hire purchase agreements.

annual report The report sent out each year by a company to its members, usually accompanied by or including the annual accounts. It may include the chairman's report and, where applicable, consolidated accounts.

annual return 1 A report required by law from incorporated companies, to be completed within a specific period after each year's annual general meeting, showing details of ownership of shares and debentures, and changes in ownership. It must also contain a copy of the balance sheet. 2 A form on which a taxpayer enters his annual income and reliefs and allowances claimed in order that an assessment of his tax liability can be calculated.

annuity A type of pension in which an insurance company pays an annual income in return for a lump-sum payment. This annual income may be for a certain period only, for the individual's lifetime, or in perpetuity.

annul To cancel an agreement, or to stop a legal contract.

answering machine A machine which answers the telephone automatically with a recorded message, when someone is not in an office and cannot take the call.

answering service An office which answers the telephone and takes messages for someone or for a company.

antedate To date (a document) earlier than the date on which it is issued. Generally such a document still operates from the date of issue. Also called **backdate**. Compare **postdate**.

anti-trust laws A body of US legislation designed to prevent or prohibit monopolies. The first such law to be enacted was the Sherman Anti-Trust Law of 1980.

AOB 'Any Other Business', an item at the end of an agenda, where any matter can be raised.

AOQL see **average outgoing quality level**

appeal The quality in a product, service or advertisement which attracts a customer and leads to a purchase.

application form A form, usually issued with a prospectus, on which application for stocks, shares, etc. issued by a company is made.

application money Money payable upon an application for stocks or shares, etc., being all or a proportion of the total issue price of the stocks or shares etc., applied for.

applied economics A branch of economics which relates the principles of economic theory and the techniques of economic analysis to the practical problems of business, government, etc.

apportionment The allotment of portions of cost to several departments of a business on some basis, usually an arbitrary one.

appraisement The valuation of an object.

appreciation 1 An increase in the value of an asset over its purchase price or book value. 2 The process of valuing an asset.

apprenticeship A contractual period served by a trainee under an employer in return for training in the relevant trade. Normally, the wage the apprentice receives will be comparatively low.

appropriation

appropriation 1 A sum set aside from earnings for a specific purpose. 2 The setting aside, by a personal representative, of property to satisfy a gift.

appropriation account 1 That section of the financial statement of a business for a given accounting period, which shows how the profits have been distributed. In the case of a company this may include allocation to reserves, taxation, dividends and retained profits. Thus, it is the setting apart of, rather than a charge against, profits. 2 A statement showing sums authorized by Parliament for government expenditure, contained in the Appropriation Act. Also called **appropriation statement**.

Appropriation Act The Act of Parliament which gives the British government the power to spend money to the limit and in the way approved by the Supply Resolutions.

appropriation-in-aid An item in the estimates of a government department which indicates a source of revenue obtained by the sale of goods or services by the department, thereby reducing its total financial requirement for the coming year.

appropriation of payments The allocation to a particular debt of a sum paid by a debtor. The debtor has the initial right to determine which debt he is paying. Otherwise the creditor may decide how the payment is to be appropriated, and may, for instance, allot the sum to pay off a gambling debt (which is not recoverable through the courts) rather than a debt for goods received (which can be sued for). In the absence of appropriation by either debtor or creditor, the payment is assumed to apply to the earliest debt incurred.

appropriation statement see **appropriation account** (def. 2)

approved society see **friendly society**

APR see **annualized percentage rate**

aptitude test A test designed to determine the type of work to which a person is potentially suited.

AQL see **acceptable quality level**

arbitrage 1 Buying shares in companies whose share price is likely to rise because of possible takeover deals. 2 The moving of funds from one market to another to benefit from price differentials. The price differential must be large enough to cover any transaction costs. Arbitrage ensures that currency exchange rates are in harmony throughout the world, since otherwise there would be wholesale movements of capital between the world's financial centres.

arbitrageur A person who specializes in arbitrage deals.

arbitrated exchange rate see **cross rate**

arbitration The settlement of a dispute by the decision of an independent person or group of people without recourse to the courts. The process may be voluntarily agreed upon or may be legally imposed, as in disputes concerning pay in various nationalized industries.

arithmetic mean An average computed by totalling all the values concerned and dividing by the number of values concerned. This is the most common of all averages.

arrears Debts which are due but unpaid.

articled clerk A clerk who is bound by contract to work in a lawyer's office for some years to learn the law.

articles of association The rules which govern the internal constitution and procedures of a limited company, detailing such items as the manner of conducting company meetings and the procedures relating to the issue of share capital. The articles must be registered, together with the Memorandum of Association, upon the formation of the company. In the United States these are called articles of incorporation.

articles of partnership The clauses contained in a partnership agreement. See under **partnership**.

artisan One skilled in an industrial art; a craftsman or mechanic.

ASA see **Advertising Standards Authority**

A shares Ordinary share capital issued by a company but not carrying voting rights.

asking price The price which a seller asks for the goods which he is offering for sale.

assay mark A hallmark, the mark stamped on gold or silver items to show that the metal is of the correct quality.

assembly line A means of manufacture in which assembly of the product is carried out in stages in a continuous flow, the work itself moving from one group of workers or machines to another in a predetermined sequence.

assessment 1 The valuation placed on property for rating purposes. 2 The taxation due on income or profits as determined by the Inland Revenue. 3 The estimate of damages awarded by a jury. 4 (US) A levy on shareholders used to raise further capital.

asset 1 Any business resource – both tangible and intangible – acquired at a monetary cost and which is expected to be of benefit to the business for a period of time, such as buildings, machinery, etc. 2 Any resource of a deceased or insolvent person from which claims may be met.

asset life The time period during which an asset is expected to contribute value to the operations of a business.

asset ratios The relationship that exists between the appropriate asset value on the balance sheet, and the total valuation of all assets.

asset stripping The taking over of a company with share values below their asset value, usually for the purpose of closing it down and selling off the assets.

asset value The value of a company calculated by adding together all its assets.

assignation A legal transfer of property or a right.

assigned revenue Income derived from taxes, duties, etc., transferred from the central government to local authorities.

assignee A person to whom property or contractual rights or obligations are transferred.

assignment 1 The transfer of property or contractual rights or obligations to a third person, usually requiring the consent of the other contractual party. 2 The document by which such transfers are effected.

assignment record A list showing the principal duties of a clerical worker, generally suitable for work of a non-routine nature.

associate company A company which is partly owned by another.

associate director A director who attends board meetings, but has not been elected by the shareholders and cannot vote.

assurance A type of contract which provides for a fixed sum of money to be payable to a person (the assured) on the occurrence of a stated event, in return for the payment of regular premiums. Unlike insurance a contract of assurance does not depend on a possible occurrence. Assurance contracts take two main forms: life assurance, a sum payable on the death of the assured; and endowment assurance, a sum payable at a certain stated date. Compare **insurance**.

at arms' length The term used to describe a transaction between two or more parties made on a strictly commercial basis, such parties acting without favour.

at best An instruction to a stockbroker to obtain the best selling or buying price for a share, commodity, etc. without restricting him to a specific price. When a stockbroker receives this instruction he must carry it out immediately, no matter what the current market price.

at call see **call money**

at par Denoting a stock or share which has a market price equal to its face value. See also **above par; below par**.

at sight (Of a bill of exchange) payable on presentation. Compare **after date; after sight**.

attachment order 1 A court order obtained by a judgement creditor whereby money due to the debtor by third parties becomes the property of the creditor. The order may also prevent the disposal of the debtor's goods which are held by third parties. 2 An order for the imprisonment of a person who is in contempt of court.

attested copy A certified copy of an original document, which may be introduced in evidence in a legal action.

attorney general The principal government law officer. He is a member of Parliament with a seat in the cabinet.

attorney, power of A deed whereby one party, the principal, empowers another, the donee or attorney, to represent him or act on his behalf. Such power is often used when attempting to obtain payment from a debtor in a foreign country.

attributable profits Profits which can be shown to come from a certain area of a company's operations.

auction The sale of property by competition. Subject to a possible reserve price, the property is sold to that party making the highest bid, the contract being binding upon the fall of the hammer. See also **Dutch auction**.

auctioneer A person licensed to sell goods or property by auction. Until the time when the contract is made he acts as the agent of the seller, but thereafter he is deemed to be the agent of both the seller and the buyer, and can bind both parties. His remuneration is generally commission on the price realized.

auction ring A group of people who collude in their bidding at an auction in order to obtain the article being auctioned at a low price. Subsequently the article is privately auctioned within the group, the surplus between the finally agreed price and the earlier auction price being distributed between the members of the ring. Such rings are illegal.

audience All the people who listen to a radio commercial, who watch a TV commercial or who read printed advertisements in magazines or displayed as posters.

audit 1 The systematic examination of the records, books of account and financial documents of a business in order to determine the accuracy of the recording of transactions and to verify the statements and reports prepared during the period under review. The audit is particularly concerned with ascertaining that the summary financial statements shows a true and fair view of the state of affairs of the business at the date stated. Under the Companies Act (1948) every British company must keep a proper set of books and ensure they are regularly examined by an independent auditor. 2 Examination of a computer transaction to make sure it is correct. 3 Examination of sales outlets to obtain information about sales.

audit block stamp A rubber stamp used to mark a document to show that it has been examined by auditors, who may initial the impression.

auditor An accountant whose task it is to carry out the examination of the records of a business on behalf of the shareholders.

auditor general see **Comptroller and Auditor General**

Austrian School of Economics A group of late 19th-century Austrian economists who developed a subjective theory of value, suggesting that value is determined by the interaction of the marginal utility of demand

and supply. Its principal exponents included Eugen von Böhm-Bawerk (1851–1914) and Ludwig Edler von Mises (1881–1979).

autarky A policy of complete national economic self-sufficiency and independence from imports. Such a policy has never been fully implemented (although 18th-century Japan is one nation which approached such a condition). However, autarky is valuable to study as a comparison with models of international trade.

authorized capital The maximum amount to be subscribed by the public in a company. The maximum is indicated in the company's Memorandum of Association and is usually divided into shares of specified quantity and value. Procedures prescribed by law are required if a company wishes to issue shares beyond the authorized limit. Also called **nominal capital; registered capital**. See also **capital clause**.

authorized clerk A stockbroker's clerk who under Stock Exchange rules is permitted to deal on the Exchange on his principal's behalf.

authorized dealer A person or company (such as a bank) which is allowed to buy and sell foreign currency.

automatic vending machine A machine selling products such as cigarettes, chocolate and drinks, which functions automatically when the purchaser inserts a coin.

automation The automatic control of mechanical processes, generally by electronic means, with little human intervention.

available capital Capital which is ready to be used.

average adjuster The person responsible for preparing claims on insurance policies, especially in marine insurance, and for determining the proportionate share to be borne by each underwriter prior to final adjustments by the underwriters themselves. Also called **average stater**.

average bond An undertaking given by a person receiving cargo from the master of a vessel that he will bear his proportionate share of any general average insurance claim that may arise from losses sustained during the voyage.

average clause A clause in an insurance policy which states that where the full value of the property is not insured, then the sum recoverable from the insurers will be the same proportion of the loss as the value bears to the total value of the property. If, for example, a house is insured for only half its value because of inflation and the house is totally destroyed by fire, then the insurers will not pay out half the value of the house but merely half of what it was insured for.

average cost The total cost of production divided by the quantity produced. The disparity between average cost and the commodity's price represents the unit profit or loss at that level of production.

average cost pricing A pricing method used to evaluate materials issued to production and stock balances, based on the average prices paid for materials during a time period. If a firm sets its sale price to equal its average cost it will always break even. The more perfectly competitive the market, the closer average cost is to marginal cost and the closer this strategy is to optimizing profits.

average due date The date on which a single payment may be made in settlement of a series of debts due at different dates without loss of interest to either party.

average outgoing quality level The highest proportion of defectives that will be found, on average, after a product has passed through the inspection phase. There are several different plans for calculating this, depending upon the way in which the rejected lots are disposed of. Also called **average outgoing quality limit**.

averager A person who buys blocks of shares in the same company at various times and at various prices, in order to establish an average price for the portfolio.

average statement The statement prepared by an average stater in which are computed the proportionate shares of an insurance loss to be borne by the underwriters. Final adjustments are then made by the underwriters.

averaging A form of Stock Exchange speculation in which the volume of transactions is increased when prices move unfavourably. The average price at which stocks or shares are sold would thus be higher than the original sale for a bear speculation which is faced with unexpected price rises. The average prices at which stocks or shares are bought would be lower than the original purchase price for a bull speculation which is faced with unexpected price falls.

avoirdupois The system of weights commonly in use in the United States, Great Britain and the Commonwealth, in which the lowest unit is the grain (based on the weight on one cubic inch of water) and the highest, the ton.

award The decision of an arbitrator, which has the standing of a legal judgement if the arbitration has been properly conducted.

B

baby bonds US government bonds in small denominations (such as $100) which the small investor can afford to buy.

back bond A bond given by the owner of property to a creditor as consideration for a loan. The bond reduces the owner's rights on the property to those of a trustee, the original rights being restored upon repayment of the loan.

backdate see **antedate**

backed note A document endorsed by a ship's broker indicating that freight charges have been or will be paid. It authorizes a ship's officer to take on board water-borne goods and also indicates the responsibility for demurrage. Also called **broker's order**.

backer A person who helps a businessman financially.

back-freight The money paid by a charterer to a shipowner for the extra costs incurred by a cargo during a voyage. This may be payment for: carriage beyond destination because of incorrect case markings; the return carriage of the goods due to non-acceptance at the port of delivery; the disposal of the goods if the consignee fails to take delivery within a reasonable time.

backhander A bribe, or money given to someone in secret to help a business deal.

back office The section of a stockbroking office which deals with the preparation of the paperwork involved in buying and selling shares.

back to back credit An arrangement used to finance a series of related trading transactions based on the provision of credit by a finance house to the final purchaser, made out in favour of his immediate seller. This credit facility acts as security for a chain of similar credit arrangements which extends backwards to the initial supplier of the goods.

back-up copy A copy of a computer disk or file, which is made and kept separate in case the original disk is damaged.

backwardation 1 The rate of interest paid by a speculator on the London Stock Exchange when he wishes to postpone the settlement of his account until the next settlement date. It is usually undertaken by a 'bear' speculator who expects that the price of the shares concerned will soon fall. 2 The difference in price in commodity markets between a good's present or 'spot' price and its future or 'forward' price. Normally the spot price is the higher. Compare **contango**.

backward integration The merger of one firm with another that is nearer the beginning of the manufacturing process. Examples are a brewery with a hop-grower or a publishing company with a paper manufacturer. Backward integration may ensure constant supplies in a time of crisis but cannot add to the organization's monopoly power.

bad debt A debt which is irrecoverable and is therefore written off as a loss in the accounts of a company.

bad delivery A situation in which an invalid transaction has taken place as a result of faulty documentation and good title of ownership is not transferred. Bad delivery occurs where documents are not genuine, or where they are damaged or where the coupons attached to a bond or share certificate are not in order. Compare **good delivery**.

bailee A person who is entrusted with the goods of another, the **bailor**, under a contract. Examples of bailees are garages and dry-cleaners. The bailee must take and maintain a resonable standard of care, depending upon the circumstances.

bailment The delivery of goods to a bailee, or the possession of such goods, for the performance of an action which forms part of a contract.

bailor see **bailee**

balance The net difference outstanding or to the credit of an account after all debits and credits have been accounted for.

balanced budget A government budget in which current expenditure equals current revenue. In the 19th and early 20th centuries it was standard policy always to balance the budget. However, under the influence of John Maynard Keynes it was realized that unbalanced budgets would affect employment and output and that, in certain circumstances, this could be beneficial to the economy.

balance brought forward; balance carried forward The amount entered in an account at the end of a period to balance the expenditure and income, which is then taken forward to start the new period.

balance of payments A comprehensive set of accounts recording a country's transactions with other countries and with international organizations. It can be divided into two parts: the current account and the capital account.

The current account is composed of visible trade (the import and export of tangible goods such as raw materials and machinery) and invisible trade (services such as banking, insurance and tourism).

The capital account deals with the flow of funds out of and into the country through investment abroad and internal investment by foreign countries and organizations.

If the balance of payments is persistently in deficit or in surplus the exchange rate of the country's currency will be liable to fall or rise accordingly.

balance of trade The difference between the value of a country's exports

balance sheet

and imports, including both goods and services, but excluding the movement of capital and currency.

balance sheet An accounting statement of the financial position of a business presented at a specific point in time, usually at the end of an accounting period. Such a statement must show assets, liabilities and capital and is now commonly presented in a vertical form which easily identifies net current assets and capital employed. It is sometimes shown with assets on one side and liabilities and capital on the other, the balancing of the statement being immediately apparent.

ballot A method of deciding which applicants shall receive shares in a new issue which has been oversubscribed.

Baltic Mercantile and Shipping Exchange An association of merchants meeting in London which deals in the chartering of ships and aircraft and is also a commodity exchange in grain and timber. Also called **Baltic Exchange**.

band chart A graphical representation of quantitative data in which information relating to each characteristic is shown in bands, one above the other.

banded pack Two or more items banded together and generally sold at a price lower than the sum of the individual items purchased separately.

bank 1 A financial institution which receives deposits from customers, handles their financial transactions and lends or invests the funds deposited with it. See also **joint stock bank; savings bank**. 2 To deposit money in to a bank account, or to have an account with a certain bank.

bankable paper A document which a bank will accept as security for a loan.

bank account An arrangement which an individual or company has to keep money in a bank.

bank balance The state of a bank account at a particular time, such as at the end of a month or year.

bank base rate The basic rate of interest which a bank charges on loans to its customers.

bank bill A bill of exchange issued or accepted by a bank. The security which is associated with such a bill makes it more acceptable in the market than a trade bill and accordingly it is subject to lower discount rates.

bank book A book, given by a bank to a customer, which shows the amounts of money which are deposited or withdrawn from a savings account.

bank charges The charges which a bank makes for carrying out transactions.

bank charter The official document by which a bank is established in law.

bank credit Facilities extended by a bank to a customer permitting the drawing of money up to a specified amount, interest being charged and security required for money actually advanced.

banker's cheque A cheque which one bank has drawn on another bank and handed to a customer in order to permit the remittance of money between banks. It may also be used in order to settle a balance between two banks arising from the operation of cheque clearance procedures. See also **clearing house** (def. 2).

banker's draft A draft drawn by, or on behalf of, a bank upon itself and payable on demand.

banker's order see **standing order**

bank giro (In the United Kingdom) the system used by clearing banks to transfer money rapidly from one account to another.

Bank for International Settlements A financial institution in Basel whose members are the central banks of Western Europe, North America and Japan. Its original purpose of promoting co-ordination between the central banks has now been almost entirely taken over by the International Monetary Fund.

bank holidays Public holidays on which banks are closed.

bank loan A stated sum of money which is loaned by a bank to a customer and repayable at a stated future date or in instalments in the case of a personal loan. Bank loans bear a specified fixed rate of interest on the amount of the loan and security is usually required. Also called **advance**.

bank mandate A written order allowing someone to sign cheques on behalf of a company.

Bank of England The central bank of the United Kingdom, initially formed as a private company, but since 1946 under state ownership and control. The bank performs a wide variety of functions including normal banking operations as the government's banker and the banker for overseas central banks, the British commerical banks and some private bodies. The bank acts as the agent of the government in the pursuit of economic and monetary policies in its control of the banknote issue, in its manipulation of the minimum lending rate and its general advice to the money market. It also acts as the agent of the government in the management of the national debt and the raising of short- and long-term loans. It acts as the registrar of government stocks, Commonwealth stocks, and those raised by local authorities and nationalized industries.

bank of issue A bank which is able to issue its own banknotes as legal tender. The right to issue banknotes for England and Wales is vested solely in the Bank of England, but Scottish banks are still able to issue notes for Scotland.

bank rate (Formerly) the rate of interest at which the Bank of England rediscounted first-class bills of exchange. All other interest rates were geared to bank rate, which was consequently used as an instrument of government economic policy. In October 1972 it was superseded by the minimum lending rate.

bank reconciliation The process of agreeing the balances as recorded in the cash book of a business and as shown by its bank account. Adjustments may be required for cheques which have not been presented for payment. See also **reconciliation statement**.

bank return A weekly statement issued by the Bank of England showing its financial position.

bank statement A document which records the transactions which have occurred in a customer's bank account during a particular period and the closing balance. The statement may be sent to customers on demand or at periodic intervals.

bankrupt A person who has been declared by a court not to be capable of paying his debts, and whose affairs are put in the hands of a trustee.

bankruptcy 1 The condition of being unable to pay one's debts. 2 Legal proceedings designed to declare a person formally bankrupt and to provide for the administration of his property in order to discharge his debts. The proceedings may be initiated either by the debtor or by his creditors.

bankruptcy, act of The performance of an action by a debtor on which bankruptcy proceedings may be based, such as filing in court a declaration of inability to pay debts or giving notice to a creditor that payment of debts has been suspended.

bar chart A diagrammatic presentation of quantitative or qualitative information in which data is shown as lines or rectangular blocks against a scale of values. In a compound bar chart two or more bars parallel to each other provide comparison. In a component bar chart the lines are subdivided (as by differential colouring) to show how each is composed and the area of the constituent parts.

bar code A system of lines printed on a product which, when read by a computer, give a reference number or price.

bareboat charter An arrangement for hiring a vessel whereby the charterer obtains complete control of the vessel during the voyage in return for the payment of all the expenses of the voyage.

bargain 1 Purchase made at a lower price than normal. 2 Any transaction taking place on the London Stock Exchange.

bargaining position A statement of the position adopted by a group during negotiations.

bargaining power The strength of one person or group during negotiations over prices or wages.

bargain purchasing The practice of buying in bulk with prompt delivery and payment, thereby earning cash and quantity discounts, while also intending to gain from reselling at an increased price.

bargains done The number of deals made on the Stock Exchange during a day.

barratry The wilful act of a ship's master or crew that is against the interests of the shipowners. Losses arising from such an action may be insured against in marine insurance policies.

barrier to entry Any phenomenon which hinders or prevents new firms entering an industry. Its existence reduces competition (at least potentially) and so encourages higher prices than would otherwise occur.

There are six major types of barrier: government prohibition (for example, by rationing airwaves to a specific number of television stations); patent restrictions; exorbitant initial costs of creation; resistance on the part of existing firms (for example, by tying contracts with customers and the threat of unprofitable price wars); established consumer preferences; and economic restrictions (such as the unavailability of a scarce resource).

barter The exchange of goods and services in return for other goods and services without the use of money or other media of exchange.

Basel Group An association of leading European central banks and US monetary authorities which takes measures to avoid disruptions in the international short-term capital market. These measures include the co-ordination of domestic economic policies so as to avoid the creation of interest rate differentials leading to short-term movements of funds, and agreement by the group's members, in the event of movement of capital, to hold one another's currency rather than to convert it into gold.

base rate see **bank base rate**

base stock system The system of replenishing stocks when existing amounts have fallen to some specified level. Compare **periodic reordering system**.

base year Statistically, the year selected as the starting point in the compilation of a series to measure the extent of changes in a particular variable or variables over a period of time. Frequently the base year is taken as having an index of 100 and subsequent years are measured accordingly.

BASIC 'Beginner's All-purpose Symbolic Instruction Code', a simple language used for computer programming.

basic salary, basic wage The normal salary for a job, without bonuses, commission or overtime payments.

basic standards Standard costs which remain in force for several years without revision. Compare **current standards**.

basis period The time period, the profits, gains or income of which form the basis of the assessment to tax for the relevant chargeable period.

basket A group of prices or currencies taken together as a standard for comparative purposes.

batch A group of generally identical items manufactured together or forming the output of one or more separate stages of production, while maintaining their identity throughout. **Batch production** is the type of production in which identical articles are manufactured or processed in groups rather than singly. Thus, shoes are generally produced in batches.

batch costing A type of costing in which the cost unit is the batch rather than the individual items.

batch processing A computer management system where information is collected into batches before being loaded into the computer and processed by it.

bear A dealer on the Stock Exchange who, in anticipation of a fall in price, sells stocks or shares at the current price for payment at the next account settlement date. If the price falls the bear may purchase the stock at a lower price, taking his profit from the price difference.

A bear need not actually possess the stocks or shares when he technically makes a sale, having to cover himself by a later purchase of shares when the price falls. Compare **bull**. See also **backwardation**; **bear squeeze**; **covered bear**.

bearer bond A bond which is payable to the bearer and does not have a name written on it.

bearer security Any stock, share, debenture, etc., whose document or title is made out 'to bearer' rather than to a named individual. Ownership of the security is thereby transferred by exchange of the documents without the need for endorsement.

bear market A period when Stock Exchange prices are falling because shareholders are selling shares.

bear raid Selling a large number of shares in a company to try to bring down the share price.

bear squeeze A situation which arises when a bear has sold shares which he does not possess and needs to buy shares before the settlement date in order to carry out the initial sale transaction. The bear may have to buy at an unfavourable price, in which case he is 'squeezed'. This squeeze is generally applied by bulls who purchase the shares which the bear originally sells. See also **cornering a bear**.

bed-and-breakfast deal An arrangement where shares are sold one day and bought back immediately in order to establish a profit or loss for tax declaration.

Bedaux system A system of remuneration based upon time saved against a measured allowed time for the appropriate job. The unit of measurement used is called the B – that amount of work normally performed by one operative in one minute. Thus, a rate of $80B$ would mean that the operation is being carried out at 133% of normal rate, since 80 is one third greater than 60 – the number of seconds in each minute.

beggar-my-neighbour policy The strategy of a country in protecting its own industries to another country's disadvantage. This may include the imposition of tariffs on imports or the refusal to import certain products. Such a policy reduces international trade and invites retaliatory action. It was pursued during the Depression of the 1930s and undoubtedly exacerbated it.

below par A term applied to the price of a stock or share when its market price is less than its face value. See also **above par; at par**.

below-the-line advertising Any advertising which does not use orthodox media, such as the press, newspapers, and television. Below the line advertising includes direct mail publicity and special offers. Compare **above-the-line advertising**.

below-the-line payments and receipts 1 That part of a government budget which deals with revenue raised by borrowing and expenditure on the redemption of government loans. 2 Business revenue or expenditure of an extraordinary nature which is separated from the normal trading performance, as indicated on the income statement of the company's accounts. Also **below-the-line expenditure**. Compare **above-the-line**.

bench mark 1 A known point of reference against which characteristics may be measured, especially used for testing computer programs and equipment. 2 A selected job against which others may be assessed.

beneficial interest The advantage derived from an interest in property which is established by a trust or other private arrangement. Possession of an interest confers the right of enjoyment of property but does not confer the rights of ownership.

beneficiary 1 The recipient of a beneficial interest. 2 One who benefits under the terms of a will.

benefit Payment which is made to an individual under a national or private insurance scheme.

benefit in kind A gain or entitlement other than money given to employees, generally as an incentive, such as assistance in purchasing a house, the use of a car, etc.

benefit theory of taxation A theory of taxation based on the principle that the state should levy taxes and return to the taxpayer an equal value in services. This implies that those who use the most services (often the poorest) should pay the most taxes. With heavy defence and social expenditure such a principle is difficult to apply in modern societies.

Benelux A customs union formed between Belgium, The Netherlands and Luxembourg in 1948. It provided a standard tariff framework which has been widely adopted elsewhere. These countries were founder-members of the European Economic Community, which has the same principles.

berthage The amount charged for the use of a berth for a vessel when in port.

berth note A document issued by ship brokers which details the terms of the contract for the chartering of cargo. These usually exclude the brokers from liability for freight or demurrage.

Bertrand duopoly A market situation in which there are only two producers in an industry supplying a large number of consumers, each of whom supposes that the other will not alter his price and that he could capture the whole market by reducing his price only slightly. The outcome is a price war which ends only when the break-even point is reached by each producer.

'best before' date The date stamped on an item of food, which is the date after which the item may not be good to eat. Compare **sell-by date**.

BES see Business Expansion Scheme

best profit equilibrium The level of operations at which the marginal costs of production equate with the marginal revenue from sales. It is at this level of output that profits are greatest.

beta shares Shares in 500 major companies listed on the Stock Exchange, but which are less frequently traded than the alpha shares.

betterment An increase in the value of land and buildings which results from nearby property development or from restrictions enforced by authorities on the use of land elsewhere. Such an increase is merely notional until the land is sold.

bid The offer of a price for an object which is for sale. On the London Stock Exchange the bid price is the lesser of the two prices of any share that are quoted by a jobber. This is the price at which he will buy.

bidding The action of making offers to buy, usually at an auction sale.

bid filing A procedure whereby firms who have submitted tenders for a contract notify a central agency of their tenders after the contract has been awarded. The agency then circulates the details of all tenders to member firms.

Big Bang The change to computerized share dealing adopted by the London Stock Exchange in 1986. As a result of Big Bang, share trading is now conducted by telephone or on the computer monitor in stockbroking offices, with the eventual closure of the Stock Exchange trading floor.

Big Board The New York Stock Exchange.

Big Four The four largest clearing banks in the United Kingdom: Barclays, Lloyds, the Midland and the National Westminster.

bilateral monopoly An industry in which the only purchaser of a commodity or service deals with the only producer of that commodity or service. Since both cannot use their monopoly power, the possible outcome of bargaining is indeterminate. One possibility is that the two organizations would act so as to maximize joint profits and then negotiate on how to divide them.

bilateral trade Trade between two countries to the exclusion of others. For instance, a developing country may buy machinery from Britain on condition that the payment received is used by Britain to buy that country's produce rather than buying elsewhere.

bill 1 An invoice stating the money due in payment for goods or services provided. 2 A bill of exchange. 3 A small poster.

billboard (US) see **hoarding** (def.2)

bill broker A dealer in bills of exchange, treasury bills and government bonds, etc., either acting on his own behalf or as an intermediary for another. One particular activity is the discounting of bills with borrowed money, subsequently rediscounting at a more favourable rate of interest.

billing The process of preparing and despatching invoices to customers.

bill of entry A document which records the nature and value of goods being exported or imported. The bill is prepared by the merchant for the customs authorities and, once certified by them, permits the loading or unloading of the goods.

bill of exchange As defined by the Bills of Exchange Act (1882) 'an unconditional order in writing, addressed by one person to another, signed by the person giving it, requiring the person to whom it is addressed to pay on demand or at a fixed or determinable future time, a certain sum in money, to, or to the order of, a specified person, or to the bearer'. In fact, it is a type of mammoth IOU which represents a company's acknowledgement of a debt to another company.

bill of exchange, clean 1 A bill of exchange which is free from any defect, qualification, etc. 2 A bill of exchange which is independent of other documentation, such as shipping documents.

bill of exchange, rebated A bill of exchange which has been discounted but subsequently taken back by the person who discounted it. A proportion of the discounting charges is rebated to him by the discounting institution.

bill of exchange, retired A bill of exchange which is withdrawn from circulation before it is due by a party liable on it.

bill of exchange, short A bill of exchange which has less than ten days before maturity or which is payable on presentation.

bill of health A certificate indicating the state of health of a port prepared by a consul or other authority and given to a ship's master on his departure. The bill may be required before permision to enter a new port is granted. See also **clean bill of health; foul bill of health; touched bill of health**.

bill of lading A document prepared by a shipowner or his agents which acknowledges the receipt and consignment of goods and contains details of the agreed conditions about the transport of the goods. The bill, which forms good evidence of the contract of carriage, is sent to each shipper of goods.

bill of sale A document, generally given as security for a loan, by means of which the debtor, mortgagor or grantor transfers the title of goods to his creditor, mortgagee or grantee. Such assignment is usually conditional and, if all the conditions are fulfilled, the property in the goods will be retransferred to the original owner. Bills of sale must be registered.

bill of sale, absolute A bill of sale in which there is an absolute and unconditional transfer of title to the transferee. The transferor cannot retake the title.

bill of sight A temporary document prepared by an importer of goods when he has only incomplete details of the cargo. The document serves as a formal request for permission to land the cargo and for inspection by customs officials when the full details of the goods may be ascertained and documented in the bill of entry. See also **bill of entry**.

bill of store A document issued by the customs authorities which permits the reimportation of goods previously exported. Such goods are not classified as foreign and thus are free of both customs duties and the general terms of trading to which foreign goods are subject.

bill of sufferance A document issued by the customs authorities which permits coastal vessels to carry dutiable goods between ports. The goods must be warehoused in a bonded warehouse or on a sufferance wharf.

bill on London A bill of exchange whose drawer is in the United Kingdom, the bill being payable in pounds sterling.

bills payable Bills which a debtor has to pay.

bills receivable Bills which a creditor will receive in due course.

bimetallism A currency system which uses the coinage of two metals (usually gold and silver) as legal tender, rather than only one. This was common in the nineteenth century, but virtually ended following its abandonment by the United States in the 1870s. Compare **monometallism**.

bin 1 A container in a shop, where goods can be piled to attract customers. **2** Section of a warehouse in which stock of an item is stored.

bin card A record showing the actual quantity of material in a specific store. It is updated whenever material is received or issued.

black To boycott (goods, services or organizations) in support of industrial or political action by others.

black economy An illicit system of trade running in parallel with normal trade but operated in order to avoid the payment of taxes, for example by not issuing invoices, payment normally being in cash.

blackleg An employee who continues to work while other employees are out on strike.

black list A list of goods or individuals or companies which have been blacked.

blacklist To put goods or individuals or companies on a prohibited list.

black market A market where goods or services are bought and sold illegally and usually at relatively high prices.

blank bill A bill of exchange which does not state the name of the person to whom payment is to be made.

blank cheque A cheque which has been signed and dated but in which the amount payable has not been filled in. This is left for the payee to insert.

blank endorsement An endorsement which transfers the title to a bill of exchange or similar document but which does not specify the name of the recipient. The bill becomes payable to the holder on maturity. See also **endorsement; special endorsement**.

blanket agreement An agreement which covers many different items.

blanket policy An insurance policy which covers many types of risk, such as a household policy which insures against fire, burglary, public liability, etc.

blank transfer A document transferring property rights, shares, etc. to an anonymous recipient. This form of transfer may be used where shares are given as security for a loan or where shares are held by a nominee on behalf of some other party.

blind filing A system for filing records in cards or folders, where index tabs are used for each section of files, several files being kept behind each guide card. Compare **visible filing**.

blind test A test where several different products are tested by a panel, with none of the products being identified to the testers.

blister pack A pack in which the item for sale is covered by a transparent plastic cover attached to a card backing.

blocked account A bank account from which payments are restricted by law. The most common restriction is to bar the transfer of the account abroad.

blocked currency A currency which cannot be taken out of a country because of exchange controls.

block grant A sum of money allocated by the central government to local authorities who have discretion as to the manner of its expenditure on the various services which they provide.

Blue Book The informal name of an annual publication by the Central Statistical Office – *National Income and Expenditure*. It provides statistics for the previous eleven years about personal income and expenditure, the relative shares of wages and profits in the national income, the aggregate profits of each industry, etc.

blue button clerk A stockbroker's clerk who is authorized to enter the floor of the Stock Exchange. The clerk's duties include collecting and distributing market price quotations but he is not permitted to deal on his broker's behalf. Also called **unauthorized clerk**. Compare **authorized clerk**.

blue chip An ordinary share which is considered safe both from loss of capital and of income. Blue chip shares are generally the shares of large, reputable companies, and the term is often used with reference to the shares of the 30 companies in the Financial Times Ordinary Share Index.

board (of directors) Those persons who have the ultimate powers of control and direction of an organization; the directors of a company.

boarding station A location appointed by customs authorities for the boarding of vessels by officials in the course of their duties.

body corporate A group of people who have formed a corporation. The corporation possesses a legal identity separate from that of its individual members.

bona fide (*Latin*, 'in good faith') A term used to describe the nature of a person or an action. Good faith, or honesty of intent, is a fundamental prerequisite for the creation of most valid contracts.

bonanza A very profitable business venture.

bond A written undertaking to perform an action (such as the repayment of money), to act as guarantor for another party, or to refrain from performing a certain action.

bond creditor A creditor whose debt is secured by a bond given by the debtor.

bonded goods Imported goods on which duty is payable and which are stored at a bonded warehouse pending payment or re-exportation.

bonded stores Normally dutiable goods which are exempt from duty because they are intended for use on board ship.

bonded warehouse A licensed warehouse where goods liable to duty may be stored, but removed only on payment of the duty.

bond note A customs document prepared by a shipper with details of goods to be taken from a bonded warehouse. The note certifies that the formalities relating to bonded goods have been complied with and that a bond has been given for the goods to ensure their proper disposal. When signed by a customs official the note acts as authority for removing the goods from the warehouse. A bond note is used for transfers of bonded goods between warehouses, for goods about to be exported, and for goods about to be loaded on board ship.

bonds Long- and medium-term loans issued by central or local governments or by companies. Such bonds generally bear a fixed rate of interest until redemption and are usually payable to bearer, permitting the transfer of title by simple delivery. See also **active bond; deferred bond**.

bond washing The selling of US Treasury bonds with the interest coupon attached and then buying them back ex-coupon so as to reduce tax.

bonus 1 A special allowance or gift paid to an employee over and above his normal remuneration. 2 That part of the profits of a life assurance company added to a policy upon the valuation of all policies in force.

bonus issue An issue of shares to existing shareholders free of charge, the shares being created by a transfer from company reserves. Shareholders receive bonus shares in proportion to their existing shareholding. Also called **scrip issue**.

bonus pack A large pack of a product, with the extra contents being apparently given free to the customer.

bonus share An extra share given free to an existing shareholder.

book balance The balance on an account.

book debts Amounts showing, in the books of account of a business, as being owing to the business from debtors.

bookkeeper One who keeps the financial records of a company.

bookkeeping The recording of the financial transactions of a business or organization.

books of account Any bookkeeping record forming part of an accounting system. It need not be in book form, but may be on cards, as computer output, etc.

book value The value of assets or investments as recorded in a company's financial records.

boom That part of the trade cycle characterized by rising prices, a high level of employment and a high level of business activity.

borrowings The total amount of money borrowed by customers from banks.

borrowing power The amount of money which a company may borrow if needed.

bottom line 1 The last line on a profit and loss account, showing a profit or loss. 2 The most important result of a business deal, especially in regard to the potential profit.

bottomry bond A bond issued by a ship's master pledging the ship and/ or cargo as security for a loan, in circumstances where money is required to complete a voyage, e.g. for repairs. Repayment of the borrowed money, together with interest, is conditional on the safe arrival of the vessel and cargo at their destination. See also **respondentia**.

bought ledger The ledger in which expenditure is recorded.

bought notes and sold notes Documents which constitute the contract made between brokers, merchants, etc., usually acting on the instructions of a client. Details of the article bought and sold, the price (if agreed) and the names of the contracting parties are recorded. The bought note is delivered to the client of the buying broker and the sold note to the seller.

bounce (Of a cheque) to be returned to the payee, because there is not enough money in the payer's account to cover it.

bounty A payment made by a government to a producer or exporter operating in a particular field of activity as a means of encouraging the development of that activity.

bourse Any stock exchange on the continent of Europe. Originally the term was applied only to the Paris Stock Exchange.

boursier An official member of the Paris Stock Exchange.

box number A reference number to which replies to an advertisement are sent. It can be either a newspaper box number, where replies are sent to the newspaper offices, or a post office box number, in which case the replies are addressed to a post office.

boycott 1 A refusal to buy certain products or deal with a certain supplier, usually on political grounds. 2 To refuse to buy or deal with certain products (on political grounds).

brainstorming A process in which a group of people, frequently from different disciplines, meet and discuss problems, hoping to solve these problems through insights gained in their exchange of ideas.

branch The local office of a bank or large business; a local shop forming part of a large national chain.

branch banking A system of banking, as typified in the United Kingdom, where a few institutions operate a nationwide service through local offices.

brand 1 A distinctive sign, trademark or tradename used to identify a product or its manufacturer or distributor. 2 A distinctive sign made upon property to indicate ownership. 3 A distinctive sign made upon goods or their containers to indicate quality.

branded goods Goods marked as, and sold under, patent or trade names, having the name of the brand clearly displayed.

brand image The idea of a certain product which is associated with the brand name.

brand loyalty The attitude of customers who always buy the same brands of products.

breach of contract A failure to perform the terms of a contract. The injured party has various possible courses of action, including suing for damages and applying to a court of law to secure the performance of the contract.

breach of warranty of authority An action of an agent which is outside the authority granted to him by his principal. Generally the principal is not liable for contracts made by his agent in breach of his authority, the agent himself being liable to the third party.

breakdown 1 Stoppage of negotiations or of working machinery. 2 The detailed analysis of items of expenditure.

break even To balance costs and revenue, but without making a profit.

break-even analysis A technique for studying the profitability of a business or a venture by applying the concepts of marginal costing to the anticipated levels of activity and constructing a break-even chart or otherwise determining the level of activity at which the enterprise makes neither profit nor loss.

break-even chart A chart which shows the profit or loss of a business or activity at various levels of output/sales. It may be plotted by determining the relationship between total cost of sales to sales or fixed costs to contribution.

break-even point That level of activity of a business at which neither profit nor loss is incurred, total costs equating with total revenue. Also called **break-even performance**.

breaking bulk The reduction of large unit sizes of goods to smaller unit sizes, undertaken by wholesalers in order to meet the limited requirements of retailers and by retailers to provide goods for sale to customers.

Bretton Woods An international conference held in New Hampshire, United States, in July 1944. It largely determined the postwar system of international monetary control which existed until the 1970s. The conference was directly responsible for the creation of the International Monetary Fund and the International Bank for Reconstruction and Development.

bridging loan A short-term loan which provides temporary finance in order to secure the completion of two related transactions.

brief A summary of a client's case which is prepared by a solicitor and forms the basis for a counsel's opinion or for the conduct of a client's case in a legal action.

British Standards Institution The agency which sets standards for all types of products, such as BSI specifications for electrical goods. Consumer goods which conform to BSI quality standards carry the kite mark.

broken stowage Cargo space which is wasted through the storing together of numerous kinds of cargo of different size and shape.

broker An intermediary or agent for one or both parties who are making or performing a contract. Brokers operate in many fields of activity, such as the stock market, shipping, etc. On the Stock Exchange broker –dealers themselves hold stocks which they sell to clients, or buy to hold. Compare **market maker**.

brokerage The payment charged by brokers for their services in arranging a contract. It is usually expressed as a percentage of the monetary value of the contract.

brokers' contract notes Bought notes and sold notes signed by brokers and forwarded to their principals.

broker's order see **backed note**

broker's return A list of a ship's cargo that is prepared by a ship's clerk and sent to the ship's brokers either daily during loading or on its completion. It is used for reference when completing the bill of lading and as proof that the goods have been loaded.

B shares Ordinary shares which bear special voting rights.

BSI see **British Standards Institution**

bucket shop 1 A firm which tries to promote the shares in dubious companies. 2 A type of travel agency that specializes in the sale of cheap air tickets.

budget 1 A forecast of the government's expenditure and revenue for the forthcoming year together with an announcement of its proposed changes in taxation. The budget is the government's main instrument of economic policy. 2 A financial statement which evaluates the level of activity planned by a business for a future time period.

budget account A bank account where the client plans income and expenditure to allow for periods when expenditure is high, by paying out a set sum each month.

budgetary control 1 The continuous comparison of actual results against budgeted results in order to secure the objectives of a company's policy or to provide a basis for its revision. 2 The formal control by the British Parliament over the contents of the budget presented to it by the Chancellor of the Exchequer. Before becoming law the budget must be agreed to by both Houses of Parliament.

budgetary requirements The income and expenditure required to meet a budget forecast.

budget deficit The situation where a country's budget is in deficit, i.e. it spends more than it raises in taxes.

budget line 1 A line on an economic graph which shows the maximum quantity a consumer with a given income could obtain of either of two products as well as of all possible combinations of the two goods. By combining the budget line with that consumer's indifference curves it is possible to discover if he is making the best possible choice. To do so he must choose that combination which is both on the budget line and on the highest possible indifference curve. 2 That level of business activity used for establishing budgeted revenues and costs.

budget period The period of time to which a given budget relates, varying according to circumstances.

buffer stocks Those stocks maintained to meet emergency demands, such as arise from late delivery of orders, unexpected scrap, abnormal production demand, etc.

building society A financial institution whose principal activities consist of receiving deposits from customers and advancing money for the purchase of homes, obtaining the deeds of the property as security for the loan.

built-in obsolescence see **planned obsolescence**

built-in stabilizers Policies and institutions which automatically dampen down fluctuations in the level of income, employment, etc. without direct government action. For instance, a rise in unemployment increases the amount paid out in unemployment benefit, while simultaneously revenue from income tax decreases. Taken together, the net effect is to increase government spending and to reflate, however slightly, the economy (so causing the process to reverse).

bulk cargo A cargo which consists of a single commodity in an unpacked condition. It must be fairly homogeneous and relatively inexpensive. Examples are wheat and coal.

bulk discount Special discount allowed by a supplier to a purchaser who buys a large quantity of a product.

bulk purchase The buying of large quantities of a product at a lower price than normal.

bull A dealer on the Stock Exchange who buys stocks or shares for settlement at the next account settlement at the current price, anticipating a rise in the market price of the stocks. The bull then resells the stock at a higher price, and makes a profit from the price difference at which he bought and sold. Compare **bear**.

bulldog bond A loan raised by a foreign bank in sterling.

bullion Uncoined gold and silver, usually in bar form, which is regarded as a commercial commodity at recognized degrees of purity.

bullion market A market in which deals relating to gold and silver are transacted. The London Bullion Market comprises firms of brokers who meet daily to set an official price for bullion.

bull market A period when share prices rise on the Stock Exchange, because optimism about the economy encourages people to buy shares.

burden A general term for company overheads.

bureau de change

bureau de change An office or bank which exchanges foreign currency or travellers' cheques for the currency of the country in which the bureau is located.

burster A machine which separates continuous stationery into its individual sheets, in some cases also removing any interleaved carbon paper.

business 1 A person, partnership, or corporation engaged in the supply of goods and/or services with a view to making a profit. 2 The level or volume of trade, in general terms.

business cycle see **trade cycle**

Business Expansion Scheme A system where individuals can invest money in a new business free of tax, provided they have no personal connection with the company.

business games Training techniques in which business activities and decisions are simulated. Many different types of game are used, but generally they tend to be competititive and supervised by an independent participant who may determine market fluctuations, etc. Sophisticated games may be played using a computer programmed with appropriate econometric models.

business interruption see **consequential loss**

business name The title under which a business is conducted, requiring registration with the Registrar of Business Names in the following circumstances: where the business is a limited liability company; where the business name does not contain the surnames of all the proprietors; where the business name includes additions other than the first names or initials of the proprietors.

buyer's market A situation in which potential buyers of a commodity have an advantage over the sellers, because of over-production, etc., and are accordingly able to dictate terms, such as a lowering of the price, favourable credit arrangements and quicker delivery dates.

buyer's over A situation which occurs on the Stock Exchange or commodity markets when the number of potential buyers exceeds the number of sellers. Compare **seller's over**.

buying in The process by which a stockbroker obtains from the market stocks or shares on behalf of a buyer to whom a seller has failed to deliver stock he had contracted to deliver. The costs of this operation are charged to the defaulting seller. Compare **selling out**.

buyout see **leveraged buyout, management buyout**

by-product 1 Residual material or incidental product created during, or remaining after, a manufacturing process. 2 A product made from such residue. Thus, sawdust is a by-product of the timber trade and animal bones of the meat trade. Compare **joint products**.

byte A storage unit in a computer, equal to one character or eight bits.

C

call 1 A request by a company to its shareholders to pay an instalment due on their holding. 2 A request made by the liquidator in a company winding up to contributories for the payment of unpaid money on shares. 3 A deposit paid to secure an option to buy stock/shares at a predetermined price at a future specified date. See also **call option**. 4 A visit made by a salesman on a customer.

callable bond A bond which must be repaid at notice.

called bond A bond whose repayment date has been notified to bond holders. After this date the bond ceases to bear interest.

called-up capital That part of the nominal value of ordinary shares issued by a company on which payment has been requested. In the event of a winding-up the holders of ordinary shares are liable for the uncalled portion of their shares. Compare **paid-up capital**.

calling cycle The order in which a salesman visits customers, and the time which elapses between calls.

call money Money which is loaned, with repayment on demand without notice. See also **money at call**.

call of more The right to request the same quantity of stock or commodity as has previously been purchased. The right must be exercised on a specific day during the settlement period. Compare **put of more**.

call option The right to buy a commodity or share at a given price within a stipulated time. The option is bought, profit being earned if the option is taken up following a favourable price movement. The extent of the loss which may arise should the option not be taken up is limited to the payment made when acquiring the option. Compare **put**.

call rate The number of calls made by a salesman in a day or week.

cambist 1 A money changer, especially of foreign money, or a dealer in foreign currency and bills of exchange. 2 A book which contains details of the weights, measurements and currencies of various countries, with their conversion into units of one particular country.

Cambridge equation An expression of the quantity theory of money which seeks to establish the relationship between the supply of money and the level of prices:

$$P = \frac{MW}{KR}$$

where P=price level; M=total supply of money; R=total real income; K=demand to hold money in the form of wealth.

Cambridge School A group of late 19th-century economists headed by Alfred Marshall, who developed a theory of value based on the interaction of the forces of demand and supply. From detailed analysis of these forces the school established various economic concepts, including that of elasticity.

campaign An organized plan of marketing and publicity, involving promotion in various media.

canons of taxation see **taxation, Adam Smith's canons of**

canvass To talk to a selected group of people, either to ask their opinion about a product or to try to sell them the product.

canvasser A person who canvasses.

CAP see **Common Agricultural Policy**

Cape scrip Any stock or share issued from South Africa.

capital 1 All resources which have been produced by mankind and which themselves are used in the process of production. Capital is thus different from land, since this is a natural rather than a manmade resource. 2 The total resources of a person or business. 3 The sum of money subscribed by the members of a company, by partners or by an individual when starting a company.

capital account 1 The bookkeeping record of transactions which relate to the partners or proprietor of a business. The account may record only the initial sum subscribed by the individual if a current account is also used. See also **current account** (def. 2). 2 The account in a country's trading which shows the movement of capital in and out of the country (in the form of international loans, overseas investments, etc.).

capital allowances A system of reliefs against a firm's profits chargeable to taxation. Capital expenditure on such items as plant and machinery can be offset against accounting profit for the year when calculating taxable profit. Current procedure is normally for the whole of the expenditure to be offset against the first available accounting profit, although in certain cases a portion of the total expenditure – called an annual allowance – is offset each year against profit for a number of years.

capital assets see **fixed assets**

capital bonus An extra payment by an insurance company as a result of capital gains.

capital clause The clause in a company's Memorandum of Association which details the authorized capital, stating its amount and its composition by share type, quantity and value.

capital employed The sum of all the resources used in a business as represented by their accounting values. The sum may be reduced by the value of current liabilities, loan capital and preference share capital, depending on the purpose for which the computation is to be used.

capital employed, return on The expression, usually in percentage terms, of the relationship between the accounting profit and the value of resources employed in a business. The expression is used as an indicator of a business's performance for comparison with the return yielded by competitive businesses.

capital equipment The equipment in a factory or office which is used to produce goods or to further the business.

capital expenditure The purchasing of long-lasting assets which will be used in the process of production. The accounting treatment is to charge for each year, as an expense, a portion of the total cost of the resource, depending on its expected life. In this case the balance of expenditure is depicted as an asset on the balance sheet. Compare **revenue expenditure**.

capital formation The increase of fixed assets in a company. Gross capital expenditure includes expenditure on the replacement of existing assets.

capital gains A realized profit made by a rise in the value of a capital asset. Such gains may be subject to taxation.

capital gains tax A tax paid on the gains arising from the disposal (whether by sale, exchange, etc) of assets. Certain assets, including private cars and household goods, are exempt from the tax.

capital gearing The relationship between the equity capital and other debt capital of a business. Where the extent of preference and loan capital is proportionately high, the financial structure is termed 'highly geared'.

The manner of capital gearing affects a company's cost of capital and also the profits available for ordinary shareholders.

capital goods see **producer goods**

capital intensive A description applied to those forms of production in which a comparatively large amount of capital equipment is used in relation to the number of employees, e.g. in oil refining.

capitalism An economic system in which there is minimal government interference in production and in which the means of production, distribution and exchange are largely in private hands. According to Karl Marx, capitalism is the stage in political development following feudalism and to be succeeded in turn by socialism and finally by communism.

capitalization 1 The process of converting the reserves built up by a business (chiefly undistributed profits) into paid-up share capital. 2 The accounting treatment given to the capital expenditure of a business.

capitalization ratio An expression of the relationship between each class of a company's capital and its total capital employed.

capital levy A tax on the value of a person's property and possessions.

capital loss A loss made when assets are sold for less than their book value.

capital market The market for long-term sources of capital. Those seeking loans on the capital market are industry, commerce and government. They are supplied by commercial banks, the Stock Exchange and savings institutions such as unit trusts and pension funds.

capital outlay Expenditure on fixed assets, such as property, machinery, office equipment etc.

capital reserves see **reserve capital**

capital transfer tax A tax applied to transfers of assets either by way of a gift during the donor's lifetime or at death. Different rates of tax are applied to these two types of transfer.

captain's entry A document which contains details of cargo being unloaded. The document is prepared by the ship's captain and issued to the customs authorities in order to comply with clearance procedures.

captain's protest An official declaration made by a ship's captain concerning any damage sustained by his ship or cargo during a voyage.

captive market The market for a certain product or service which is provided by only one supplier, the purchaser thus having no freedom of choice.

carat 1 A measurement of the purity of gold. The maximum of 24 carats indicates pure gold. 2 A unit of weight which is used in diamond transactions. It is equal to 0.2 grams.

cargo book 1 A book which is maintained by ship-brokers detailing the goods taken on board ship, whether from land or from a barge. 2 A book which is maintained by the master of a coastal vessel, detailing voyages and goods loaded and discharged.

carnet An international document which allows dutiable goods to pass through countries by road without paying duty until the goods reach their final destination.

carriage 1 The transport of goods from one place to another. 2 The cost of transporting goods.

carriage forward A sale where the customer will pay for the shipping of the goods bought when they are delivered.

carriage free A sale where the customer does not pay for shipping the goods bought.

carriage in and out see **freight in and out**

carriage paid A sale where the seller pays the shipping to the customer's warehouse.

carrier A company which transports goods.

carry over (On the Stock Exchange and commodity markets) to postpone the settlement of an account when due.

cartage The transport of goods by road.

cartel An informal association of companies which pursues policies designed to reduce or eliminate competition between members through the establishment of price, production and marketing controls. Cartels may be national or international, government-owned or privately controlled. One international cartel is OPEC.

cart note A document used by customs authorities when dutiable goods are transported either for shipment or to a warehouse.

carton A light cardboard box for transporting packs of individual items.

cash Ready money in the form of banknotes or coin. The meaning is frequently extended to include documents payable on demand and readily convertible into notes or coin, and deposits held with banks.

cash against documents A term in commercial contracts that indicates that the documents which give title to goods will be released to the purchaser only when the money due for the goods has been paid.

cash-and-carry warehouse Warehouse where purchasers can buy goods retail for cash, paying a lower price than in normal shops.

cash bonus A share of profits earned by an insurance company distributed to policy holders instead of being added to the amount of the policy.

cash card A special plastic card with computer-readable codes, used by a customer to obtain money from a cash dispenser.

cash cow Part of a company or subsidiary company in a group, which provides reliable profits year after year.

cash desk The counter and till at the exit of a shop, where purchasers pay for their purchases.

cash discount A reduction from the specified price of goods granted to the buyer in consideration for payment of the debt within an agreed time period.

cash dispenser A machine outside a bank which automatically provides cash when a special card is inserted and special instructions are given.

cash flow The record of the movement of cash into and out of a company's account, as payments are made and receipts received. See also **negative cash flow, positive cash flow**.

cash on delivery A method of selling goods whereby the customer pays on receipt of the goods, the payment being transmitted to the seller by the carrier of the goods. The Post Office provides a cash on delivery service. Often abbreviated to **C.O.D.**

cash ratio 1 The relationship between a firm's cash and bank position and its current liabilities. 2 The ratio between the cash reserves, i.e. cash in hand and held at the Bank of England, maintained by commercial banks and their total deposits: by custom the ratio is kept at about 8%.

casting vote

casting vote An extra vote given to a chairman at a meeting and exercised by him in the event of votes being equally divided. In common law no casting vote rights exist: the privilege must therefore be conferred by the regulations which govern the meeting, for example, a company's Articles of Association.

casual labour Workers who are hired for short periods and paid in cash.

catalogue A printed list of products and prices, often with illustrations.

caveat emptor 'Let the buyer beware', phrase meaning that the purchaser is responsible for checking that the goods bought are in good condition.

CBI see **Confederation of British Industry**

CD see **certificate of deposit**

central bank A bank, usually state-owned, whose operations are directed by the government as an instrument of financial policy. Typical functions of a central bank include acting as banker to the state and the commercial banks, controlling the note issue and managing the state's currency and credit policies.

certificated bankrupt A person who has been declared bankrupt by a court and who holds official release from his bankruptcy in the form of a certificate issued by the court indicating that it has cancelled his debts.

certificate of damage A document prepared by a surveyor on behalf of dock authorities when goods are received from a ship in a damaged condition. The document gives details of the nature and cause of the damage and is required to assist in the recovery of losses from either the insurance underwriters or the shipowners.

certificate of deposit A certificate from a bank showing that a company has an amount on deposit. Such certificates can be sold at a discount to raise cash at short notice.

certificate of incorporation A document issued by the Registrar of Companies to evidence that a company, having completed the formalities, has been registered and is entitled to the privileges attached to registration.

certificate of inspection A document which certifies that goods are in a sound condition. The document is prepared by an appropriate authority to meet the terms of a contract or the legal requirements of an importing country.

certificate of origin A document which states the country from which goods have been exported. It is prepared by the exporter and is used by the importer to obtain entry for the goods (at preferential rates of duty where appropriate).

certificate of registry A document issued by the Registrar of Shipping which certifies that a vessel has the status of a British ship, having fulfilled the requirements of the Merchant Shipping Acts. The certificate details changes in the ownership or captaincy of the vessel, and is kept on board ship, Also called **ship's register**.

certificate of survey A document which details the external condition of goods landed from a vessel. The document is prepared by a surveyor and issued to support an insurance claim on the goods.

certified accountant An accountant who has passed the professional examinations and is a member of the Association of Certified Accountants.

certified cheque A cheque which contains a statement by the banker on whom it has been drawn that the cheque is in order and will be paid. Also called **marked cheque**.

certified transfer A transfer form which contains an endorsement by a company secretary indicating that share certificates which are the subject of a sale have been received by the company. A certified transfer procedure is used especially when a person sells only part of his holding.

cesser clause A clause in a charter agreement which absolves the charterer from liability on a cargo once this has been loaded on board.

cession The act of giving property to someone, especially to a creditor.

CGT see **capital gains tax**

chain store One store in a large group of similar retail stores.

chairman The person appointed to preside over the board of directors of a company and who bears prime responsibility for the conduct of the affairs of the body of which he is chairman.

chamber of commerce An association of firms engaged in a variety of business activities which seeks to promote and protect the trade interests of member firms. The dissemination of statistical and commercial information is also an important function.

chamber of shipping An association of shipowners and allied bodies which represents the interests of the shipping trade.

Chancellor of the Exchequer (In the United Kingdom) the chief finance minister in the government.

charge account An account which a customer has with a retail store, allowing purchases to be made on credit, the purchaser settling the account at the end of a certain period.

charge card A plastic card, used by a purchaser to buy goods on a charge account.

charges forward A term used on documents to indicate that the carriage charges on goods are to be paid by the purchaser only when he obtains them.

charging order A court order that stops a debtor from disposing of his property. The order allows the property to be sold by the creditor if the debt is not paid within a specified time.

charter A document issued by the Crown, which confers special rights and favours on a body such as a company or an institution. See also **chartered company**.

chartered accountant An accountant who has passed the professional examinations and is a member of the Institute of Chartered Accountants.

chartered company A company which is established by grant of a Royal Charter by the Crown. Originally used to set up trading concerns, Royal Charters are currently applied for to establish a formal company structure for the governing bodies of non-trading organizations, such as professional associations.

charterer A person who hires a vessel or part of a vessel's cargo space. The sum he pays is known as the freight. See also **charter party**.

charter party The contract for the hire of a vessel or of cargo space for the carriage of goods. The contract is made between the shipowner and the charterer, and contains, among other things, details of the charges, lay days allowed and demurrage provisions. See also **demurrage; lay days; time charter; voyage charter**.

chartist A person who studies stock market trends and forecasts future rises or falls.

chattel A moveable resource or property right other than freehold land. Leasehold land is called *chattels real*; other resources are called *chattels personal*.

cheap money Finance and credit facilities which can be obtained at comparatively low interest rates. Governments often create cheap money artificially to stimulate the economy, by increasing the amount of money in the banking system, which in turn lowers interest rates.

check sample A sample which is tested to see if a whole consignment is of the right quality.

cheque A written order to a banker authorizing him to pay a specified sum of money to a person named in the order, to his order or to bearer from funds deposited with the banker. See also **cheque to bearer; cheque to order; crossed cheque**.

cheque guarantee card A plastic card from a bank which a customer presents at the time of signing a cheque, and which guarantees payment of a cheque up to a certain maximum sum.

cheque to bearer A cheque made payable 'to bearer' is one which does not name the payee. Anyone holding the cheque may thus present it for payment. If the cheque is crossed the money payable must be entered into the holder's bank account. If the cheque is uncrossed payment may be paid over the bank counter upon endorsement by the holder. A bearer cheque does not require endorsement when transferring title to the cheque. Compare **cheque to order**.

cheque to order A cheque made payable to a named person or to his order. Payment may be made into the bank account of the payee if the cheque is crossed or over the counter if it is uncrossed. A cheque to order requires endorsement when transferring title to the cheque. Compare **cheque to bearer**.

Chinese walls An arrangement whereby different departments in a large finance corporation do not inform one other of deals they are engaged in, to prevent insider dealing.

chose in action A right to property held by a person who does not possess the property itself but who can recover it by legal action, e.g. mortgages, warrants. Such rights are assignable, although the consent of the person possessing the property is normally required. Compare **chose in possession**.

chose in possession A legal right to property which is held by the person who actually possesses the property. Compare **chose in action**.

c.i.f. see **cost, insurance and freight**

circular letter of credit A letter of credit sent to all branches of a bank which has issued it.

circulating assets Cash and those assets (e.g., debtors and finished goods) which in the short run are transformed into cash. The cash is then used to continue business operations through the purchase of fresh stocks.

circulating capital see **working capital**

circulation 1 Money which is in use by the public. 2 The number of copies of a newspaper or magazine which are distributed.

City Code on Takeovers and Mergers A code of conduct relating to company take-overs and mergers which was compiled in 1968 by leading financial institutions of the City of London including the Accepting Houses Committee, the British Insurance Association, the clearing banks and the Stock Exchange. A panel appointed by the institutions supervises the conduct of mergers and take-overs in relation to the code, but the code currently has no legal force.

Civil List The annual sum voted by Parliament payable to the sovereign for the maintenance of the Royal Household.

classified advertisement An advertisement which is listed in a newspaper under a special heading, such as 'jobs wanted' or 'businesses for sale'.

claw back The taking back of funds or shares which have already been allocated.

clean acceptance see **general acceptance**

clean bill see **document against acceptance**

clean bill of health A certificate indicating that a port is free of infections or contagious disease. The bill is given to a ship's master on leaving port, since it may be required before permission is granted to enter a new port. See also **bill of health; foul bill of health**.

clear (Of a cheque) to pass through the banking system, with money being transferred from the payer's account to that of the payee.

clearance 1 The performance of various functions by shipping agents relating to the forwarding of goods from the port of arrival, including receipt of goods, processing of documents, observance of customs regulations, etc. 2 A customs document which details the charges paid by a ship and certifies that all customs formalities have been observed. The document acts as authority for the ship to leave port.

clearance sale The sale of old stock by retail shops at special inducement prices.

clear days 1 Those days forming the time period to which a contract relates, excluding the days on which the contract begins and ends. 2 Those days forming the time period required for due notification of a meeting, excluding the day on which the notice is given and the day on which the meeting takes place.

clearing banks Those commercial banks which are organized with the London Bankers Clearing House.

clearing house 1 A place where firms with many transactions or dealings among themselves can settle their net receipts or payments. 2 A banking arrangement whereby the joint stock banks settle daily among themselves the debts arising from the cheque transactions of their customers. See also **banker's cheque**.

clear profit The profit remaining after all expenses have been paid.

client A company or individual who uses the services of an advertising agency.

clock card A card on which is recorded the time at which an employee books into and out of his place of work. Where remuneration is on a time basis this record forms the basis of calculation of gross wages. Also called **time card**.

clock in To register entry on works premises by punching or inserting one's clock card.

close company A privately owned company, where the general public may own a small number of shares.

closed shop A business or industry in which only members of the particular and appropriate trade union (or unions) may work.

closing bid The last bid at an auction, the bid which is successful.

closing prices The buying and selling prices quoted for stocks and shares at the end of daily dealings on the Stock Exchange. Compare **markings**.

COBOL A computer-programming language that is especially suitable for commercial uses. Unlike more sophisticated programming languages such as ALGOL, COBOL is based on simple, untechnical words and phrases. Its name is an acronym for *c*ommon *b*usiness-*o*riented *l*anguage.

C.O.D. see **cash on delivery**

cold call A sales visit where the salesman has not made an appointment and the client is not an established customer.

cold start The starting up of a new business where there was none before.

collateral security Documents giving title to property rights which are deposited with a creditor as security for a loan. The documents are returned on repayment of the loan.

collection The receipt of money due, a service performed by a bank on behalf of its customers. The nature of the service may vary, but includes receipt of money due by way of a cheque, bill of exchange, interest on debentures, etc.

collective A group of people who work together in a business which they all own and manage.

collective bargaining The meeting of representatives of employees and employers to establish and set down certain conditions of employment and to provide orderly methods of taking up and settling wage claims, complaints, disputes, grievances, etc.

collective bargaining agency The individual or group which meets an employer and conducts bargaining on behalf of the employees included in the bargaining unit.

collective ownership The ownership of a business by the people who work in it.

collision clause A clause in a marine insurance policy in which the insurers indemnify the insured against damages to another vessel arising from a collision for which the insured ship is responsible. Also called **running down clause**.

collusive tendering The practice by firms competing for contracts of agreeing among themselves on the tender prices each which will submit for a contract. The firms thereby effectively allocate contracts among themselves.

commercial An advertisement on radio or television.

commercial attaché A diplomat attached to an embassy, who represents and promotes the business interests of his country.

commercial bank see **joint stock bank**

commercial property Buildings used for business purposes, such as factories and offices.

commission A fee paid to an agent or representative, which is a percentage of the sales achieved.

committee of inspection A committee appointed by the creditors of a business on its winding-up in order to supervise its liquidation.

commodity exchange A trading centre where the titles to ownership of commodities are dealt in. One of the most important is the London

commodity futures

Commodity Exchange, which is the world's major market for the international sale of sugar, coffee, cocoa, soya bean meal, vegetable oil and wool.

commodity futures Trading in commodities for delivery at a later date.

Common Agricultural Policy The collective agricultural policy of the European Economic Community. It has three main targets: to provide a stable and acceptable standard of living for the farming community; to encourage the modernization of backward farms; to encourage the movement without restriction of agricultural produce within the EEC. Prices are agreed for a range of produce including milk, butter and cereals. These prices are maintained by a levy on imports of agricultural produce from outside the EEC and also by intervention buying on the part of the European Commission when the price of a product is likely to fall below the agreed price.

common carrier A person or business which undertakes the conveyance of goods for hire.

Common Market see **European Economic Community**

common pricing The illegal fixing of prices by several businesses so that they all charge the same price for competing products.

common stock (In US usage) the ordinary capital of a business, in the form either of stock or shares.

Companies Act An Act of the British Parliament which states the legal limits within which companies may act.

Companies House The office where all documents referring to registered companies (such as copies of annual accounts) must be deposited and can be inspected.

company A commercial organization which conducts a business. There are three types of company: chartered companies (those set up by Royal Charter); statutory companies (set up by an Act of Parliament); and registered companies (registered with the Registrar of Companies). The last is the most common and also covers limited companies. In law, a company is a legal entity and can sue, be sued, enter into contracts, etc.

company law The laws which refer to the ways in which companies may work.

company promoter A person who performs the functions necessary to secure the formation or flotation of a company, e.g. arranging the preparation of the Memorandum and Articles of Association, arranging registration of the company and drafting the prospectus.

company secretary The chief administrative officer of a company, whose responsibilities include various statutory duties such as maintenance of the minute book for board and company meetings, maintenance of the share register, and administration of the payment of dividends to shareholders and interest to loanholders.

compensation trading The supply of goods or services as repayment of a debt or liability. It is particularly common when an exporter deals with an importer in a country where foreign currency payments are restricted. The importer will supply the exporter with goods or services which are directly associated with the imported items (direct compensation trading) or with other goods which have no relation to the original transaction (indirect compensation trading).

competition 1 In business, the activity in which firms engage to attract customers to their product or service including price differentials, advertising, after-sales-service, etc. 2 In economics, a system of economic relationships between numerous buyers and sellers of goods and services. Each person acts independently to maximize satisfaction or profit within a pricing mechanism which is subject to the free play of the market forces of demand and supply. See also **imperfect competition; monopoly; perfect competition**.

competitive price A specially low price, which aims to compete with a rival product.

complaints department A department in a company which deals with complaints from customers about products or service.

complaints procedure The official methods of presenting complaints formally by a trade union to management.

complementary good A product which is used in association with another product and whose demand and supply pattern is closely linked with the pattern of the other product, e.g. pen and ink, cameras and film. Accordingly, if the price of one rises, demand for its complement should fall even though its own price is unaltered. See also **joint demand**.

compliance department The section of a securities house which makes sure that confidential information is not leaked.

composite demand The aggregate demand position for a product which has a number of alternative uses and thus a number of separate demands. For example, rubber has several uses and thus demands – for tyres, balls, etc.

composition The payment of a debt at a specified rate of repayment per £ of the debt in full settlement of the debt. See also **compounding with creditors**.

compounding with creditors A means of settling debts whereby the creditors agree to accept payment of a proportion of the full value of what they are owed in full settlement. The proportion of debt repaid would depend on the debtor's assets, and is expressed as a rate per £ of debt, so that creditors receive payment proportionate to the value of what they are owed.

compound interest Interest which is calculated on the original capital sum plus the interest already accumulated. For example, compound interest of 10% on a capital sum of £100:

End of year 1 – interest 10% × 100=£10

End of year 2 – interest 10% × (100+10)=£11

End of year 3 – interest 10% × (100+10+11)=£12.10

Compare **simple interest**.

comprehensive insurance An insurance policy which covers against a large number of possible risks.

Comptroller and Auditor General The person directly responsible to the House of Commons for the examination and audit of the Appropriation Accounts passed by Parliament.

compulsory liquidation The liquidation of a company which is ordered by a court.

computer-readable (Codes or text) which can be read and understood by a computer.

concealment of assets The hiding of assets so that creditors do not know of their existence.

concert party The action of several companies which act together to plan the takeover of another company.

concessionnaire A person who has the right to be the only seller of a product in an area.

conditional order An instruction to a banker authorizing the payment of a certain sum provided that a receipt is obtained from the person to whom payment is to be made.

conditions of employment The terms of the contract by which an individual is employed by a company.

Confederation of British Industry An organization which represents the management of British industry. It was formed in 1965 from the merger of the Federation of British Industry, the National Association of British Manufacturers and the Union of British Employers Confederation.

confirmation note A document sent with a contract or order to be signed by the recipient as an acknowledgement of receipt of the contract, etc. and as confirmation of the contract.

confirmed credit see **documentary credit**

confirming house A business institution which acts on behalf of the overseas buyers of British goods by supplying expert local knowledge of trading conditions, by placing the order for goods, by handling documentation and by providing credit facilities.

conflict of interest A situation where an individual may profit personally from decisions which he takes in an official capacity.

conglomerate A group of subsidiary companies making very different types of product linked together into an organization.

consequential loss Loss arising from the curtailment of business due to fire, etc. Such loss may be insured against. Insurance may cover net profit loss and expenses (such as salaries) which must still be paid despite the disruption. Also called **business interruption**.

consideration The undertaking by one party to perform an action or to pay a sum of money in response to an offer or promise made by another party, thus establishing a valid contract. Generally, consideration must be 'valuable', i.e. it must involve some liability or loss to the party giving the undertaking or involve some benefit or gain for the other party.

consideration money The sum of money exchanged for the purchase of stocks or shares and which is indicated on the share transfer form. This sum need not be the amount received by the original seller of the stocks or shares, because for purposes of stamp duty any subsequent sale must be entered on the share transfer form at its transaction value.

consignee The person who is to receive goods, being either a purchaser or agent.

consignment The sending of goods to an agent who holds them and sells them on behalf of the sender.

consignor The person who owns goods and sends them on consignment to a consignor to sell.

consolidated accounts The accounting statements (profit and loss, balance sheet) required by law from companies owning subsidiary companies. The details of all the companies in the group are merged into a single statement of profit or loss and a single balance sheet. Also called **group accounts**.

consolidated fund The central banking account of the British government, held at the Bank of England, into which all revenues are deposited and from which all expenditures are paid. See also **consolidated fund services**.

consolidated fund services The part of government expenditure which is fixed by statute and does not require annual authorization by Parliament, e.g. the Civil List, judges' salaries, charges on the National Debt. See also **civil list**.

consolidated shipment Shipment of goods from different companies grouped together into a single load.

consolidation of shares The process or result of raising the nominal value of issued shares by merging a number of shares into one share of a larger unit value. The process of consolidation requires the passing of an ordinary resolution at a general meeting of the company, or as otherwise required by the Articles of Association.

consols Funded government securities, redeemable at its discretion but in practice irredeemable. Holders of consols thus purchase the right to receive an annual payment of a stated interest for an unlimited period, although the stock may be sold on the market. Also called **consolidated stock**.

consortium A group of companies (sometimes from different countries, and often offering very different services) who join together to work on a single large project, such as building a railway system or a tunnel.

constant returns A term used to describe the manufacturing situation which arises when the increased quantity of production is directly proportional to the proportional increase in the factors of production employed in creating the product. Compare **diminishing returns**; **increasing returns**.

constructive total loss (In marine insurance) a cargo or vessel damaged beyond economic restoration and whose loss therefore represents a claim on the insurers.

consular invoice An invoice which requires the signature of the consul whose country is to receive exported goods. The procedure is designed to ensure that the laws of the importing country, especially customs requirements, are correctly observed by the exporter.

consumables Goods which are bought and eaten or otherwise destroyed in use. These include foodstuffs or household cleaning products, and also paper and typewriter ribbons used in an office.

consumer credit Credit given to individual purchasers by banks or shops in the form of overdrafts, loans or special credit facilities.

consumer durables Solid items bought by the general public for use in the house. These may include washing machines, cookers and refrigerators, which are likely to be in use for several years.

consumer goods Commodities or services consumed directly to satisfy a want rather than one used to produce something else. Compare **producer goods**.

consumer legislation Laws which have been passed to protect consumers from unscrupulous businesses.

consumer panel A group of consumers who report on goods they have used, so that the manufacturer can improve the goods or use the panel's comments in advertising.

consumer price index (In the United States) the index which measures the rise in retail prices of consumer goods, used as a way of measuring inflation and the cost of living.

consumer protection Laws for the protection of consumers against unfair or illegal traders.

consumer resistance The lack of interest shown by consumers in a certain product, either because of price or bad quality, or because the product is unsuitable for the market.

consumer's behaviour, principles governing A set of factors, revealed by economic analysis, which influence the pattern of the distribution of a consumer's income over the goods and services available. Thus: **1** Expenditure is arranged so that the marginal utility of goods or services equates with price. **2** A fall in price increases consumption, and vice versa. **3** A rise in real income increases consumption, though not necessarily proportionately.

The principles are established upon various economic assumptions, notably that consumers behave rationally and seek to optimize their expenditure patterns.

consumer sovereignty The power which consumers have to dictate to manufacturers the terms on which they will give their custom, such as types of product to be produced and acceptable prices. Sovereignty exists only where there are free market conditions and freedom of choice.

consumer surplus The difference between the price which a consumer pays for a good or service and the highest price he would be prepared to pay in order to secure the good or service.

consumption The using up of goods and services in the satisfaction of one's needs or in the manufacturing process.

container A large box of steel, aluminium, glass-reinforced plastic, etc. in which a large quantity of goods may be transported by road, rail, canal or sea without intermediate loading and unloading. Containers are generally standardized so that uniform handling equipment can be used at ports, freight terminals, etc.

containerization The putting of goods into containers for shipping.

contango A charge paid by the buyer of securities on the Stock Exchange as consideration for the seller's agreement to postpone settlement of the transaction. Compare **backwardation**.

contango day The first day of the Stock Exchange settlement period, during which arrangements for carrying over transactions to the next settlement period may be made.

contested takeover A takeover bid where the board of the company does not recommend the offer to the shareholders and actively fights to prevent the takeover.

contingent liability A liability which may arise if a future event occurs, e.g. an adverse decision in a legal action, dishonour of a bill which has been discounted, etc.

A business is required to state as memorandum information in its published accounts the nature and value of any contingent liabilities.

continuation clause A clause contained in a marine insurance policy wherein the insurers agree to extend the insurance cover on a ship to the completion of its voyage, in circumstances where the policy otherwise elapses while the ship is at sea. The insurers charge a pro-rata rate of premium for extending the insurance cover.

continuous inventory

continuous inventory see **perpetual inventory**

continuous manufacture The production of a single item by continuous process or of multiple standard products all by the same sequence of operations.

continuous stocktaking The checking, counting and recording of physical stock quantities throughout the year. This may obviate the need for one major check at the end of the financial year by spreading the work load over a wider timespan. It also provides updating information for a system of perpetual inventory.

contra account An account which offsets the balance in another account.

contraband Goods which are brought into a country illegally, without paying customs duty.

contract note A brief statement of the terms of a contract relating to the sale of goods.

contra entry An entry made in the opposite side of an account to make an earlier entry worthless, for example a debit against an earlier credit.

contributories Persons who are liable to contribute towards paying a company's debts upon its winding-up. Liability arises through current or recent (i.e. within 12 months) membership of the company, and extends to the balance unpaid on shares held by the member or transferred by him.

control chart see **quality control chart**

controlled economy An economic system where all business activity is planned and directed by the government.

convenience foods Ready-prepared food, bought from supermarkets, in a form which requires little or no further work on the part of the purchaser.

conversion The process of substituting for a loan bearing one rate of interest another loan bearing a different (usually higher) rate of interest. The holders of the original loan are entitled either to convert their holding or to request its redemption.

convertibility The ability of a currency to be exchanged for gold or for another currency. The rate of exchange may be fixed at a certain point, or fixed within certain limits, or may be determined by market forces of demand and supply.

convertible loan stock Loans raised by a company or by a government which carry the right to be exchanged for company ordinary or preference shares or exchanged for a further loan issue. The right of exchange is set at some stated future time, which may be at the redemption date of the loan. Also called **convertible debenture stock**.

conveyance 1 The transfer of property rights relating to land, wills, etc. Such transfers can only be undertaken by qualified legal practitioners, e.g. solicitors. 2 The document which proves such a transfer has taken place.

co-operative A business run by a group of workers who own it and share the profits equally.

copywriter A person who writes the text of advertisements.

corner To obtain a monopoly in the control of the supply of a commodity, stock, share, etc. through large purchases of the item over a period of time.

cornering a bear The procedure undertaken by bulls on the Stock Exchange of purchasing the shares being sold by bears and insisting upon delivery at the settlement date. Frequently the bears have made a fictional sale of shares they do not possess and delivery of the shares on settlement requires purchases on the holders' (i.e., the bulls') terms. The bears are 'cornered' and are then 'squeezed' by the bulls for the purchase price of the stocks or shares.

corn exchange Any large cereal market.

corporate image The idea which a company would like the public to have of it, and which is promoted by the public relations department.

corporate plan An overall strategy adopted by a company for its activities over several years.

corporation tax The tax on profits made by companies.

correlation The state that exists when two sets of variables are found to be linked in some way. See also **regression analysis**.

cost accountant An accountant who analyses the costs of a business to provide information on the basis of which managers can make decisions.

cost centre A physical location, item of machinery, person or process for which costs may be ascertained and used for cost control.

cost-effective Which brings the most profit for the lowest cost.

cost, insurance and freight A term used in commercial contracts to indicate that the contract price includes the cost of the goods, freight charges and insurance to the port of delivery. The seller's responsibility extends up to the arrival of the goods at the port of delivery. Compare **free on board**.

cost-of-living index The index which measures the cost of living by comparing the prices of a range of consumer goods against the prices at an earlier date, and expresses the difference as a percentage.

cost of sales account A ledger account in which is recorded the cost of goods transferred from finished goods stock accounts.

cost of sales adjustment see **current cost accounting**

cost price A selling price which is the same as the price the seller paid for the item, that is either the manufacturing cost or the wholesale price.

cost-push inflation Inflation caused by an increase in the price of goods which itself results from a rise in production costs. See also **demand-led inflation; inflationary spiral**.

counter A flat display surface in a shop.

counterfoil A detachable slip on a share certificate, cheque, postal order, etc. on which details of issue may be recorded and retained for the information of the issuer.

counterpack A display pack which can be placed on the top of a counter in a shop.

countersign To sign a document which has already been signed by another person.

countervailing duty A duty imposed on importers into a country as a response to similar duties imposed by other countries or to ward off unfair competition.

country of origin The country where a product has been manufactured.

country of residence The country in which one lives or is deemed to live for tax purposes. It is possible to be liable to tax as a resident of a country even though that country is not one's normal habitual residence.

coupon 1 A slip attached to a bond which, on presentation to the company on the stated date, entitles the holder to dividend or interest due. A bond will normally contain a number of dated detachable coupons which are formed into a coupon sheet. See also **talon**. 2 A section of an advertisement or leaflet, which the reader cuts out and sends to the advertiser, either requesting further information or ordering goods.

covenant 1 An undertaking to perform or refrain from a specified action. The undertaking acquires legal validity when made under seal. 2 To sign an agreement to pay a sum of money each year by contract. See also **deed of covenant**.

cover 1 The documents of title to a property, marketable securities, etc., which are deposited with a creditor as security on a loan. Cover is frequently requested by stockbrokers who are asked to undertake a speculative transaction on a client's behalf. The documents provide security for the broker's own liability on the transaction. 2 The number of times a public company's profit after tax which is available for dividend distribution exceeds the actual distribution. For instance, if a company has £500,000 profit available but distributes only £100,000, then the dividend is 'covered five times'. Dividend cover is one pointer to a company's health.

coverage 1 The extent or value of risks covered by an insurance policy. 2 The value of provisions held to meet liabilities.

covered bear A person on the Stock Exchange who pursues a bear transaction, i.e. selling, then repurchasing at a lower price, actually having possessed the shares he has originally sold. Also called **protected bear**. Compare **bear squeeze; cornering a bear**.

covering letter A letter sent with documents, explaining why they are being sent.

cover note A document issued by an insurance company prior to the issue of the formal policy on which the company indicates that it has accepted and insured the subject matter from the date stated.

crawling peg exchange rate A structure of rates of exchange for a country's currency in which rates of exchange alter only slowly and in stages from an existing fixed rate to a new predetermined rate. This type of movement permits change without the usual severe financial and economic disruption that accompanies a substantial change of rate in a single step. However, in most cases such a slow process is almost impossible to maintain.

credit 1 The time period extended by a seller (or taken by a purchaser) before payment on a transaction is required. 2 A bookkeeping term for an entry in accounting records which creates a liability or reduces the value of an asset. 3 The provision of funds to customers by means of loans, overdraft facilities, etc.

credit account An account which one business has with another, allowing the first to buy goods or services and pay for them at a later date.

credit balance A balance in an account showing that more money has been received than is owed.

credit base A term which refers to the deposits held by a commercial bank at the Bank of England and to cash held at the commercial bank's branch offices, which together are maintained at a fixed proportion of the bank's total deposits. The balance of deposits are available for the provision of credit by way of advances to customers, loans and investments. The size of the base, currently about 30% of total deposits, affects the extent of a bank's credit formation.

credit card 1 A document issued by a bank or finance house to a subscriber, enabling the holder to obtain goods and services from businesses accepting the card, without payment of cash. Precise arrangements vary but the issuing authority usually guarantees a cheque drawn by the card holder up to a limit stated on the card or guarantees payment in some other way. 2 A card issued by a wholesaler or retailer, enabling the holder to obtain goods or services without immediate payment.

credit clearing A system operated by the commercial banks which provides for the transfer of the account of a customer of one bank of money paid into another bank.

credit control The activities associated with the attempt to regulate the extent of money outstanding to a business through its trading operations. Such activities include the initial determination of a potential customer's ability to meet debts, the establishment of credit limits for customers and the securing of prompt payment of monies due.

credit limit A fixed amount which is the maximum a customer can use as credit.

credit note A document issued by the seller of goods giving an allowance to the purchaser for goods returned, short weight on goods invoiced or an incorrect invoice, etc.

creditor A person whom payment is due for money previously loaned or for goods or services provided without immediate cash settlement. Compare **debtor**.

credit rating The amount which a credit agency states a borrower is capable of repaying.

credit squeeze The process of restricting credit facilities or of making credit more expensive by raising interest rates. The credit squeeze is initiated by governments acting through monetary policies in response to adverse economic conditions. Standard features of a credit squeeze are a limit on bank lending and restrictions on hire-purchase.

credit transfer 1 A means of transacting payments other than by cheque, operated by the commercial banks. Various forms of credit transfer are employed including standing orders. 2 A document made out by a seller with details of bank account number, address, etc, which is completed by the purchaser. The document acts as an instruction to the purchaser's banker to pay the sum stated and to charge the purchaser's account. 3 See **trader's credit**.

critical path analysis see **network analysis**

crossed cheque A cheque on which markings or instructions have been added to ensure that payment may be made only into a bank account. See also **account payee; general crossing; not negotiable; special crossing**.

cross holding A situation where two companies each own shares in each other, as a protection against takeover bids.

cross rate The rate of exchange between two currencies obtained by comparison of each currency with a third or with a number of intermediary currencies. For example, the rate of exchange between the pound and the dollar may be determined by expressing the rate with the franc or deutschmark as intermediaries. If there were a significant difference between the direct exchange rate and the cross rate, then dealers would take advantage of it through buying and selling, and this would bring the two rates together. Also called **arbitrated exchange rate**.

cum all A term used to describe the market quotation of a share which carries all rights.

cum bonus 'With bonus.' The market quotation of a stock or share, the rights to bonus which the share possesses being transferred to the buyer. Compare **ex bonus**.

cum coupon 'With coupon attached.' The market quotation of a bond which is sold with the interest coupon still attached.

cum dividend 'With dividend.' The market quotation of a stock or share, the right to receive the dividend immediately due being transferred to the buyer. Compare **ex dividend**.

cum drawings 'With drawings.' The market quotation of a bond at or near a repayment period, the right to receive any benefits resulting from the repayment being transferred to the buyer.

cum interest 'With interest.' The market quotation of an interest-bearing security, the right to receive the interest payment immediately due being transferred to the buyer. Compare **ex interest**.

cum rights 'With rights.' The market quotation of a stock or share, the rights to any bonus or rights issue offered by the company being transferred to the buyer. Also called **cum new**.

cumulative interest Interest which is added to capital each year.

cumulative preference share A unit of a company's capital which bears a fixed rate of dividend to which the holder is entitled from profits before any distribution among the ordinary share capital.

Preference shares also have a prior claim, in relation to ordinary shares, to repayment in the event of a winding-up. If a dividend is not paid, the right to dividend accumulates until sufficient profits in future years permit the payment of dividends.

currency The money in coins and notes which is legal tender in a particular country.

currency of a bill The time period between the date on which a bill of exchange is drawn and the date on which the bill becomes payable. Where the bill is drawn 'after sight' the time interval begins with the date of acceptance of the bill. When it is drawn 'after date' the time interval begins from the date on the bill.

current account 1 The account held by a bank which records transactions made by a customer. Payments by the customer may be by cheque, interest on the balance of the account being generally not given. Compare **deposit account**. 2 The bookkeeping record of the transactions during an accounting period which relate to a partner or proprietor of a business. The account is frequently maintained where capital accounts are held at fixed amounts. See also **capital account**. 3 In a country's balance of payments, the record of movements of money caused by sales to and purchases from overseas countries.

current assets The working capital of a company, such as stock used to create more income, cash, debts owed to the company, bills receivable, etc.

current cost accounting A system of accounting which is designed to reflect in the determination of profit and in the balance sheet the impact of the change in the input price of goods and services used by the business. Profit is split into two major components in this system.

1 Current cost operating profit – this compares the current cost of resources consumed with revenues earned for a period. It will usually be determined by applying three adjustments (deductions) to the trading profit which is calculated on a historic cost basis.

(a) A depreciation adjustment which represents the difference between the value to the business of the part of fixed assets consumed in the period, and the amount of depreciation charged on a historic cost basis.

(b) A cost of sales adjustment which reflects the difference between the value to the business of stock consumed (usually its current replacement cost) and the cost of stock charged using historic costs.

(c) A monetary working capital adjustment which reflects a charge for the additional debtors and creditors created for the business as a result of increases in the price of goods and services.

2 Current cost profit attributable to shareholders – this is derived from 1 above after an adjustment which reflects the manner in which the business is financed. To the extent that the business is financed by borrowing, the full allowance for price changes made in determining operating profit may not be required. Accordingly, a gearing adjustment adds back a portion of the adjustments made to historic cost profit in 1 above.

The gearing proportion is determined as a percentage thus:

$$\frac{\text{average net borrowing}}{\text{average net borrowing} + \text{average equity}}$$

The current cost balance sheet comprises assets and liabilities as usual, but with assets valued on the basis of 'value to the business'. This generally means that fixed assets and stock will be valued at their current replacement cost (rather than at their historic cost).

current liabilities The debts which a company has to pay within the next accounting period.

current ratio The ratio between the value of current assets and current liabilities.

current standards Standard costs which are established for use over a short time, being related to current conditions. They are generally revised annually if annual budgets are set. Compare **basic standards**.

current yield The dividend calculated as a percentage of the price paid for a share.

curriculum vitae A brief account of an individual's educational qualifications and professional career, usually included in a job application.

customer service department The department in a company which deals with complaints, orders, after-sales service and other services related to customers.

customs barrier A heavy customs duty, imposed with the intention of discouraging imports.

customs bill of entry A document issued daily by the customs authorities, which is divided into two lists. Bill A details ships inwards, with lists of cargoes of port of entry. Bill B details the classification of goods imported and exported.

customs broker A person who clears goods through the customs for a shipping company.

customs clearance A document given by customs officials to a shipper to show that customs duty has been paid and the goods can be shipped.

customs debenture A certificate issued by the customs authorities on which the exporter declares that goods on which he is claiming drawback have actually been exported and are not intended to be reimported.

customs declaration A statement of the nature and value of the contents of a parcel sent by post to a foreign destination, the statement being attached to the parcel.

customs drawback see **drawback**

customs duty A tax which is levied on an imported good, being administered by the Customs and Excise authorities. The tax may be specific or ad valorem. See also **ad valorem; excise duty; specific duty**.

customs entry A document which lists goods being loaded or shipped abroad with details of weight, value and description. It is prepared by an importer or shipper and handed to the customs authorities in order that the customs may clear the goods and authorize importation or shipment abroad.

customs union A single customs region formed by a number of countries in which tariff and other trade restrictions are eliminated as between the member countries and a common tariff policy is maintained against other countries. The European Economic Community is an example of a customs union.

cut-price Sold at a very low price.

cybernetics An inter-disciplinary science drawing on the fields of biology, economics, management, etc. to produce theories relating to the control and management of complex human organizations and machine systems.

cycle billing The preparation and despatch by a firm of customers' statements throughout an accounting period, as opposed to despatching all statements together. The sales ledger is usually split into a logical sequence, e.g. alphabetically, and divided into cycles. In this way peaks and troughs of work are avoided.

cyclical unemployment Unemployment caused by fluctuations in the trade or business cycle. It is usually thought to be short-term in nature and to disappear as the economy revives. It is thus less serious than structural unemployment.

cy près (*French*, 'as nearly as possible'.) An instruction in a court order relating to the administration of a trust whose terms cannot be precisely carried out.

D

damages, nominal A small amount of money awarded by a court or arbitrator as recognition that a breach of contract of a minor character has taken place, and generally where no real loss has been incurred.

dandy note A customs document which allows delivery of the goods stipulated in the document from a bonded warehouse.

data Information in the form of figures and words which is stored in a computer.

data bank A store of information which can be easily accessed and displayed on a computer screen.

data base A store of data which can be processed by a computer to provide information to users.

data processing The systematic sequence of operations performed on facts and figures with the object of extracting or revising information. The term is applicable to both manual and mechanical handling of information, but is now mostly used to signify the manipulation of data by computer.

data reduction The elimination of superfluous or spurious information to minimize the amount of information available for processing without distorting the results.

Data stream An outline information service about stocks, currencies and other financial information.

dawn raid The sudden buying of 15% of the shares in a company at the beginning of a day's trading, as a prelude to making a takeover bid.

days of grace The extra time allowed for payment of a bill of exchange or insurance premium beyond the date on which payment is due. Three days' grace are allowed on bills of exchange.

dead account A ledger account which has a nil balance and has not carried any transactions for a long period, and can be treated as closed and removed from the ledger.

dead freight Freight charges payable by a charterer for cargo space which he does not use, but which he stops others from using.

dead letter 1 A letter which fails to reach its destination and is not reclaimed by the sender. See also **dead letter office**. 2 A document whose terms are invalid or no longer relevant because of lapse of time or changed circumstances since the preparation of the document.

dead letter office A department of the Post Office where undelivered letters are examined to see whether they may be returned to the sender.

dead rent (In mining leases) the rent which is payable according to the terms of a leasing arrangement, whether the leased asset is used or not.

dead security An asset, such as a mine, which has no value as collateral on a loan unless it is utilized.

dead weight A ship's cargo which is charged by weight rather than by measurement and serves the function of ballast, thereby securing the stability of the vessel.

deadweight debt That part of the National Debt which is not offset by productive assets. It was created mainly through wartime loans for the purchase of war materials. Compare **reproductive debt**.

deadweight capacity; deadweight tonnage The maximum amount or weight of cargo which a ship can carry safely.

dealership The position of being a dealer, either retail or wholesale, in a brand product.

dealing floor The area of a securities firm's offices where marketmakers deal in shares.

dear money Finance and credit facilities which are available at a high rate of interest.

death duty see **estate duty**

debenture This is, formally, the document which describes the terms of a loan raised by a company. In general usage it refers to the loan itself. A debenture is a long-term loan rather than part of a company's share capital, bearing a fixed rate of interest and being redeemable at a specified date or else irredeemable. It is usually secured on the assets of a company, which ranks the debenture holder as a preferential creditor in the event of winding up. Registration of debentures is required by law for the charge on assets to be valid. See also **debenture, all monies; debenture, fixed charge; debenture, floating; debenture, naked**.

debenture, all monies A debenture which is secured on both the fixed and floating assets of a company raising a loan. In the event of a winding-up the debenture has prior claim to the assets in order to secure the redemption of the loan.

debenture, bearer A debenture which can be transferred by simple delivery. It is not necessary for notice of transfer to be given to the company which originally issued the debenture.

debenture, customs A certificate issued by customs authorities to exporters in respect of goods which have previously borne import duties. The certificate permits the exporter to claim drawbank. See also **drawback**.

debenture, fixed charge A debenture which is secured on specified fixed assets of the company raising the loan. In the event of a winding up the debenture has a prior claim to the specified assets in order to secure the redemption of the loan.

debenture, floating A debenture which is secured on the circulating assets of the company raising the loan but without attachment to any specified asset. In the event of a winding-up the debenture has a first claim on these circulating assets in order to secure the redemption of the debt.

debenture, naked A debenture which is not secured on any of the assets of the company raising the loan, the debenture holder ranking with other creditors in the event of a winding-up.

debenture, registered A debenture which is repayable only to its registered holder or his personal representative. Any transfer of the debenture to another party must be registered by the company which originally issued the debenture.

debit 1 A bookkeeping entry of an amount owing by the account so debited. It represents value received by that account which may be either a personal or an impersonal account. In Britain, a debit entry is made on the left-hand side of an account. 2 To charge a customer's account with the cost of goods or services supplied.

debit balance A balance in an account which shows a debit, that is more money is owed than has been received.

debit note A document showing that a recipient's account has been debited in respect of some transaction. Thus a customer may raise a debit note on his supplier in respect of defective goods returned. It is usually supplementary to an invoice.

debt/equity ratio The relationship between a company's long-term borrowings and the value of its share capital including reserves.

debtor A person from whom payment is outstanding for money previously loaned or for goods and services provided but not paid for. Compare **creditor**.

debug To test (a computer system) in order to trace faults and eliminate errors, particularly with reference to programs.

deck cargo Any cargo carried on the deck of a ship rather than in the hold.

declaration The announcement of a dividend by the directors of a company, usually made at the annual general meeting. A dividend is not payable until the formal declaration.

deed A written document which formally sets out a contractual agreement. The document requires the signature under seal of the contracting party and delivery to the other party in order to establish a legally valid contract. A deed is required for certain forms of contract, such as mortgages, and for contracts containing an undertaking which is not exchanged for any consideration.

deed of arrangement A deed whereby an insolvent debtor seeks to organize a settlement with his creditors. The deed must be registered and must conform to certain regulations. Various forms of deeds of

deed of assignment

arrangement are common, such as deed of assignment and deed of inspectorship.

deed of assignment A form of deed of arrangement whereby an insolvent debtor contracts to transfer his property rights to his creditors in settlement of their claims upon him.

deed of covenant A deed whereby a person contracts to pay a fixed sum to a named person or organization for a specified period of time. The payer may deduct tax from the gross payment. If the covenant is in respect of a charity and extends for at least four years tax paid may be recovered by the charity.

deed of inspectorship A form of deed of arrangement whereby an insolvent debtor contracts with his creditors to transfer the control of his business to trustees (inspectors) appointed by the creditors. The trustees may wind up the business or continue operations in order to provide funds for the repayment of creditors' debts.

deed of transfer see **transfer deed**

defalcation The illegal use of funds by someone who is not their owner, but has been entrusted with them.

default To fail to carry out the terms of a contract, used especially with reference to the failure to pay a debt.

defeasible Denoting an interest which is terminable if a specified event ever occurs.

defence document A document drawn up by a company which is the object of a takeover bid, in which the company tries to persuade its shareholders not to accept the offer.

deferred annuity An annual income which begins at a specified future date. The income is provided for by the payment of a capital sum at the present date.

deferred bond A bond which is issued at a rate of interest increasing annually up to a specified date, upon which the bond is often exchangeable for active bonds. Compare **active bond**.

deferred charge A charge against profits in respect of deferred expenditure.

deferred credit Any income which is received and credited to an account during one accounting period but is attributable to a subsequent period. Such income is omitted from the computation of profit for the current period and carried forward for inclusion in the profit statement of the relevant period.

deferred creditor A creditor who is owed money by a bankrupt, but who can only be paid after all other creditors.

deferred expenditure Any expenditure not attributable to any one accounting period. An example is expenditure on research and development, which may be charged over those accounting periods which it may benefit. Compare **deferred expense**.

deferred expense An expense incurred during a current accounting period which relates to a subsequent period. Such an expense is omitted from the computation of profit for the current period but carried forward for inclusion in the profit statement of the relevant period. Also called **prepaid expense**. Compare **deferred expenditure**.

deferred liability An amount owing, e.g. a loan, mortgage, etc., but not due for a considerable period.

deferred ordinary shares; deferred stock That part of a company's capital which is entitled to a distribution from profit after all prior claims have been met including preference and ordinary share dividends at a specified rate of dividend.

deferred taxation Taxation which a company must eventually pay but which need not be noted in current tax assessments.

deficiency account A document which records the estimated or actual loss incurred by the owners or creditors of a business. The document is frequently prepared in connection with bankruptcy proceedings. Also called **deficiency statement**.

deficit An excess of liabilities over assets or of expenditure over revenue.

deficit financing The issuing of government securities to provide funds to cover a budgeted excess of expenditure over revenue.

deflation 1 A decrease in the general price level caused by a fall in the economic activity of a country. Output, employment and real prices will all fall. Governments introduce deflationary policies in order to cut the level of imports or to tackle a state of inflation. Compare **inflation**. 2 The conversion of a factor from a nominal to a real amount by allowing for inflation. For example, the comparative level of salaries over a decade can only be meaningful after inflation has been allowed for.

defunct company A company which has been struck off the register of companies because it is not carrying on in business.

degearing A reduction in a company's loan capital in relation to the value of its ordinary shares.

delay theory see **queuing theory**

del credere agent An agent who guarantees to his principal that goods sold by him will be paid for, receiving as consideration an extra commission on the goods sold.

delegation 1 The practice of conferring duties, powers and responsibilities on subordinates while retaining overall responsibility and control. 2 An agent's act of entrusting a person to perform the agent's duties. Such delegation generally requires the permission of the principal but it may also be assumed where necessary to ensure the proper performance of the duties.

delegatus non potest delegare The doctrine that a person to whom powers have been delegated cannot generally delegate them to another, except with the authority of his principal, or unless it is the custom of the trade.

delivered price The price of goods which includes packing and transport.

delivery book A book maintained by the carriers of goods which lists goods forwarded by the carrier. The signature in the book of the person who receives the goods acts as an acknowledgement of receipt and of delivery of the goods.

delivery note A document which is sent with goods to a customer, one copy usually being retained by him and another signed by him and returned to the despatcher as evidence of delivery.

delivery order A document prepared by the owner of warehoused goods authorizing the warehouse to release the goods to the person either named in the document or named thereon by way of endorsement.

demand 1 The quantity of a commodity or service which a person is both willing and able to purchase at a given price. 2 The sum of individual demands aggregated to form the demand situation for a particular commodity or service. This may be graphically represented by a demand curve. 3 The presentation of a debt for payment upon its maturity or according to the terms of an agreement.

demand bill A bill of exchange which is payable on presentation.

demand curve A line linking the quantities of an article a person will buy at every possible price. Price is normally plotted on the vertical and quantity on the horizontal axis. A normal demand curve will slope downwards from left to right.

demand deposit Money in a bank account which can be withdrawn on demand or by writing a cheque.

demand draft A bill of exchange on which no acceptance is required and which is payable on presentation by the holder.

demand-led inflation; demand-pull inflation Inflation that exists when too much money chases too few articles. In effect, their price is 'bid up' (since demand exceeds supply).

demand schedule A list which details the quantity of a commodity or service demanded at different price levels, either for an individual or for the total of individual demands. It can be charted as a demand curve.

demand theory The economic theory that the preferences of customers will affect and control the types of products and services which are available.

demarcation dispute Any dispute between two or more trade unions (rather than between unions and employers) as to whose members should carry out certain functions.

demise charter A contract for the hire of a vessel by the terms of which the charterer engages the crew and assumes full rights and control over the vessel during the charter period.

demography The statistical study of human populations, including their birth rate, death rate, occupational distribution, etc., and the investigation of trends and influences upon their size and classifications.

demonetization The removal of a particular coined metal from use as legal tender.

demonstration The action of showing how a machine works. This may be demonstrating a food processing machine to potential customers in a department store, or demonstrating a new fax machine to a potential business user in his office.

demurrage A penalty charge levied against a contractor or charterer for failing to complete the terms of a contract within the stipulated time. It is contained in the contract and is usually levied at a daily rate on days in excess of the agreed period, excluding legal holidays and Sundays. Compare **dispatch money**.

denationalize To transfer a nationalized industry from public ownership to private ownership.

Department of Trade and Industry British government department dealing with businesses. The secretary of state for trade and industry can intervene in takeover bids by referring them to the Monopolies and Mergers Commission.

department store A shop which has numerous sections, each selling specialized goods and services, in an attempt by the retail unit to satisfy a wide range of customer requirements.

depletion The reduction in the value of a natural resource through the extraction of its reserves. The extent of the reduction is charged as a business expense.

deposit 1 A part-payment of the purchase price of goods, securing the goods for the purchaser provided that the balance of the price is paid within a specified time. 2 The money placed with a bank or similar institution to establish or add to an account. 3 A sum of money paid over as proof of the intention to complete a contract. 4 The placing of goods or securities with a bank, etc. for safekeeping.

deposit account An account formed by the deposit at a bank of money on which interest is normally earned. Withdrawal from the account is permitted only after giving a specified period of notice. See also **current account** (def. 1).

deposit slip see **paying-in slip**

depreciation 1 The reduction in the value of an asset through wear and tear, obsolescence, etc. 2 An accounting device by means of which the value of an asset is converted into an expense for each of the accounting periods during which the asset is expected to contribute value. See also **depreciation fund**.

depreciation fund A bookkeeping record of the annual depreciation charge for an asset. This annual charge represents an equivalent annual figure invested, loaned or used as premiums on an endowment insurance policy. Income from the investment is reinvested and credited to the depreciation fund. The policy of annual investments or premiums, together with reinvestment of income, is designed to provide ready money (by cashing the investments, redemption of the loan or receipt of the endowment) for the purchase of a new asset when the existing asset requires replacement.

depreciation provision The bookkeeping record of the accumulated portions of the cost of an asset which have been written off as an expense in each of the accounting periods with which the asset is associated.

depressed market A market in which there is little trading and in which prices tend to fall.

depression A period of economic crisis with high unemployment and sharp fall in trade.

deregulation The reduction in the level of government controls over the way an industry operates; the deregulation of the airline industry in the United States resulted in lower fares and higher competitiveness between airlines, some of which collapsed or were taken over.

derived demand The demand which exists for a commodity because of its contribution to the manufacture of another product. For example, the demand for steel or wood pulp is derived demand.

destructive tests Quality control tests which by their nature result in the destruction of the sample under test, such as are used in determining breaking strains, inflammability, etc.

devaluation The reduction in the value of a currency in terms of other currencies, usually effected by a change in the official rate of exchange. A policy of devaluation may be employed by a government in order to rectify a severe imbalance in the balance of payments.

developing country A country whose economic activity is at a basic and low level, characterized by a concentration on agriculture, little or no industrial investment, and low living standards, with high fertility and mortality rates.

development area An economically depressed area of a country to which the government encourages firms to move through financial and other inducements. Such areas are often those with traditional heavy industry, e.g. coal mining and steel production.

development cost The expense incurred by a business on a product or on an improved method of production from the research stage to the implementation of formal production, including cost of design, testing, test production and trial runs.

deviation 1 The circumstances in which an insured vessel may alter course without affecting its insurance cover. These include altering course for the safety of the vessel or its cargo, to save life or to save a distressed vessel. 2 (In statistics) the positive square root of the variance of a sample.

dies non A day on which business cannot be transacted on the Stock Exchange.

difference The practice of both buying and selling shares within a single account period, taking profit on the price difference and avoiding the need to handle the securities at the settlement.

differential costing A method of comparing products, projects or policies by reference to and evaluation of the elements of cost which are peculiar to each product, project or policy or differ as to their incidence.

differential piece rate system A method of remuneration of employees which relates earnings to work produced, remuneration being based on an increasing scale of payments for units produced.

dilution of equity A situation where the ordinary share capital of a company has been increased, but without an increase in assets, with the result that each share is worth less than before.

diminishing returns A manufacturing situation which exists when production expands at a rate which is less than proportionate to the rate of increased use of the factors of production. This usually occurs in conditions of maximum capacity or excessive use of facilities, producing breakdowns, wastage, etc. Compare **constant returns; increasing returns**.

direct assistance The aid given to the liquidity position of discount houses through the purchase of bills of exchange from them by the special buyer of the Bank of England. In providing assistance the special buyer prevents a possible rise in interest rates, which might occur through lack of liquidity.

direct cost An element of material, labour or overhead expense which is directly associated with a particular unit of production. Major direct costs are production wages, raw material costs and power costs. Compare **fixed cost**.

direct costing see **marginal costing**

direct debit A transaction in banking by which the account of a debtor is charged with a claim at the instigation of the creditor directly.

direct exchange The process of exchanging two currencies at their related rate of exchange without recourse to a third currency for the computation of the optimum exchange rate. Compare **cross rate**.

direct labour cost The labour cost which can be indentified with, and allocated to, cost centres or cost units. Also called **direct wages cost**.

direct mail advertising An advertising technique whereby the advertising message is sent by post to a wide range of potential customers.

direct marketing The promotion of products or services directly to the potential customer by mail or TV advertising, without using retail outlets.

direct materials cost The cost of materials which can be identified with, and allocated to, a cost centre or a cost unit.

director A person who takes part in the management of a company or other organization at the highest level. The first directors of a limited company are named in the Articles of Association. Subsequently directors are appointed by the shareholders as specified in the articles. A director acts as trustee for the company's property on behalf of its shareholders. Various statutory obligations are demanded of the body of company directors, including ensuring the maintenance of proper books of account and the submission of annual accounts to the shareholders and the Registrar of Companies.

directors' emoluments All sums of money and benefits in kind received by directors.

directors' fees Payments made to directors in respect only of their role as directors. Such payments do not include their salary or other benefits.

directors' report A statement compiled by the directors of a company and required by law to be submitted with the annual accounts to the Registrar of Companies and to shareholders. The statement must, among other things, provide details of the company's affairs, its principal activities, the names of directors and their shareholdings, the recommended dividends and any proposed transfer to reserves.

direct selling The selling of products or services directly to the customer, such as by door-to-door salesmen.

direct taxation Taxation levied on individuals, assessed on their income from a variety of sources, such as wages, salaries, profits, and interest. The tax may be collected from the individuals personally or deducted from their earnings and collected by their employer. See also **indirect taxation; PAYE**.

direct wages cost see **direct labour cost**

dirty bill see **foul bill of health**

dirty money The extra remuneration paid to workers for handling difficult or objectionable cargo or for working under physically disagreeable conditions.

disappreciation The reduction of the price of a product to its long-term equilibrium level, usually a delayed corrective reaction to a previously excessive price rise.

discharge The release of a person from his obligation.

discharged bankrupt A bankrupt who has been released by a court order from further liability to pay off debts which were the subject of bankruptcy proceedings.

discharge of a bill The nullification of all rights and liabilities on a bill of exchange as by payment, cancellation, etc.

disciplinary procedure The method, laid down in an agreement between management and workers, by which a worker is warned if his work is unsatisfactory.

disclaimer A legal refusal to accept responsibility.

discount 1 The charge or profit made by a bank or other institution as consideration for the purchase of a bill of exchange before its maturity. The charge is expressed as a rate of interest applied to the face value on the bill and the time before maturity. 2 The reduction in the price of a product or service, either as part of trade practices, or in order to sell more units at a faster rate.

discounted value The difference between the face value of a share and its lower market price.

discount house A financial institution whose principal activities are the discounting of bills of exchange and investment in treasury bills. It is financed chiefly with funds borrowed from the commercial banks.

discounting 1 The evaluating of future income flows in terms of their present value. 2 The process of obtaining payment on a bill of exchange before its maturity, taking a lower sum than the face value of the bill. This difference represents the 'discount' on the bill. See also **discount**. 3 The anticipation of a movement in the price especially of a commodity or security which, through the resultant buying or selling activities, induces a price movement, although not necessarily the same as that anticipated. The process of anticipating price movements is held to assist the evening out of daily fluctuations in many markets.

discount market The market formed by dealings relating to bills of exchange and treasury bills, operated by financial institutions, especially discount houses.

discount store A commercial retail/wholesale organization which sells goods to the public at reduced prices, chiefly for cash.

discretion 1 A client's instruction to a broker to complete a transaction for stocks or shares above or below the price specified by the client. 2 The extent of the variation from the specified price authorized by the client.

discretionary order An order made to a broker for the purchase of stocks or shares, etc., to a specified value, but allowing the broker to select the stocks or shares. The order is usually accompanied by the appropriate cover.

discriminating monopoly A monopoly which increases its profit by selling its product at different prices to different sections of its market. One such discriminating monopoly is the Electricity Board, since it levies different prices for commercial and industrial consumption.

discrimination see **price discrimination; trade discrimination**

diseconomies of scale A situation in which the production of larger quantities of a product involves higher costs, as if new equipment is purchased or more workers engaged.

disguised unemployment Unemployment among those who want to work but who do not appear in unemployment figures for various statistical reasons. They include housewives, young school-leavers and the handicapped. Unemployment figures invariably underestimate the number of unemployed but by how much is a matter of dispute.

dishonour The refusal either to pay a bill of exchange when it is presented for payment upon maturity or to accept a bill of exchange which has been drawn on oneself. The holder of the bill may attempt to recover his debt from any party to the bill, having first complied with the various procedures required upon dishonour, such as giving proper notice of dishonour to the drawer and each endorser.

disinflation The process or policy of removing pressures on the economy which are forcing prices upwards and the real value of the monetary unit downwards. Pressure may be removed by curtailing expenditure through credit restrictions and a dear money policy, and by taxation.

disinvestment The reduction in capital assets by not replacing old equipment. The reluctance on the part of the investor to invest in new industry.

disk drive The part of a computer which spins the magnetic disk and positions the read/write head.

dismissal The termination of an employee's contract of employment. Such termination must usually be accompanied by the appropriate notice or payment in lieu of notice. See also **dismissal, summary**.

dismissal procedure The correct and legal method by which an employee is dismissed, following the rules laid down in the contract of employment.

dismissal, summary A dismissal which is effective immediately and without notice or payment in lieu of notice. Such termination must be justified by the employer, common grounds being disobedience, theft, etc.

dispatch money An allowance paid to a contractor or charterer for completing the terms of a contract within the stipulated time. Compare **demurrage**.

dispatch note A document completed by the sender of a parcel to post to a foreign country giving such details as the name and address of the addressee, and the name of the sender.

display advertisement An advertisement which is designed to attract the attention of the reader, being set in larger type and usually surrounded by a box.

disposable personal income The income which an individual has left, after tax and social security contributions have been deducted.

dissentient member Any shareholder of a company who has voted against a successful special resolution recommending a company reconstruction. He may require the company liquidator to purchase his shares at an agreed price or at a price to be determined by arbitrators.

dissolution The termination of a partnership, occasioned for example by the voluntary retirement of a partner, the completion of the terms of the partnership agreement, and the legal dissolution on numerous grounds following an application to the court by a partner.

distraint A legal remedy available to a creditor to recover outstanding debts, especially rent due, by which he can enter premises, seize the debtor's property and hold it until the debt is paid.

distress The act of seizing a debtor's property in order to secure payment of outstanding debts.

distress merchandise Goods which have been seized and are sold to pay a company's outstanding debts.

distribution 1 The business activity concerned with transporting finished goods to customers. 2 A payment made by a company to its shareholders in the form of cash dividend, a bonus share issue, etc. 3 The process of allocating the resources of a person who has died without making a will after debts and costs have been met. 4 A field of economic study which examines the forces determining the payments received by the various factors of production.

distributor A person or company which transports goods from a warehouse to the customer. Also, a company which stocks and sells goods for an overseas manufacturer.

district audit The examination of the accounting records maintained by local authorities by an official appointed by the central government. Accounting records are examined both for accuracy and for validity of expenditure.

Any expenditure by the authority which is beyond its powers may be disallowed, the council members responsible for authorizing the expenditure being held personally liable.

diversification Expansion of a firm into an unrelated industry. Reasons for diversification include risk-spreading, the avoidance of seasonal trade fluctuations, or ensuring increase of growth-rate. Diversification, unlike vertical integration with which it otherwise has similarities, cannot increase monopoly power. See also **horizontal integration; vertical integration.**

diversity factor The probability that a number of pieces of equipment will be used simultaneously. If, for example, the expected utilization of 100 units is 20 units at any one time the diversity factor is 1:5.

dividend 1 A share of a company's profits distributed to shareholders, usually expressed as a percentage of the nominal value of shares. A dividend need not be paid, although the right to a dividend may be accumulated. See **cumulative preference share**. **2** A share of the debtor's realized assets, distributed to creditors, usually expressed as a rate per £ of debt. **3** The annual interest distributed to holders of the National Debt.

dividend cover The ratio of the dividend paid to the net profit out of which it is paid.

dividend mandate An authorization given by a shareholder to the company to pay dividends into the shareholder's bank account.

dividend stripping The practice of distributing accumulated reserves to shareholders as dividends from funds provided by the sale of assets.

dividend warrant A cheque issued by a limited company to pay a dividend to a shareholder. It is accompanied by a document showing the net dividend payable to shareholders, the tax liable on the dividend and whether or not it has been deducted.

dividend yield The dividend expressed as a percentage of the price of a share.

division of labour A method of organizing the production process which involves the specialization in separate operations by different individuals. This assists the expansion of output through the development of operator skills and dexterity, the minimizing of delays involved in transferring to other operations and the potential for mechanical assistance arising from the simplification of work. Such concentrated monotonous work arising from specialization may, however, have adverse psychological effects on operatives.

dock warrant A document, completed by a warehouse official of a dock authority on the instructions of the owner of goods, which details the weight of goods warehoused, the date from which rent is chargeable, and to whom the goods are to be delivered. The warrant gives title to the goods and, on presentation of the warrant, the goods are released from the warehouse. Property in the goods may be transferred by endorsement of the warrant.

document against acceptance A bill of exchange whose documentation of title to the goods must be surrendered to the drawee when he accepts the bill. Also known as **clean bill**.

document against payment A bill whose documents of title must not be surrendered until the bill has been paid.

documentary bill A bill of exchange with documents to title to goods, such as the bill of lading, invoice and insurance policy, attached as security. The documents are exchanged only when the bill is accepted or paid.

documentary credit A credit facility extended, usually by banks, to importers whereby the bank agrees to settle creditors' accounts. Settlement chiefly involves payment on bills of exchange drawn on the importer, the bank requiring that certain documents of title are presented with the bill and that certain other conditions are complied with. Also called **confirmed credit; irrevocable credit.**

dole Money paid by the government to the unemployed.

dollar gap The postwar international shortage of dollars, which were required to finance an adverse trading position with the United States or dollar area. Traditionally, reserves were run down or loans were made by the United States, but the international currency problem was eased by the forms of assistance operated by the International Monetary Fund and other institutions.

dollar stocks Shares in US companies, traded on the London Stock Exchange.

domicile A country where an individual is deemed to live permanently or where a company has its registered office.

domiciled bill A bill of exchange whose payment is to be made other than at the acceptor's usual place of business. The location of payment is notified by the acceptor on the bill at the time of acceptance.

door-to-door selling The direct selling of goods or services by salesmen calling on potential customers in their homes, used in particular for selling items of household necessity.

dormant balance An account held at a bank on which no transactions have been recorded over a long period of time.

dormant partner see **sleeping partner**

double account system An accounting system prescribed by law for public undertakings, which maintains separate balance sheets for capital and general transactions.

double entry A system in bookkeeping of recording transactions which reflects the duality of each transaction as it affects business, that is, the receipt of value in exchange for the giving of value. An account is debited with that part of a transaction which concerns the receipt of value, and an account is credited with that part of the transaction which concerns the giving of value. The method of double entry facilitates the compilation of accounting data, especially the profit and loss, and balance sheet statements.

double option An arrangement which gives an investor two rights – to buy or to sell shares at a given price at a future date, the choice of right to be exercised depending on circumstances at the future date. The investor may choose not to take up either right, in which case he pays only the fee which had been charged for the double option.

double taxation relief A system of tax relief extended to individuals and businesses by arrangements with other countries, designed to prevent income from abroad being taxed twice; as income earned in a foreign country being taxed by that country, and as income of the recipient in the United Kingdom taxed by the UK tax authorities.

Commonly a rate of tax is applied by the UK authorities which brings the total tax payable to that level which would apply if the normal UK tax rates were applied to the whole income.

Dow Jones Industrial Average The index of share prices on the New York Stock Exchange, based on a group of 30 major companies.

downmarket Aiming at a less wealthy sector of the market, entailing higher unit sales at lower unit prices.

downside factor The possibility of an investment leading to a loss.

down time The time during which machines or plant are not available for operating because of mechanical failure or non-availability of labour or materials.

downturn A movement towards lower prices or lower trading activity.

draft 1 An order to a bank to pay a specified sum to a named person or to the bearer of the order. 2 A bill of exchange. 3 An allowance granted by manufacturers or wholesalers to retailers for losses arising through evaporation, etc.

draw The preparation of a bill of exchange or other order instructing a bank to pay a sum of money.

drawback A rebate of the duty paid on imported goods allowed to manufacturers, etc. who subsequently export the finished article. See also **debenture, customs**.

drawee The person on whom a bill of exchange is drawn, requiring him to pay a specified sum of money at a future date. The drawee does not assume liability on the bill until he has accepted it. In the case of a cheque, the drawee is the bank which holds the account of the drawer.

drawer The person who prepares a bill of exchange which, once accepted, may be retained by the drawer until maturity or may be discounted for earlier payment. If the bill is dishonoured the drawer may be liable on the bill.

drawn bill A foreign bill of exchange which may be negotiated by the drawer directly with the drawee's banking agent. Compare **made bill**.

drawn bond A bond which ceases to bear interest once its redemption date, advised to holders, has been exceeded.

drop shipment Shipment of goods direct to a customer's warehouse, without going through an agent or distributor.

drug on the market A situation in a market where a commodity is in excess supply and is therefore unsaleable.

dry goods Goods such as textiles, drapery, etc., as opposed to perishables, such as grocery articles.

DTI See **Department of Trade and Industry**

due date The date on which a debt is payable, especially with reference to bills of exchange. For documents containing payments specified as 'on demand', 'at sight' or 'on presentation' the due date occurs whenever the debt is presented for payment, without days of grace. Other documents have a specified date inserted on the document for payment, in which case days of grace are allowed beyond the date specified.

dummy pack An empty pack which is used for display purposes.

dumping The practice of selling a product in different markets at different prices. The term is more generally used to describe the practice of selling goods abroad at prices below the cost of production or below the competitive price level in order to achieve some income. Dumping is one of the few practices which, it is generally agreed, may be protected against by the imposition of import duties.

duopoly A market situation in which only two sellers operate, each having a significant impact on the market. The reactions of each seller must always be considered by the other when deciding upon pricing policy, etc.

duopsony An industry with only two buyers and many sellers. It is the direct opposite of a duopoly.

durables; durable goods Goods which may be expected to have a long period of use, such as washing machines, cookers, etc.

Dutch auction A method of selling goods by public sale, the auctioneer beginning with a high price, which is reduced until an offer is made. See also **auction**.

duty-free shop Shop at an airport or at a frontier between two countries, where goods are sold without duty being payable.

duty paid A price quoted for goods, which includes the payment of import duties.

E

e. and o.e. (errors and omissions excepted) A phrase, without legal significance, included on business invoices and statements to indicate that the business is not liable on a clerical error or omission but reserves the right to amend details.

earmark To reserve allocated funds for a special purpose.

earned income Any income from which is derived from employment, in the form of wages or salaries. It thus excludes income from shares, savings, rents, etc.

earnest money A sum of money handed over by a prospective party to a contract as evidence of his intention to proceed with and complete the contract.

earning potential 1 The amount of dividend which it is expected that a share should produce. 2 The amount of money which a person is capable of earning.

earnings 1 Any remuneration from employment in the form of wages or salaries. 2 The profits of a business, either before or after tax.

earnings per share The relationship between business earnings after taxation and preference dividend and the number of ordinary shares. This measurement is a useful guide to the performance of a company.

earnings profile 1 The forecast phasing of revenue for each year of the expected life of a project. 2 A record of the profits after tax and preference dividends of a company over a period of years.

easement A legal right to the use of property, which is enjoyed by a person or persons other than the owner (a right of way) or owned in common (as is air).

easy money policy A government economic policy which encourages the expansion of the economy by making money more easily available for investment.

easy terms The terms of repayment of a loan which is either spread over a long period or is granted at a low rate of interest.

EC see **European Economic Community**

ECGD see **Export Credit Guarantee Department**

ECI see **Equity Capital for Industry**

econometrics The study of the statistics of national economies.

economic cycle The period during which an economy expands, then slows down, and then expands again.

economic growth The process of development and the policies designed to achieve economic development. Growth may be measured by a variety of criteria, such as per capita improvement in living standards, increase in the volume and value of capital investment, production, etc.

economic life The period over which an asset is expected to contribute value. It is influenced by such factors as the rate of usage, obsolescence, etc.

economic man A hypothetical individual who always behaves rationally in the disposition of his resources, seeking to obtain the maximum satisfaction of his wants. The concept does not necessarily describe the nature of consumer behaviour in reality but is useful in economic analysis.

economic model A computerized plan of a country's economic system used by governments and research institutes to forecast future economic trends.

economic order quantity That quantity of material or items which is most economic to order and to stock, taking into account all relevant factors. Thus, it would reflect quantity discounts, costs of tied-up capital, spoilage, transport costs, etc.

economic rent The amount which must be paid for a unit of a factor of production in order to retain its use. It is equivalent to the amount of money that factor of production could earn in its most profitable alternative use.

economics The scientific study of human behaviour relating to the allocation of resources in order to satisfy personal and national requirements.

economic sanctions Restrictions on trade with a country, imposed by another government with the aim of changing that country's political system or of restricting that country's activities on the international scene.

economy 1 The legal, political and social framework within which economic activity is conducted. 2 The process of satisfying maximum wants through the optimum use of personal and business resources and effort.

economy of scale The benefit of an increase in production through a lower unit cost which results from expansion of the size either of inputs of factors of production or of operations.

Production economies may arise from mechanization which is facilitated by specialization and simplification of procedures. Technical economies may arise through the use of large plant. Additionally, other economies may arise from a large scale of operation, as through quantity discounts on purchases or the establishment of specialized activities such as market research. See also **constant returns; diminishing returns; increasing returns**.

economy pack A specially large pack of a common domestic item, such

ECU

as washing powder, which appears to give better value for money than the normal packs.

ECU see **European Currency Unit**

EDP see **electronic data processing**

EEC see **European Economic Community**

effective demand The actual demand for a product at the price at which it is for sale.

EFTA see **European Free Trade Association**

EFTPOS Payment system where a customer pays for purchases at a cash desk with a card similar to a credit card, but which automatically debits the customer's bank account and credits the store with the value of the sale. Abbreviation for **electronic funds transfer at point of sale**.

EGM see **extraordinary general meeting**

elasticity A measurement in economics of the degree of response of a change in one factor to a change in a related factor, expressed in a price-demand, price-supply or demand-income relationships.

Where a change in one factor occasions a proportionately equal but opposite change in the other factor, elasticity is described as unitary. Where the response is greater than the original change then the situation is described as elastic. Where the response is less than the original change the situation is described as being inelastic.

elasticity of demand The extent of a response of demand for a product to a change in its price. It may be expressed mathematically by dividing the percentage change in demand by the percentage change in price.

Elasticity of demand is affected by such factors as the availability of substitutes and the nature of the product, i.e. a necessity or a luxury.

elasticity of income The extent of a response of demand for a product to a change in the level of personal or collective income.

It may be expressed mathematically by dividing the percentage change in demand by a percentage change in income.

elasticity of supply The extent of a response of supply for a product to a change in its price. It may be expressed mathematically by dividing the percentage change in supply by the percentage change in price.

electronic data processing The processing of data (financial, scientific, etc.) using electronic equipment, chiefly computers.

electronic funds transfer at point of sale see **EFTPOS**

electronic mail A system of sending messages from one computer terminal to another, using telephone lines.

electronic point of sale see **EPOS**

eligible paper Those forms of investments, such as treasury bills, short-term gilt-edge securities and first-class bills of exchange, which are held by discount houses and on which the Bank of England is prepared to advance money.

embargo 1 A prohibition placed on goods or ships entering or leaving a country. The prohibition may be aimed specifically at one country or may be general in its application. 2 A court order which prevents the removal or disposal of property while relevant judicial proceedings are being conducted.

embezzlement **The unauthorized appropriation of money belonging to an employer or his business.**

emoluments The pay, salary or fees of directors who are not employees of a company.

employee share ownership plan A scheme to encourage employees to acquire shares in the company that employs them, the scheme being a tax benefit to both the employee and the company.

employers' association An association of firms within an industry, which seeks to develop common policies and represent members' interests in negotiations with other organizations.

employer's liability The legal responsibility which an employer bears for the negligent actions of his employees which cause injury to fellow employees.

employment exchange see **job centre**

EMS see **European Monetary System**

enclosure A sheet of publicity matter, a circular or other document put into an envelope with a letter.

endorsement 1 The act of writing one's signature on a document e.g. a bill of exchange, signifying the transfer of title in the document to another person. The signatory (endorser) is thereby liable to all subsequent endorsers and holders of the document in the event of non-payment of the bill on its maturity. 2 A note showing that someone (usually a celebrity) has used a product and approves of it, used as advertising copy for the product.

endowment mortgage A mortgage backed by an endowment policy. The borrower repays the interest on the mortgage, but not the capital, which is covered by an endowment policy for the amount of capital borrowed.

endowment policy A contract made with an assurance company whereby the company agrees to pay a fixed sum at a specified future date or upon the death of the assured in return for the payment of an annual premium.

end product A manufactured product which is the result of a production process.

end user The person who actually uses the product which has been bought. In a business situation, the end user may well not be the same as the purchaser of the product.

engineered cost A business expense, for example material or labour,

entered in; entry in

which is part of the specification for a product. Compare **managed cost**.

entered in; entry in see **entry; entry for home use; entry for warehousing**

entered out, entry out see **entry; specification**

entrepôt 1 A centre for the distribution of goods over an extensive area. 2 A commercial port whose principal activities relate to the re-exportation of goods previously imported without the imposition of duties. 3 A place similar to a bonded warehouse where dutiable goods may be stored.

entrepreneur A person who both manages a business and assumes the financial risks involved in business, standing to make a profit or to lose the capital he has invested. He is considered by conventional economic theory to be the prime catalyst in the market system.

entry The procedures involved in securing passage for a vessel either in or out of port and in obtaining permission to unload or load cargo. Entry requires the observation of customs regulations and the completion of the appropriate customs documentation.

entry for home use The customs procedures required to secure permission to unload dutiable goods upon which the duty is to be paid immediately. If in the examination on prime entry of the goods it is found that insufficient duty has been paid then a further entry procedure, post entry, is required.

entry for warehousing The customs procedures required to secure permission to unload goods and place them in a bonded warehouse.

EPOS A payment system where the cash desk in a store is fitted with electronic equipment such as bar code readers and light pens. These automatically record sales and alter the stock quantities as items are purchased. Abbreviation for **electronic point of sale**.

equilibrium price The price at which quantity demanded equals quantity supplied. In a free market the price is set by reference to the interactions of the forces of demand and supply. In this situation there is no impetus for the supplier to alter his output or for the consumers to change their buying habits.

equity 1 The total interest in a business, including capital and reserves, which is attributable to the ordinary shareholders, partner, or proprietor. 2 A body of legal principals and remedies which have been developed through the application of the concept of justice to the operation of statute and common law. Principles of equity are applied in specific legal areas, especially in securing the performance of the terms of a contract.

equity capital The amount of a company's capital which is owned by the shareholders in the form of ordinary shares.

Equity Capital for Industry A fund established in 1976 by financial institutions of the City of London. Finance in the form of loans and share stakes is provided for medium-sized or small manufacturing companies.

equity of redemption The right of a mortgagor to recover his legal interest in the property even after the stipulated time for repayment of the loan has elapsed. The loan, interest and costs must however be repaid.

ergonomics The scientific study of people at work. It attempts to obtain greater efficiency from both men and machines through improvement in the design of machines, in work routines and in the working environment.

errors and omissions excepted see e. and o.e.

escalator clause; escalation clause A clause in a contract which allows for regular price increases because of increased costs.

escape clause A clause in a contract which allows one of the parties to avoid carrying out the terms of the contract under certain conditions.

escrow The safe keeping of money by a third party.

escrow account An account where money is held in escrow until a contract is signed, or until goods are delivered.

ESOP see **employee share ownership plan**

establishment charges The costs of people and property in a company's accounts.

estate 1 The resources of a person, especially a deceased person. 2 The nature of a person's legal interest in land.

estate duty A tax on the value of property which passes to others on the death of a person. This form of tax has been replaced in the United Kingdom by the Capital Transfer Tax.

estimate A price quoted for a good or service before a contract is made. In certain circumstances the estimate is a valid contractual price.

estoppel A legal concept which prevents a person denying knowledge of a particular theory, or from denying a relationship with another person, in circumstances whereby his conduct has caused others to believe he has such knowledge or relationship.

Eurobond A long-term loan (usually for more than five years) to a government or company made by a foreign bank or banks.

Eurocheque A cheque drawn on a British bank which can be cashed in a bank in another European country.

Eurocurrencies Currencies of European countries used for trade within Europe, but outside their countries of origin.

Eurodollars Dollar funds held in European commercial banks. The funds provide a source of short-term international loan finance and supplement the currency reserves of the European central banks.

Euromarket 1 The European Community seen as a potential market for goods or services. 2 The trading market in Eurocurrencies.

European Currency Unit The unit of account used by the European Monetary System. Its value is equal to the aggregated value of the member-nations' currencies.

European Economic Community A customs union comprising 12 countries: Belgium, Denmark, Greece, Ireland, France, Italy, Luxembourg, the Netherlands, Portugal, Spain, the United Kingdom and West Germany. The purpose of the Community is to achieve eventual unification through the integration of economic and political activity.

European Free Trade Association An association which originally comprised seven countries: Austria, Norway, Portugal, Sweden, Switzerland, Denmark and the United Kingdom. EFTA was designed to eliminate tariff and trade restrictions between member countries, each, however, retaining its own trade policies in relation to non-member countries. The entry of the United Kingdom and Denmark into the EEC in 1973 undermined EFTA as a free trade area.

European Monetary System A system designed primarily to limit the fluctuations of exchange rates of member-countries within prescribed limits. Agreement must be reached in advance before a currency can be revalued or devalued to a greater extent than permitted under the system, and financial support for currencies is provided by the European Monetary Fund to which all members contribute. The EMS was formed in 1978 and its original members were Belgium, Denmark, France, Luxembourg, the Netherlands and West Germany. Ireland and Italy joined later the same year. The United Kingdom has not as yet joined.

evasion see **tax evasion**

evolutionary operation A technique for plant improvement by experimentation on the plant while causing the minimal disturbance to normal operating conditions.

ex all 'Without the attached rights to dividend, bonus issue, new issue of shares etc.' A term used to describe the market quotation of a stock/share where such rights are retained by the seller. Compare **cum all**.

ex ante A description of a future event which has been extrapolated from present data. Compare **ex post**.

ex bonus 'Without the attached right to the bonus just announced.' A term used to describe the market quotation of a stock/share where such a right is retained by the seller. Compare **cum bonus**.

ex capitalization 'Without the right to any attached bonus or scrip issue.' A term used to describe the market quotation of a share where such a right is retained by the seller.

exceptional items Items in a balance sheet which do not appear each year. Such items may be redundancy payments, sale of property, etc.

excess capacity A situation where a producer is able to make more product than he is actually producing.

excess profits Profits which are considered to be more than is normal for the type of business concerned.

exchange 1 The process of transacting business through the giving and receiving of value by the contracting partner. 2 The location where merchants transact business, particularly in a specialized commodity, such as a stock exchange or a corn exchange.

exchange at a discount The exchange rate between two currencies in circumstances where the current market rate of exchange for one currency is below its official rate. This may occur when a devaluation is believed to be imminent and consequently no one wishes to suffer a loss by holding the currency.

exchange at a premium The rate of exchange between two currencies in circumstances where the current market rate of exchange for one currency is above its official rate. This can occur with hard currencies in areas such as Eastern Europe and the Third World which suffer from a lack of foreign exchange.

exchange control The governmental regulation of foreign currency transactions in order to ensure the strength and stability of the national currency and to protect gold and foreign currency reserves.

exchange equalization account A fund in the United Kingdom which comprises the country's sterling, gold and foreign currency reserves and which is managed by the Bank of England.

   The fund finances transactions for the purchase or sale of sterling, which are conducted to stabilize short-term fluctuation in the rate of exchange of sterling.

exchange of contracts The point in a sale of a property when the buyer and seller both sign the contract of sale which then becomes binding.

exchange premium Any extra charge which is above the normal rate of exchange when buying foreign currency.

exchange rate The price relationship between two currencies at which they are convertible.

exchange rate parity The fixed price relationship at which two currencies are convertible. Parity is determined by government policy and maintained by various measures, including, for example, the operation of the exchange equalization account. Compare **floating exchange rate**.

Exchequer In the United Kingdom, the government department dealing with public revenue.

exchequer accounts The accounts held at the Bank of England, consisting of deposits produced from inland revenue and customs collections, and from the proceeds of borrowing.

exchequer bills and bonds The loans raised by the Treasury to provide temporary or short-term finance. Bills are issued for temporary loans extending from three to twelve months, while bonds are issued to provide slightly longer-term funds.

exchequer return A weekly statement issued by the Treasury which gives details of the week's revenue and expenditure, accumulated totals to date for the financial year and details of the receipts and issues relating to treasury bills, ways and means advances, national savings and other forms of government borrowing.

excise duty A tax levied on domestically produced goods at the production stage, such as beer, spirits, and tobacco, or raised as fees for licences permitting the manufacture of such goods. Excise duties are collected and administered by local authorities and the Customs and Excise authorities. See also **customs duty**.

exclusion clause A clause in an insurance policy or warranty which lists items not covered by the insurance.

exclusive agency An arrangement where a company is appointed the sole agent for a product in a certain market.

exclusive dealing An arrangement between two parties which limits the extent to which one party will transact business with other persons. An exclusive arrangement may require registration and investigation as a potentially restrictive practice.

ex coupon 'Without the right to the attached interest coupon.' The market quotation of a debenture, bond, etc. where such a right to interest is retained by the seller.

ex dividend 'Without the attached right to the dividend just due.' The market quotation of a stock/share where such a right to dividend is retained by the seller. Compare **cum dividend**.

ex drawing 'Without the attached right to any drawings due.' The market quotation of a security where such a right is retained by the seller. Compare **cum drawings**.

executive A senior member of a business with commensurate management duties and responsibilities.

executive director A director of a company who works full-time in the company and has the power to make decisions in a certain area of the company's activities.

executor A person appointed by the maker of a will to secure the performance of the terms of the will. The executor has the power to act until probate is granted by the court. Compare **administrator**.

executor and trustee corporation A specialist company established by banks and other financial institutions to perform the functions of trustee, administrator or executor for clients.

executor's year A period ending one year after the death of the person who has appointed an executor, during which year traditionally the executor should attempt to complete his duties.

executory A contract in which a person undertakes to perform or to refrain from a particular action at some future date.

ex gratia payment A payment made without legal obligation and not forming part of a contractual relationship.

exhibition A type of promotional activity where companies show their goods or services to prospective customers. If the purchasers are exclusively other companies and the general public is not admitted, the exhibition may be called a **trade fair**.

ex interest 'Without the attached right to interest just due.' The market quotation of a debenture especially where such interest on it is retained by the seller. Compare **cum interest**.

ex-officio membership Membership of a committee which derives not from election but from the position which the person holds within an organization.

expense A resource acquired by a monetary expenditure which has been used up during an accounting period and is charged against that period's revenue.

expense account Allocation of money which a businessman is allowed by his company to spend personally on travelling and entertaining clients in connection with his business.

export Any good or service which is sold abroad.

export bounty A payment made by a government to exporters as a means of encouraging them.

Export Credit Guarantee Department A department of the British government which insures manufacturers and traders against the risk of loss arising from exporting goods. Cover is normally extended beyond those commercial risks usually borne by insurance companies to provide against political risks such as civil war in the importing country or the imposition of exchange controls by the importing country, as well as the insolvency of the buyer. The Department also helps exporters to obtain finance for exported goods or services, if necessary by guaranteeing loans.

export duty A tax levied on exported goods.

export licence A formal document issued by the Department of Trade and Industry which is required to authorize the export of certain types of goods, such as armaments, works of art, etc.

export of capital The outflow of domestic currency which is used to finance investments in foreign countries.

ex post Actually realized; seen in the light of the previous expectations based on earlier data. Compare **ex ante**.

exposure 1 The amount of risk which a lender runs of losing the money lent. 2 The number of people who are likely to see an advertisement.

ex rights 'Without the attached rights to new shares issued by the company.' A term used to describe the market quotation of a stock/share where such rights are retained by the seller.

extended credit Sale of a product on credit, where payment is deferred beyond the normal date. In the home market, this might be 60 or 90 days, as opposed to the usual 30 days. In the overseas markets, credit terms will be considerably longer.

extended guarantee A guarantee of the good working order of a machine, which covers a longer period than the usual guarantee, for example two years as opposed to twelve months.

external account An account held in a British bank by someone who is domiciled in another country.

external audit The examination of company accounts by agents from outside the company in question, with a view to reporting to shareholders that the statements provided by the business to shareholders give a true and fair view of the company's performance and financial position. External auditing is required by law for limited companies by persons legally qualified to conduct such an audit. The auditors' report is added to the published accounts of the company. Compare **internal audit**.

external sterling The sterling funds held by people resident outside the sterling area.

extractive industry An activity which exploits mineral or other natural produce of the land and sea, such as coal-mining and fishing. The produce of an extractive industry is finite and cannot be replaced by man's efforts.

extraordinary general meeting A meeting of the shareholders of a company, which may be called by a member of the company who gives due notice to all members and an indication of the business to be conducted. There is no legal limit to the number of such meetings which can be held in a year.

extraordinary resolution A motion at a company meeting which, in order to be passed, requires a majority of at least 75% of the members actually voting. Due notice of the motion and of its extraordinary nature must be given to the shareholders and must be filed with the Registrar of Companies.

ex warehouse 'Sold from a warehouse', the buyer of the goods providing and paying for transport from the warehouse or paying the costs thus incurred.

F

face value The value printed on a document, such as a share certificate. The printed value need not represent the issue price, redemption price or current market value. Also called **nominal value; par value**.

facility planning The scientific analysis of future requirements of production capacity, capital, manning, etc. to ensure the smooth functioning of future strategies.

factor 1 A person who deals on behalf of the owner of goods, the transaction being made in the factor's name. The factor usually has possession of the goods and is legally authorized to pass title to the purchaser. **2** A firm that buys the trade debts of a client and collects them on its own behalf. The price the factor pays is less than the face value of the debt, but if the debt is successfully collected the balance will be paid to the client, less a service charge. The factor may also advance money to the client using the debts as security. **3** A constant element in a series of mathematical calculations.

factor comparison A system of job evaluation in which each of a number of key jobs is analysed under the headings of skill, responsibility, physical requirements, etc. The pay for each job is then apportioned over the factors and this data is used to fix the pay for other jobs.

factor cost The cost of using any unit of a factor of production (capital, land, labour or entrepreneurial skill) in one process rather than another.

factoring The performance, by an independent firm, of the credit control functions of a business and the assumption of responsibility for debts and their collection. Periodic payments are made to the business, representing sums collected from debtors less the firm's fee, which is usually charged as a percentage on turnover. Money may be advanced to the client, using the debts as security.

factors of production The resources which are combined to produce goods and services: they comprise land, labour and entrepreneurial skill.

Factory Acts A series of legislative enactments which regulate the conditions of employment in factories in relation to hours of employment (especially for women and children) and the provision of standards for heating, lighting, safety, etc.

factory inspectorate A government department responsible for the inspection of every part of a factory or workplace, examination of

facultative endorsement

registers, certificates and other documentation, etc. to ensure that the provisions of the Factories Acts and any other relevant instruments are being complied with.

facultative endorsement A form of endorsement written on a bill of exchange by which the endorser waives certain duties otherwise required by the holder from him, e.g. providing notice of dishonour.

facultative reinsurance The reinsurance of individual risks. The party who reinsures may select any or all of the original contingencies covered by the original policy.

faculty theory of taxation see **taxation, faculty theory of**

failure The act by an individual or business of suspending payment of goods and services received while awaiting bankruptcy proceedings.

fair dealing The legal buying and selling of shares.

fair trade An international trading situation in which goods are exchanged on equal terms. Thus, duties and restrictions imposed by one country are met by reciprocal duties and restrictions by other countries. Duties may also be imposed on imports to nullify any price advantage they possess over home-produced goods. Compare **free trade**.

fair wages clause A clause inserted in contracts (especially government contracts) ensuring that wage rates and other conditions of labour are no less favourable than those commonly accepted in the particular area or in the industry. This, and certain other provisions, must apply to all those employed by the relevant contractor and by any sub-contractors.

falling market A market where prices are coming down.

f.a.s. see **free alongside ship**

fatigue allowance The time included in a standard time to allow for losses in production which might be attributed to fatigue. It is usually expressed as a percentage of the normal time.

fax 1 To send a copy of a letter or other document using a scanning system which transmits the image to an output device along the telephone lines in the form of electronic data. 2 A message sent in this way.

feasibility study An investigation of a proposed or existing plan or project in order to determine its technical and financial viability.

Federal Reserve System The central bank network in the United States, which comprises reserve banks from 12 Federal Reserve Districts, all national banks and, optionally, state banks. The reserve banks are established with capital subscribed by member banks of a particular Reserve District.

The system is controlled and co-ordinated by a Board of Governors (the Federal Reserve Board) which influences discount rates (and thus interest rates in general), determines cash ratios for members, acts as lender to the member banks and directs foreign exchange business.

fee 1 A remuneration received for services rendered to a business, client, etc. 2 A grant of land, usually made in consideration of services rendered.

feedback The passing of information relating to operational performance, etc. back along a system so that effective action can be taken to remedy any deviation of an operation from a formulated plan.

feedback, negative The normal and essential correction necessary to bring a system into line by making a correction in the opposite direction to the original divergence.

fee simple A freehold interest in property which is at the absolute disposal of the owner, usually passing to his heir. Compare **fee tail**.

fee tail A freehold interest in property which descends in a particular, specified line.

fiat money An issue of money, either in note or token form, which the state declares to be legal tender, even though it has no inherent value but only the value assigned to it. All paper money is fiat money since it is inherently worthless. By contrast gold sovereigns are not because of their gold content.

fictitious assets Resources which have been utilized by a business but are retained on the financial statement in order to conform to legal requirements, as, for example, expenses incurred in the formation of a company. Such expenses cannot be written off against profit but may be eliminated from the financial statements by certain prescribed means.

fictitious bill see **accommodation bill**

fidelity bond A form of insurance policy that indemnifies an insured party against a misappropriation of funds. Insurance cover may be related either to particular individuals or to particular positions of responsibility within a business.

fidelity guarantee A personal guarantee of another's integrity. Such a guarantee may be required by an employer before an applicant is accepted for employment in a position of financial responsibility.

fiduciary 1 Dependent upon public confidence for value. 2 One to whom another's property is entrusted, to be held or managed. 3 Denoting the relationship between such a person and his principal.

fiduciary issue The value of notes that the Bank of England is legally empowered to issue without a gold backing. Such an issue is backed by government securities. Also known as **fiduciary note issue**.

fiduciary loan A loan given without requiring security, the personal integrity and honour of the creditor being regarded as sufficient guarantee that the loan will be repaid.

field research The gathering of information from customers, the public, etc. by means of direct contact through interviews.

field sales manager The person in charge of a sales force working in a particular geographical area.

fieri facias A writ under which a sheriff may seize and sell the goods of a debtor. Proceeds are generally paid into court and can be used to satisfy a plaintiff's claim.

fifo see **first in, first out**

file 1 A container in which documents are arranged in an orderly manner, thereby facilitating reference to them. 2 A set of related records collected together for processing as a group, particularly in data processing.

filing wheel A method of storing records on a series of platforms attached to a vertical axis. Access is then possible by rotating the required segments of files. Also called **roundabout**.

film analysis The detailed examination of work for method study by use of motion picture technique.

FIMBRA see **Financial Intermediaries, Managers and Brokers Regulatory Association**

final accounts see **annual accounts**

final discharge The last of a series of payments which settles a debt.

final dividend The dividend proposed by directors of a company which brings the dividends for the year (including any interim dividend) to the total recommended by the directors to the company members.

final notice A demand for payment which, if ignored, is followed by legal action to recover the outstanding debt.

Finance Act Any Parliamentary legislation which deals with the raising of revenue, in particular the act which gives power to the proposals set out in the annual Budget. In the United Kingdom statutory regulations restrict the power of the House of Lords to amend or reject a finance proposal passed by the House of Commons.

finance company see **finance house**

Finance Corporation for Industry An offshoot of Finance for Industry Limited that provides long-term finance for large British firms. Its primary aims are the encouragement of exports, investment in fixed assets and the supply of working capital.

Finance for Industry Limited The overall holding company of the Finance Corporation for Industry and Investors in Industry. Its major shareholders are the Bank of England and the clearing banks.

finance house An institution which normally specializes in hire-purchase finance and factoring. Also called **finance company**.

financial accounting The recording of a company's transactions, assets and liabilities in monetary terms, and the reporting of financial information to interested parties, either within the company or outside the company.

financial adviser A person or company giving advice on financial matters for a fee.

financial instrument Any investment which can be traded, such as shares, certificates of deposit, etc.

Financial Intermediaries, Managers and Brokers Regulatory Association A self-regulatory organization which monitors the actions of financial advisers and insurance brokers, who have to be registered with FIMBRA in order to practise.

financial ratio An expression of the relationships between various facets of the financial position reported by a business, such as the ratio of profit to capital employed or ratio of current assets to current liabilities.

The ratios, by comparison with past data or data of competitors, may be used as a guide to business performance and financial stability.

Financial Services Act An act passed in 1986 to regulate financial services and protect the consumer.

Financial Times Actuarial Shares Indices There are 54 share indices published from Tuesday to Saturday in the *Financial Times*. Each share index covers an individual sector of the market and is compiled daily by computer in co-operation with the Institute of Actuaries in London and the Faculty of Actuaries in Edinburgh.

Financial Times Ordinary Share Index An index which indicates price movements in industrial ordinary shares dealt in on the London Stock Exchange. The index is compiled from movements in 30 leading industrial companies and is published twice daily in the *Financial Times*. The 30 leading companies are widely regarded as being exceptionally sound and well-established.

Financial Times – Stock Exchange 100 Index An index showing price movements in the shares of 100 major companies which are traded on the London Stock Exchange. Since the index is more broadly based than the older FT Index, it can be taken as a more accurate reflection of share prices as a whole.

financial year A period for which a business draws up its accounts. While normally running for 12 months, it can be for a shorter or longer period.

finder's fee A payment made by one company to another (generally operating in an associated field) for providing information about a demand from a customer which leads to an order.

fine bill A bill of exchange which, because of its origin, for example, a treasury bill, or its backing, as by an accepting house, is regarded as especially safe and negotiable. The discount rates applied to such a bill are therefore favourably low. Also called **first-class bill**.

fineness of coin A measure of the proportion of pure to base metal content in coins of legal tender.

fine paper see **first-class paper**

finest rate of discount The interest rate charged for discounting first-class bills of exchange, being the lowest obtainable.

fine trade bill A trade bill having the backing of a well-known bank or finance house.

fine tuning The application of monetary and fiscal policy by the government to regulate fluctuations in output and employment, control inflation and help the balance of payments.

finished product A good carried in stock in completed form ready for delivery to the customer. Such merchandise may have been manufactured by the company or may be complete items purchased for resale.

fire insurance A contract of indemnity against loss by fire given by insurance companies in consideration of an annual premium.

firm Any form of business organization. While often applied to companies, the term more properly describes business partnerships, or a sole trader employing more than one employee.

firm offer An offer price made for an article, tender, etc. which, if accepted, forms the contract price.

firm, theory of the The economic study of the forces which determine the prices paid for the use of factors of production, the forces which lead to the allocation of resources to different products, and the forces which determine the revenue received from these products.

first call The request by a company to its members for payment of the first instalment due on shares after they have been allotted to members.

first-class bill see **fine bill**

first-class paper Any bill, promissory note, etc. carrying the names of well-known discount houses, banks or finance companies as acceptors or endorsers. Thus, treasury bills which are accepted by the government are classified as first-class paper. Also called **fine paper**.

first cost The initial cost incurred in setting up a business activity, introducing any change, etc.

first in, first out A common basis for valuing stock or withdrawal from stock which assumes that goods are used in the order in which they were put into stock. Thus a withdrawal would be priced at the amount paid for the first material taken into stock from which it could be drawn and stock-in-hand would be valued at more recent prices. Compare **last in, first out** (def. 1).

first-line management Managers who have immediate contact with the workforce.

first option Giving another party the right to be the first to decide something, such as an exclusive agency for a product.

fiscal 1 Pertaining to public revenues. 2 Pertaining to general financial matters.

fiscal year The twelve-month period, beginning on the sixth of April, which is used for central government accounting and taxation purposes.

five characteristics The main features of an individual which are examined when making an assessment for job suitability. They are generally: impact on others, qualification, innate abilities or skills, motivation and adjustment.

Five-Year Plan A plan for a country's economy covering a period of five years. Five-year plans are used in planning controlled economies.

fixed assets Those resources which are expected to be of continued value to a business over a number of years. The cost of such assets (buildings, plant, etc.) is generally written off against the profits of the years during which benefit is derived from them.

fixed budget A budget which remains unchanged during the budget period, irrespective of the level of activity actually attained.

fixed capital The funds which finance the purchase of assets which are to be retained more or less permanently in a business.

fixed charge 1 An interest payment on a debenture loan which is treated as a business expense and must be met before any profit is earned. 2 A recurring business expense which does not vary with the volume of production or the level of trade, such as rent or rates.

fixed costs Any costs which tend to be unaffected by variations in volume of output. In some cases major changes in volume will affect fixed costs, as when a production facility is closed down or when extra output can be achieved only by increasing production facilities.

fixed deposit A deposit account which pays an unchanged rate of interest over a stated period.

fixed income An income which does not change, such as the income from an annuity or from fixed deposits.

fixed-interest investments Investments producing an unchanged rate of interest.

fixed-price agreement An agreement where a supplier provides a product or service at a price which remains the same during the lifetime of the agreement.

fixtures and fittings Those resources which, without being part of the original building structure, are attached to a business premises, such as piping, radiators, etc.

flag discrimination Any preferential treatment, by way of charges and facilities, extended by one country to the ships of another.

flagship Most important item in a company's product line.

flap sorter A device which assists the sorting of documents into any desired order, comprising a series of hinged flaps between which papers can be quickly inserted without undue exertion.

flash-pack A package marked with a promotional price reduction to encourage sales.

flash report A report on the estimated financial performance and health of a business for a particular accounting period, which is prepared before the end of the period in order to decide whether corrective action is necessary.

flexible budget A budget which is designed to change in relation to the attained level of activity. It is therefore essential to identify and separate costs which are fixed, semi-fixed or variable, since not every cost element will change with changes in the activity level.

flexitime A system where workers can start or stop at different times in the morning and evening, provided that a certain number of hours are worked per day or per week. Flexitime systems are useful in that they may allow workers with young families to take up full-time employment. They also help to stagger peak periods of rush-hour travelling.

flight of capital The rapid movement of capital from one country to another, because of changes in exchange rates and the fear of possible devaluation.

float 1 To launch a company, scheme or enterprise. 2 To sell an issue of shares or bonds upon the formation of a company. 3 Uncollected cheques in process of transfer between banks. 4 A reserve, especially of cash.

floating capital Funds available for carrying on a business, including funds employed in marketable investments.

floating charge A restriction of the disposal of the current assets of a business, arising from a loan or debenture on which the assets are pledged as security. In the event of a winding-up the loan creditor has a prior claim to these assets.

floating debt A portion of the national debt that is repayable at short notice. It consists mainly of treasury bills and ways and means advances.

floating exchange rate The rate at which domestic currency may be exchanged for foreign currency or gold, being determined by the interactions of the forces of demand and supply for the currencies and gold. A government may, however, operate to prevent wide daily fluctuations in the exchange rate. Also called **free exchange rate**. Compare **exchange rate parity**.

floating policy An insurance policy covering goods of differing values and in varying locations, such as the stock within a manufacturer's premises, whose value cannot be accurately calculated beforehand. At the end of the year, the disparity between the cost of the floating policy and what it should have been is made up.

floor see **dealing floor**

floor to floor time The time taken to pick a component up, machine it and deposit it again upon completion of the operation.

flop (Of a share issue or a new publication) to fail.

floppy disk A small disk used for storing and sending information. Floppy disks are available in various diameters, 3.5 and 5.25 inches being the most common.

flotation The raising of capital in a company through the sale to the public of shares. Preliminary legal procedures relating to the formation of the company must first be complied with and further requirements specified by a stock exchange must be met if the company is to be quoted on the exchange and its shares dealt in.

flotsam Goods cast overboard, or parts of a shipwrecked ship or its cargo which remain floating on the sea. Compare **jetsam**.

flow chart A diagrammatic representation of a sequence of operations relating to a production process, the handling of materials or documents, office procedures, etc.

flow line The production line, along which products pass in the course of production.

flow process chart see **process flow chart**

flow production A type of mass production in which individual machines or operators are employed on the same operations and the product moves from one machine or operator to the next as it nears its completed state.

f.o.b. see **free on board**

folio **1** A page of a book of account, or two pages, facing each other and having the same reference number. **2** A certain number of words used as a unit for calculating the length of a legal document.

follow-up system A system of filing correspondence so that it is brought to notice on a predetermined date in order to initiate further correspondence or action.

Footsie see **Financial Times – Stock Exchange 100 Index**

f.o.r. see **free on rail**

forced sale A sale which takes place because a court has ordered it, or because it is the only way to avoid a financial crisis.

force majeure An unexpected event which disrupts the performance of a contract and excuses one party to the contract. Such events may include the outbreak of a war or a strike.

forecasting The prediction of the future change in a variable. Techniques for forecasting include extrapolation of growth curves, extrapolation of time series and regression analysis.

forecast interval The time interval between successive forecasts, usually equal to the period covered by the forecast.

foreclose To deprive a mortgagor of the right to redeem his property. In default of payment, a mortgagee may bring an action in the court and, if the debt is still unpaid by the date set by the court, the mortgagor loses the property.

foreign bill A bill of exchange which is not drawn upon a resident of the country or is not payable in the country in which the bill is issued. The law of the country in which the bill is issued applies in respect of drawing, acceptance and endorsement. The law of the country where presentment is to be made applies in the event of dishonour.

foreign currency account A bank account in the currency of another country, such as a dollar account in a British bank.

foreign currency reserves The reserves held by one country in currencies of other countries, used to support its own currency and pay foreign debts.

foreign domicile bill A bill drawn on an overseas institution which can be sold only on the discount market unless endorsed by a bank.

foreign exchange The process of trading one currency for another. This takes place on the international exchange markets where trading sets the exchange rates of currencies. Foreign currency is required by individuals, businesses and governments to finance the purchase of goods and services and to make loans to other countries.

foreign exchange deal A contract to exchange one currency for another at an agreed price for settlement on an agreed date.

foreman Someone in charge of a small group of workers on the factory floor or in some other manual occupation.

forex see **foreign exchange**

forfeit clause A clause in a contract which says that goods or money will be taken if the contract is not fulfilled.

forfeited share A share in a company on which a payment by its purchaser is outstanding. The company may reclaim and reissue the share in accordance with the terms and procedures specified in its Articles of Association.

forfeiture Loss of property as a penalty for the commission of a misdeed, breach of a contract, neglect of a duty, etc.

formation expenses see **preliminary and formation expenses**

form control The scrutiny and authorization of new or revised paperwork to ensure that no unnecessary work is being added and that forms in use are a necessary part of routines.

form design The studying of paperwork with a view to simplifying form completion, eliminating duplication of information and facilitating retrieval of the data.

form letter A letter printed many times over for distribution to customers, suppliers, etc.

form of words Words correctly printed out in a legal document.

for money A Stock Exchange term describing transactions that must be settled financially with the delivery of the documentation. Compare **for the account**.

for the account A Stock Exchange term describing transactions that must be settled financially with the delivery of the documentation at the next settlement period.

FORTRAN A complex computer programming language especially suitable for scientific and mathematical use. The name is an acronym for *for*mula *tran*slation.

fortunate acquisition The gaining by a business of an asset that proves to have a value significantly higher than the price paid for it. An example is if mineral deposits are discovered on land after it has been bought at a price which took no account of or undervalued the deposits.

forward buying The purchase of shares or commodities or currency for delivery at a later date.

forward contract A contract for the purchase of currency, shares or commodities for delivery at a later date.

forward dating The practice of dating documents in advance of the issue date. It is used on invoices to extend the credit period for payment of goods and on cheques to indicate that when presented on the stated date the cheque will be paid, but not before.

forward exchange A system of protecting from fluctuations in exchange rates, whereby a definite quotation in the present is obtained for the purchase or sale of a foreign currency at a future date. This can be a fixed date or an option date, which is generally at any time up to a normal maximum period of three months from taking the option to completion of the contract.

forwarding The activities and procedures relating to the transport of goods, especially exports and imports. Forwarding activities include securing customs clearance, handling and processing documents, etc.

forwarding address An address to which correspondence may be forwarded if the addressee has moved.

forwarding agent A general agent responsible for the collection and delivery of merchandise, whose duties are to ensure proper warehousing, delivery to correct destination, and transport from rail to quay when goods are being shipped.

forward integration The merger of one firm with another that is nearer the end of a production or selling process. An example would be the merger of a publisher with a bookshop chain or a brewer with a hotel group.

forward marketing The purchase and sale of commodities, securities or currency at an agreed price for delivery and payment at a specified future date. The practice is used to ensure against potential future adverse price movements, the agreed price being determined by demand and supply forces in the forward market. Also called **dealing in futures**.

foul bill A bill of lading endorsed to show that the relevant goods have been put on board in a defective condition.

foul bill of health A bill of health issued to a shipmaster indicating that infectious diseases are in evidence at the port concerned. Such a bill will usually involve the imposition of quarantine regulations for passengers or goods before permission to enter the next port is granted. Also called **dirty bill**. See also **bill of health; touched bill of health**.

founder's shares Shares issued to those who promoted a company, as remuneration for their service, or to defray preliminary expenses. Such shares are usually issued as fully paid and rank for dividend after payment of dividend to ordinary shareholders. They may carry the right to all surplus profits after ordinary dividend has been paid.

f.p.a. see **free of particular average**

fractional certificate A certificate for part of a share.

franchise 1 An agreement by which a company grants to another the right to use the company's name and trademarks, and to market the company's goods or services in return for a fee. 2 (In marine insurance) the proportion of the issued value of goods or the minimum value thereof which is disallowed for insurance claim purposes (unless the ship carrying the goods is stranded or sunk). If damage is above the minimum the whole loss is recoverable.

franco Denoting in a contract or invoice that it is the seller who is liable for all costs of transport of goods to the buyer's warehouse.

franco price A price which includes all charges up to delivery to the buyer.

franked investment income Any income which a company receives from dividends in shareholdings in other companies. It is received net of tax and consequently is not again subject to corporation tax.

The recipient company may obtain relief for the tax deducted from its income by offsetting such tax against the tax which the company is due to pay on its distributions.

franking machine A mechanical device for endorsing letters, packages, etc., instead of using adhesive postage stamps. Readings are submitted regularly to the Post Office, payment being made direct to the postal authorities.

fraud 1 Deceit and trickery in order to gain some unfair or dishonest advantage. 2 A false representation of fact (or sometimes of opinion) made knowingly or recklessly without concern about the truth of the statement. If fraud is proved to have occurred in the drawing up of a contract, the other party can rescind the contract and sue for compensation. Also called **fraudulent misrepresentation**.

fraud, actual Intentional misrepresentation of facts causing pecuniary injury to another party.

fraud, constructive A false representation of a fact made without any wrongful intention.

fraud on the minority A doctrine which, while recognizing the rule of the majority by virtue of their voting power, protects the minority against fraudulent actions.

fraud squad A special police department which investigates business fraud.

fraudulent conversion The application of property or its sale proceeds to his own use or for another's use by one who has been entrusted with such property.

fraudulent misrepresentation A false statement made to trick someone or to persuade someone to enter into a contract. See also **fraud**.

fraudulent preference 1 A deliberate preference for one creditor or surety by an insolvent debtor. Such a move can constitute an act of bankruptcy. 2 Any payment to a creditor with a view to giving such creditor preference over others. If this occurs within six months of the commencement of a winding-up of a company, such a transfer is void and the liquidator may recover the property.

fraudulent trading The carrying on of a business with intent to defraud creditors. Directors may be personally liable for debts incurred without limitation of liability if, to their knowledge, trading has continued without any reasonable prospect of the company being able to pay its debts.

free 1 Not subject to any special restrictions or regulations. 2 Without charge; not subject to payment.

free alongside ship A contract whereby the seller is responsible for all costs incurred in conveying goods to the wharf but excluding hoisting on board.

free collective bargaining Negotiations about wages and working conditions between management and union representatives.

free currency A currency which a government allows to be bought and sold without restriction.

free depreciation The freedom to depreciate assets for tax purposes at whatever rate a business may decide. Such a device acts as an incentive to invest in capital equipment.

free docks price A price which includes delivery to and unloading at the docks at the port of departure but excludes dock dues, porterage and wharfage.

free economy An economic system in which productive activity and trade are conducted without interference from external influences such as government regulations.

free enterprise A means of operating within an economic environment which is characterized by the private ownership and exploitation of the factors of production.

free entry
   Such a system does not preclude state participation in economic activity by, for example, providing a legal framework for commercial activity.

free entry   The customs procedures required to secure permission to unload goods which are not liable to duty. See also **entry**.

free exchange rate   see **floating exchange rate**

free gift   A gift given to a customer, which is not paid for by the customer. This a common promotional device and may be a gift in return for a certain level of purchase or a gift to attract an order.

free good   Anything that is naturally occurring, in abundant supply and needs no conscious effort to acquire. An example is air.

free goods   Merchandise which does not bear customs duties.

freehold   Denoting land which is owned absolutely. See also **leasehold**.

freelance   An independent worker who works for several different companies and is paid a fee, but is not employed by any of them.

free list   A list issued by customs authorities which details those goods on which duty is not charged.

free market economy   An economic system where the government does not interfere in any way in business activity.

free of all average   Denoting a marine insurance policy in which the insurer will pay only on total loss. Claims for general and particular average are not recoverable under such a policy.

free of capture and seizure   A clause inserted in a marine insurance policy which excludes liability in the event of capture, seizure, arrest and detainment of the ship or goods, and liability arising from the consequences of war or other hostilities.

free of particular average   Denoting a marine insurance policy in which the insurers are responsible for total loss or for general average loss. The goods are insured against the ship being stranded, sunk or burnt or involved in a collision.

free of tax   Denoting income received after deduction of tax. In the case of dividends so declared, the term is misleading, since the recipient must declare the gross amount and may be able to recover some or all of the tax paid. In the case of a fee or salary said to be paid free of tax the gross amount is an allowable expense of the employer.

free on board   A contract whereby the seller pays all expenses incurred in putting goods on to a ship named by the buyer. Once the goods are on board property passes to the buyer and is at his risk providing he has been notified of the shipment. Compare **cost, insurance and freight**.

free on board and trimmed   A free on board contract in which the seller is also responsible for ensuring that the goods are properly stored aboard ship.

free on rail   A contract in which the seller is liable to pay all expenses incurred in conveying the goods to the railway depot nearest the place of manufacture.

free overside A contract for the carriage of goods where the price includes f.o.b. plus freight costs to the port of destination. The seller is responsible for supplying the vessel. Property passes once the goods leave the vessel, the buyer being responsible for conveying the goods from the ship. Generally, the contract price does not include insurance on the goods since the goods are at the seller's risk until they are unloaded.

freephone An arrangement by which telephone calls are made in reply to advertisements, to place orders or to ask for information, with the seller paying for the call, not the customer.

free port A port where no duties are levied on imports or exports.

freepost A postal service where letters sent to an advertiser or to place orders, are charged to the supplier and not to the customer.

free sample A small sample of a product which is given free to prospective customers as a promotional device.

free stock The balance in stock of a particular item against which no allocations have been made.

free trade International trade unrestricted by protective duties and prohibitions.

free trade area A trading arrangement entered into by a number of countries whereby tariffs and trade restrictions between the participants are eliminated, each country retaining its independent trade arrangements with other countries outside the area.

freeze 1 To fix prices of goods or labour at a specific level, or within stated limits, usually by government order. 2 To exclude a competitor, as by severe price cutting. 3 To render collection of bank loans impossible.

freight 1 The ordinary conveyance of goods as by common carriers. 2 The payment due for transporting goods by land, sea or air.

freightage The cost of transporting goods by land, sea or air.

freighter 1 A vessel engaged primarily in the transport of goods. 2 The charterer of a vessel. 3 One who receives and forwards freight.

freight forward Freight charges which are payable at the port of destination.

freight in and out The carriage charges made by a haulier in addition to the invoice price of the materials quoted by the supplier ('freight in') or in addition to the invoice price of goods quoted by the manufacturer ('freight out'). Also called **carriage in and out**.

freightliner A national railway container service which began in Britain in 1964. Containers are loaded at the factory, sent by road to a freightliner terminal and then carried by rail and then road to their destination.

freight note A document which indicates the freight charges due on goods taken on board a vessel. The note is prepared by shipbrokers and sent to the shippers of the goods.

freight release A document prepared by a shipbrokers, or an endorsement by them on a bill of lading, which signifies that freight charges have been paid and authorizes a ship's officer to give up possession of the goods to the presenter of the document or bill of lading. Freight release is used especially when goods are shipped 'freight forward'.

frequency distribution A chart or graphical representation showing the distribution of certain characteristics among a statistical population.

friendly society An association registered under the Friendly Societies Act, 1896, which provides benefits to the elderly, infirm, orphans, etc.

fringe benefit A payment in kind in addition to remuneration for work, for example, luncheon vouchers, holiday pay, subsidized canteen services, sports facilities, non-contributory pension schemes, a company car, etc.

front-end loaded A fixed-term investment where the bulk of the management charges are paid in the first years, and not spread over the whole period of the investment.

front-line management see **first-line management**

frozen account A bank account where the money cannot be used or moved because of a court order.

frozen asset Any business asset whose disposal is restricted.

frustration The discharge of a contract where, without default by either party, the contractual obligation has become incapable of being performed because of a radical change in circumstances. Financial settlement in such a case is laid down under the Law Reform (Frustrated Contracts) Act, 1943, although this does not apply to all contracts.

frustration clause A clause in marine insurance removing any liability from the insurer in the case of a frustrated contract.

FT Index see **Financial Times Ordinary Share Index**

FT-SE 100 Index see **Financial Times–Stock Exchange 100 Index**

full costing The concept of each product bearing its share of all the manufacturing costs. This generally has the effect of including fixed costs in stock valuation.

full-cost pricing The setting of selling prices by the application of profit requirements to products costed on a full-cost basis.

full employment The level of employment at which everyone willing and able to work is employed.

full-line forcing A marketing strategy adopted by companies whereby dealers are obliged to handle the whole range of the company's products if they are to receive supplies of a particularly saleable product.

full-time Working all the normal working day (that is about 35 hours per week).

fully paid shares Shares where the full face value has been paid.

functional Denoting the position within an organization of a specialist contributing a service to managers comprising the executive members of the organization. While such a person may be in a direct relationship with his own staff, he has an advisory relationship with other managers, an example being a personnel officer or an organization and methods officer.

functional analysis see **value analysis**

functional budget A budgeted statement of income or expenditure related to the responsibility of a particular function in a business, such as personnel.

functional costing A system of analysing budgeted expenditure by reference to particular objectives. The objectives are regarded as outputs produced by the proposed expenditure (the inputs). The technique relates individual inputs and outputs in order to establish the cost of achieving different objectives. See also **output budgeting**.

functional foreman A concept whereby an individual is responsible for the correct performance of a certain function throughout the company. Thus, a functional office manager would be responsible for the clerical function in all departments.

functional responsibility Any specialist responsibility which provides primarily a service for the managers and executives of an organization. The personnel manager, for example, has specialist knowledge and skills which are used to assist the effectiveness of management throughout the organization. Also called **specialist responsibility**.

funded debt The various forms of long-term government borrowing which have no fixed repayment date, such as Consolidated Stocks with no stated redemption and principal loans, redeemable between certain dates. The funded debt forms part of the national debt.

funding 1 A process whereby the time period of indebtedness is lengthened. Funding is usually operated through the replacement of short-term loans on their maturity by longer-term loans. **2** The process of providing for the ultimate payment of a liability or for the replacement of an asset through the systematic investment of money and reinvestment of accumulated interest. **3** The provision of financial resources.

funds 1 A stock of money or financial resources. **2** Government stock. **3** Debts owed by the government on which interest is payable.

funds flow statement A statement which itemizes the movements in assets and liabilities within a specified period, being used to indicate the changes in the cash position or to explain the asset movements associated with the profit/loss achieved during the period.

funk money see **hot money**

futures Securities or goods bought or sold for future delivery. There may be no intention to take them up but to rely upon price changes in order to sell at a profit before delivery.

futures contract A contract for the sale or purchase of securities, goods, etc. for future delivery. It has the effect of minimizing extreme price fluctuations.

future tax Taxation calculated on the profits of the current accounting year but payable at some future date.

G

galloping inflation Very rapid inflation which a government finds almost impossible to reduce.

game theory A derivative of operational research and mathematical theory whereby problems can sometimes be approached as in a game, the object being to discover those strategies to beat the opponent.

gaming contract An agreement in which two parties stand to win or lose their stake as the result of a game; a type of waging contract. Such contracts are legally void.

Gantt chart A bar chart on which machine loadings or work programmes are plotted against a horizontal time scale. From such a chart planned times can be read for activities. Sometimes actual results are also plotted.

garnishee An individual or organization which holds money belonging to someone who has debts owed to other parties. The creditor may serve a garnishee order on the garnishee preventing the making of payments to the debtor until so sanctioned by the court. The most common garnishees are banks.

garnishee order A court order restraining persons owing money to a judgement debtor or holding goods belonging to the debtor from handing over the money or goods to the debtor. The order may be sought by an unsatisfied judgement creditor and is designed to prevent the debtor from applying debts or goods owed to him in any manner other than in paying his creditors.

GATT (General Agreement on Tariffs and Trade) An international commercial treaty which specifies a code of conduct for international trade, notably the elimination of discriminatory preference duties, and provides for trade conferences from which tariff reductions for wide categories of goods have resulted. Some 90 members representing over 80% of world trade subscribe to the treaty and it has now a permanent base in Geneva.

Gaussian curve see **normal curve**

gazumping (In house purchase) the practice of offering more than another purchaser whose offer has already been accepted, in order to secure the property.

g.c.a. see **group capacity assessment**

GDP see **gross domestic product**

gearing The relationship between capital having a prior charge, such as loan or preference capital, and equity capital.

gearing adjustment

gearing adjustment see **current cost accounting** (def. 2)

general acceptance The usual form of acceptance on a bill of exchange, evidenced by a signature, which indicates an unqualified backing to the bill and the drawer's order to pay. Also called **clean acceptance**.

general agency An agency arrangement by which the agent has authority to perform action in the ordinary course of his business, as agent on behalf of his principal, or to act for his principal in all matters or in all matters relating to a particular business.

general audit An examination of all the books and accounts of a company.

general average (In marine insurance) the apportionment of a partial loss of a vessel or cargo among all the owners and insurers involved in the venture. The loss must have been incurred with the intention of saving the ship and/or the rest of the cargo. Compare **particular average loss**.

general bond An instrument which gives an undertaking that the goods comprised in any number of shipments will be properly exported or otherwise accounted for to the customs authorities.

general crossing A mark added to a cheque comprising two parallel lines drawn diagonally across the face of the cheque. The marking indicates that payment of the cheque must be made into a bank account. See also **crossed cheque; open cheque; special crossing**.

general equitable charge An equitable charge unsecured by the deposit of title deeds to land. In order to preserve the holder's right it may be registered as a land charge.

general manager An executive having overall responsibility for the whole or part of a business.

general meeting A meeting of all the shareholders of a company. See also **annual general meeting; extraordinary general meeting**.

general partner see **active partner**

general strike A total withdrawal of labour within a country.

gentleman's agreement A contractual arrangement made orally and without any formal legal evidence of its existence and which is therefore binding on two parties in honour only.

Giffen good A commodity for which demand rises if prices rise and falls if prices fall, contrary to normal economic patterns. This occurs if the commodity forms so large a part of the customer's purchases that a rise in its price forces the customer to abandon consumption of more costly items in order to satisfy minimum needs. The Giffen good, still being the cheaper item, is then purchased in greater quantity. The effect was noted in the nineteenth century by Sir Robert Giffen in the consumption of potatoes by the very poor. Since it was their primary source of nutrition a rise in its price meant that the consumers had to reduce their consumption of meat, fish, etc. to pay for the same quantity of potatoes.

gift inter vivos A term used to describe a gift made during the lifetime of a donor. To be liable for a lesser rate of capital transfer tax such gifts must normally be made at least three years before the death of the donor.

gifts tax see **capital transfer tax**

gift voucher A piece of paper give as a gift, which entitles the holder to purchase goods from a certain store free of charge.

Gilbreth symbols The process chart symbols developed by Frank Gilbreth.

gilt-edged securities Securities issued by the government which earn a fixed rate of interest and are dealt in on the Stock Exchange. They may be irredeemable, e.g. Consol, or redeemable, e.g. savings bonds. This is considered a safe investment, since the government is unlikely to renege on its debts, but usually offers a relatively low rate of interest.

gilts see **gilt-edged securities**

giro A system of settling transactions between customers which is operated collectively by a number of banking institutions and by the Post Office. Customers' accounts are held at the local bank branch rather than centrally, as with the Post Office giro.

giveaway see **free gift**

give on The process of paying contango charges on a Stock Exchange transaction at the settlement period.

glut A heavy over-supply of a commodity. The market reaction is for prices to fall substantially as an inducement to purchase.

GNP see **gross national product**

goal congruence The state of affairs which exists when the aims of two or more departments, executives, companies, etc. coincide. It is usually accepted that to achieve such a position is a common aim of general management.

going concern A business in operation and carrying out normal activities.

going concern value The valuation placed on a business from the position of its continued operations with a view to earning profits. This valuation will be different to the realizable value of its individual assets and will include, for example, an evaluation of its profit-earning potential.

going rate The usual or current rate paid for a certain piece of work.

going value 1 Market value. 2 See **going concern value**.

golden hallo Special sum of money paid to entice an executive to join a company.

golden handshake Compensation paid to an executive of a company on his displacement and especially on his retirement.

gold market Any market where gold is traded.

gold point The amount by which a currency which is linked to gold may vary in price.

gold reserves That part of a country's reserves which is represented by holdings of gold.

gold standard A monetary system having gold of specified weight and fineness as the basic unit of value. It was the dominant economic system up to the end of the nineteenth century, but had largely ended by the 1930s.

golf ball 1 A metal sphere forming the typeface of a typewriter, on which all the characters are fixed. The sphere rotates and impresses a character when the appropriate key is pressed. 2 A typewriter using such a typeface. Generally the platen remains stationary and the typeface moves, producing a fast typing time.

good delivery A valid transaction in securities whereby good title to ownership is properly passed. Compare **bad delivery**.

good faith Honesty of purpose. Its existence is presupposed in most contracts, particularly insurance contracts.

good merchantable quality and condition see **Sale of Goods Act**

good root of title see **root of title**

goods Any personal chattels other than choses in action, comprising all movable, material things other than currency and also livestock, minerals and crops. Immovable things such as land, houses and anything permanently attached to land are excluded.

goods delivered free Goods which are transported to the customer's home or warehouse at the supplier's cost.

goods delivered on board Goods which are transported at supplier's cost to the ship or plane, but not to the customer's warehouse.

goods inwards note A document on which are recorded details of goods supplied, description and quantity, details of the supplier, etc. Also called **goods received note**.

goods on approval Goods which are supplied to a customer, who may return them free of charge if they are not suitable.

goods on consignment Goods which are entrusted by a principal, such as a manufacturer or exporter, to an agent for sale.

goods received note see **goods inwards note**

goodwill 1 The trading benefit which an existing business derives from its custom and reputation. This benefit may be evaluated financially when determining the purchase price of a business. 2 The difference between the purchase price paid for a business and the book value of its assets.

government broker The title given to the representative of a stock-broking firm who deals in government securities on the Stock Exchange on behalf of the Bank of England.

government stock Another name for any gilt-edged security.

grading The process or result of classifying commodities according to their quality, employing technical characteristics and features of taste, etc.

graduated pension scheme A scheme initiated by the British government in order to supplement the Old Age Pension. Varying contributions are made by each employee in relation to his earnings, similar contributions being paid by the employer. An employee who contributes to a firm's pension scheme which provides benefits at least equal to those provided by the state scheme can be exempted from the state scheme.

graduated taxation see **progressive taxation**

grants-in-aid Financial assistance given by the central government to local authorities. The forms of grant are various, including a percentage grant for approved expenditure on specified services and a lump sum grant whose disposal is at the local authorities' discretion. See also **rate support grant**.

graph A diagrammatic presentation of data used to facilitate the assimilation of information.

gratis Free, costing nothing.

gratuitous bailee One who accepts property for safe custody but without making a specific charge for so doing. He must take the same degree of care of the goods as if they were his own but his duties are not as onerous as those of a bailee for reward.

gratuity A gift, generally of money, over and above any payment due for a service.

green card 1 A special international insurance certificate for a vehicle, which extends insurance cover if the vehicle is driven abroad. 2 A US work permit for a person who is not a US national.

green clause A clause contained on a documentary credit arrangement which authorizes the seller of goods to obtain an advance payment on them from a bank or other body providing the credit facility. The advance payment is designed to enable the seller to arrange and pay for the shipment and storage of the goods.

greenfield site A site for a factory or other business premises, situated in the country and not surrounded by other buildings.

green labour Untrained or inexperienced labour. Also called **green hand**.

greenmail A method of making money, by buying a large number of shares in a company, then threatening to mount a takeover bid, and selling the shares back to the company at a profit.

green pound The unit of account in which the United Kingdom makes its contributions into the fund of the Common Agricultural Policy of the EEC. Although the green pound was originally equal to the pound sterling, currency fluctuations have caused their values to diverge.

Gresham's Law The theory allegedly propounded by Sir Thomas

grievance procedure

Gresham, councillor to Elizabeth 1, that bad money will always drive out good. If coins having the same nominal value but containing different weights of the same metal are in circulation together people will save the higher-quality coins and pass on the less valuable. Eventually these will be the only coins in circulation.

grievance procedure see **complaints procedure**

gross 1 A price value or weight before any deduction or allowance. 2 Numerically, 144 units.

gross domestic product The value of goods and services produced in an economy. The value may be measured by aggregating market values of goods and services or by aggregating incomes from employment, profits, dividends, etc. (i.e. factor cost, which is equivalent to market values less purchase tax plus subsidies). It is equivalent to gross national product less the value of net property abroad.

gross earnings Earnings before payment of tax and social security contributions.

grossing up The process of determining the gross value of a net figure. The gross value of a net receipt of £1 which has been taxed at 20% is £1.25. Net + 20% gross = gross; net = 80% gross; gross = $^{100}/_{80} \times 1 = 1.25$

gross margin see **gross profit**

gross national product The total monetary value of all the goods and services produced by a country in a year, expressed either at factor cost or at market prices.

gross output The total quantity or value of goods produced by an industry, individual firm, etc. Compare **net output**.

gross profit The difference between the sales value of an article and its purchase cost or its prime manufacturing cost, i.e. the cost of materials and labour incurred in producing the article. A business trading account usually records the gross profit earned from all sales. Also called **gross margin**.

gross receipts Total receipts before subtracting any expenses.

gross sales Total sales before taking any account of discounts, allowances, rebates, etc.

gross weight The total weight of an article, including its container or package. See also **net weight; tare weight**.

ground rent The rent paid for the use of ground or for a lease for ground which contains the right to erect buildings. The lease runs for a period of years and upon its expiry the buildings usually revert to the landlord.

group A business unit which controls a number of separate companies through majority shareholdings.

group accounts see **consolidated accounts**

group capacity assessment A technique for planning optimum manpower requirements by measuring the work performed in each of the tasks done by a group of people and using the results to control workload.

group depreciation method A way of calculating depreciation by classifying all assets having equal depreciation lives together. This saves the work involved in calculating depreciation on each individual asset.

group incentive scheme A system of remuneration whereby a group of employees share in a pooled incentive, based on the results of the group. This may be useful where it is difficult to quantify the contributions of certain classes of employees.

Group of Seven (G7) The seven major industrialized nations whose finance ministers meet regularly to discuss international financial problems. Originally the **Group of Five** (United Kingdom, United States, France, West Germany, Japan), later expanded to seven by including Canada and Italy.

Group of Ten see **Paris Club**

group trading A group or chain of retailers or wholesalers who join together to obtain the benefits of bulk-buying, eliminate wasteful distribution methods and cut administrative costs.

growth Expansion of trading activities, by increasing turnover, or market share.

growth areas Geographical areas with a higher than average concentration of industrial or commercial enterprises, which have developed rapidly, usually through the operation of local or central government incentives or following the provision of effective transport systems.

growth industry An industrial sector which is expanding rapidly.

growth market A market where demand for a product or service is growing rapidly.

growth share A share which is likely to rise in value.

guarantee A written undertaking in which a person accepts liability for the payment of a debt or the performance of an action contracted by another in the event of that person's default. Compare **indemnity**.

guarantee company A company in which the liability of its members is restricted to the amount that they have agreed to contribute in the event of a winding-up. Many professional organizations fall into this category.

guaranteed pay The minimum remuneration guaranteed to an employee who is paid on a system of payments by results. If his earnings, calculated on work performed, fall below the minimum the employee receives the guaranteed pay.

guarantee fund 1 A provision made by a business to meet any exceptional anticipated loss. 2 A fund maintained by the London Stock Exchange which is designed to meet investors' losses arising from the failure of a member.

guarantee society A firm which, in return for the payment of an annual premium, undertakes to bear the losses arising from fraud, etc. committed by the employees of a business.

guarantee stocks Stocks and shares on which the interest and/or capital sum is guaranteed either by the issuing company or by another company.

guarantor A person who gives a guarantee.

guardian One having the duty of protecting the rights, property or person of one who is incapable, either physically or legally, of managing his own affairs.

guide card A card, generally coloured or projecting from the general filing system, splitting the contents of the files into sub-divisions to facilitate access or location of individual cards or files.

guidelines Proposals from a government department indicating how something should be done, but which do not have the force of law.

H

haggle To argue over a price, with the buyer attempting to reduce it and the seller attempting to keep it the same.

Hague rules A set of internationally agreed rules related to shipping contracts and customs, especially the rights and liabilities of the contracting parties. For example, a carrier of goods is liable to make a ship seaworthy. Neither the carrier nor the vessel is liable for loss or damage arising from an act of God, etc. The rules have been adapted within the legal commercial framework of numerous countries.

half commission man A term used on the Stock Exchange to describe a person who introduces clients to a stockbroker, receiving a share of the stockbroker's commission on any share transactions that result from the introduction.

hallmark A mark made on an article of silver or gold to indicate its quality. Government assay officials or officials of the maker's organization are responsible for marking the article, which may bear up to four marks – indicating the maker (usually by his initials), the assay office (each of the five in the United Kingdom has a different symbol), the quality of the article (indicated by a carat mark) and its date of manufacture (shown by a letter which changes annually).

hammering The notification to members of the London Stock Exchange that a member is unable to meet his liabilities and may no longer deal on the Exchange. Three strokes of the hammer are used to draw members' attention to the notice.

handling charge A charge made for dealing with an order, such as for administration, invoicing, packing, insurance, etc.

Hang Seng Index The index of share prices on the Hong Kong Stock Exchange

hard cash Money in notes and coins, as opposed to cheques and credit cards.

hard copy A printed record of figures, words, etc. produced by a machine. Electronic processing of data frequently necessitates the use of readable output as a permanent record.

hard currency A currency which has a stable or upwardly mobile exchange rate. Consequently it is an acceptable medium for international trade. Compare **soft currency**.

hard disk A rigid magnetic disk, which can store more data than a floppy disk, and usually cannot be removed from the computer.

hard sell A vigorous advertising and promotional campaign which is designed to increase the sales of a product. Compare **soft sell**.

hardware The machinery which comprises a computer system. This includes the central processing unit, input and output devices, etc. Compare **software**.

hash total A total of all quantities, values, etc. on a set of documents, the total having no significance except to ensure that all the documents have been accounted for. It is often essential in ensuring that all relevant input documents have been processed.

haulage The charge made for the carriage of goods, especially by land. It does not include loading or unloading of the goods.

headhunt To approach managers and executives in order to try to persuade them to move to jobs in other companies.

headhunter A company which recruits executives for rival concerns by approaching people working elsewhere and persuading them to move.

headlease The initial leasing arrangement between the owner of property and the tenant. The tenant may subsequently sublet under a number of leasing arrangements.

heavy industry An industrial sector dealing in heavy raw materials (such as steel) or which manufactures large products, such as ships or engines.

hedge Action taken to reduce exposure to risk.

hedging An attempt to prevent losses on a transaction arising from adverse price movements in the commodity markets. A dealer who sells goods in the futures market may attempt to protect himself against a rise in price by buying in the market or by getting other dealers to take over part of his sales.

hereditament A term used by rating authorities to describe a plot of land for which a rateable value is assessed. The assessment forms the basis for the calculation of the rates due on the property. A rate poundage is applied to the rateable value to produce the rates due.

heritable bond A bond which pledges a land conveyance as security for the repayment of borrowed money.

hidden assets Assets which are given a lower value in a company's accounts than their true market value.

hidden price increase A reduction in the quality or quantity of a product or service while its price remains static. It is thought to be less immediately noticeable to consumers and so to be less likely to cause a switch in demand to rival products.

hidden reserve The assets of a business when they are greater than the valuation disclosed in the balance sheet. This could arise when assets are valued at cost price in the balance sheet rather than market price when the latter figure is higher. Also called **secret reserve**.

hidden tax   A tax that is included in the price of a good or service rather than being levied separately. Consequently, all indirect taxes are hidden taxes, one example being value added tax.

hidden unemployment   A state of unemployment characterized by a level of employment in an industry which is higher than necessary or justified, there being no alternative employment available.

high-level computer language   A programming language which uses normal words and figures in its instructions.

highly geared or **high geared**   Denoting a company, or the capital of such a company, which carries a large proportion of prior-charge capital in relation to equity capital. This has the effect of absorbing a relatively high proportion of earnings.

high-pressure salesman   A salesman who sells a product or service very actively and insistently, thinking more about the commission he will earn than about the actual requirements of the customer.

High Street Banks   The main British banks which accept deposits from individuals.

high task   The rate of production achieved by a normal worker operating at incentive speed.

high-yield investment   An investment, such as a unit trust, which aims to produce a higher than average yield.

hire   A contract whereby one may enjoy the benefit of an article or service for the contracted period in return for a single or regular payment. Ownership of the article or service, however, is not exchanged.

hire purchase   A contract for the purchase of goods, whereby in return for periodic payments of the purchase price the buyer immediately receives the article. Ownership of the good is only transferred when the contracted price has been fully paid. The procedures and documentation relating to hire purchase transactions are strictly laid down by law and provide some measure of protection for the purchaser. In the United States this is called **instalment plan**.

hire purchase finance house   A financial institution whose primary activity is the provision of funds for the purchase of goods under a hire-purchase arrangement. The usual method of financing is for the finance house to buy the goods from the trader on behalf of the purchaser and to assume responsibility for the collection of the debt from the hire-purchaser.

histogram   A graphical presentation which employs rectangles to illustrate the frequency distribution of a series of events.

historical trends   Trends in business activity, such as product sales, market share, etc., on which forecasts of future developments can be based.

historic cost   The actual price paid for an asset or resource. The balance

hive-off

sheet evaluation of an asset is frequently made on this basis rather than on its current market value or value in present or alternative use.

hive-off To split off part of a large company to form a small autonomous subsidiary.

hoarding 1 Holding on to money rather than spending or investing it. Hoarding causes a withdrawal of money from circulation and if this occurs on a very large scale the market rate of interest will be affected. 2 A very large outdoor poster site.

holder The person in possession of a bill of exchange.

holder for value The possessor of a bill of exchange on which value has been given at some time (not necessarily by the holder). Such a holder has a title to the bill only as good as the person from whom he received it and, in the event of dishonour of the bill, the holder may claim from parties to the bill only up to the last time value was given.

holder in due course The possessor of a bill of exchange on which he has given value, having received the bill in good faith and without notice of any defect on the bill. Such a holder acquires a good legal title to the bill, irrespective of the title possessed by earlier parties to it and, in the event of dishonour, the holder may claim from all parties on the bill.

holding A group of shares owned by an individual or company.

holding company A company which has a controlling interest in another company through a majority shareholding in it. Also called **parent company**.

holding deed The deed wherein ownership of freehold land is conveyed to the existing owner.

holding out see **passing off**.

home loan A loan by a bank or building society to help an individual buy a house or flat, usually secured by a mortgage.

home market The market formed by the country in which a trading company is based.

home sales Sales in the home market.

homogeneous product A product any one unit of which cannot be distinguished from another. This means that consumers have no preference between competing sellers on grounds of quality but concentrate instead on price, speed of delivery, after-sales service, etc. Compare **product differentiation**.

honorarium Money paid to a professional person, such as an accountant or lawyer, which is less than a full fee.

honour To meet an obligation when it becomes due, for example paying a bill of exchange when it reaches maturity.

honour policy A form of marine insurance policy which covers the risk of a person who has an interest in a voyage in circumstances where the

122

interest may be difficult to establish. Such a policy is not legally enforceable, but is fulfilled as a matter of honour if losses arise. See also **insurable interest**.

horizontal communication Communication between employees at the same level, as between managers.

horizontal integration The merger of firms with identical functions in an industry. There are many motives for this including the sharing of specialist facilities, benefiting from economies of scale, etc., but it is always true that the greater the degree of horizontal integration in an industry the greater the monopoly power that exists. See also **diversification; vertical integration**.

hot bill A freshly issued Treasury bill, whose maturity is too distant to make it an attractive short-term investment for many financial institutions, especially the commercial banks.

hot money Funds which are transferred at short notice between international financial centres in response to changes in relative rates of interest and in anticipation of exchange rate movements. For example, fear of devaluation will cause funds to flow out of a centre and this will be sufficient to drive down the exchange rate of the abandoned currency. Also called **funk money**.

house journal; house magazine A publication issued by a large company to give its employees news of the company's activities and encourage a feeling of loyalty.

housing bond A local authority loan which may be issued without the need for central government approval. The bond must be issued at par and the proceeds from the issue can be applied only for housing purposes.

human capital The education, experience and skills possessed by a workforce.

hype Very exaggerated claims for a product or service, made in advertising.

hyperinflation A period of swiftly rising prices, usually assumed to be a rate of 50% a month or more. Such a rate cannot be sustained and invariably leads to social breakdown and a return to a barter economy. Perhaps the worst recorded case took place in Hungary in 1945–46 when prices rose at an average rate of 19,800% a month.

hypermarket A very large supermarket. Hypermarkets are usually located outside town centres so as to allow car-drivers easy access.

hypothecation, letter of A document issued by the owner of goods in which the goods or their documents of title are charged as security for a loan. The letter is especially used in commercial shipping.

I

ICFC see **Industrial and Commercial Finance Corporation**

idle capacity The unused productive facilities of a business, especially plant and machinery.

idle capital; idle money Capital or money which is not being used productively, or is not being invested to produce interest.

idle time Any time which is lost from the available productive working day resulting, for example, from machine breakdowns.

ILO see **International Labour Organization**

image The general impression which the public has of a product, brand or company.

IMF see **International Monetary Fund**

immovable property Houses and other buildings on land.

imperfect competition A situation with a large but distinct number of sellers and buyers in which some of the conditions of perfect competition have not been fulfilled. Characteristics of imperfect competition include product differentiation, advertising and the formation of cartels. In this situation prices will be above marginal costs and consequently resources will not be allocated efficiently.

impersonal accounts Those ledger accounts of a business in which all transactions other than those relating to personal accounts are recorded. Impersonal accounts are subdivided into real accounts and nominal accounts. Compare **personal accounts; real accounts**.

import A product from a foreign manufacturer sold in another country. To control its balance of payments, a country will sometimes restrict imports by means of prohibition, currency restrictions, import duties and import quotas.

import duty A tax levied on goods entering a country. The rate of tax may be ad valorem (i.e., according to the value of the goods) or specific (i.e., a specific rate for a particular type of good). Imports which are subsequently re-exported may have any duty paid refunded.

import levy A tax levied on imports, especially a tax in the European Community on imports of farm produce from outside the European Community.

import licence A government licence which permits the unrestricted entry of types of good contained in published schedules ('an open general licence') or the entry of a specific type of good by a specified importer ('general licence').

import quota An official maximum quantity placed upon the importation of a specific type of good. The maximum may be related to the importation of a good from a particular country or to the total imports of a particular good.

imprest system A method of controlling cash expenditure, with especial reference to the petty cash of a business. A fixed cash balance is established at the beginning of a period and the balance in hand at the end of a period is replenished up to the initial balance, vouchers for payments made being presented as proof of expenditure. At any time the value of cash in hand plus vouchers received should equal the fixed initial balance.

impulse buying or **impulse purchase** The purchase of articles without prior plan, the purchaser being attracted to buy through the eye-catching packaging and display of the product.

IMRO see **Investment Management Regulatory Organization**

in bond A term used to describe goods which are stored at an official warehouse pending arrangements for payment of duty to the customs authorities.

incentive An inducement to improve performance. An example would be a bonus to an employee for extra output, or a reduction in income tax, encouraging everybody to earn extra income.

incentive scheme Any system of remuneration in which the amount which can be earned depends upon the results obtained, thereby providing the employee with an incentive to produce better results. The scheme may be based upon individual, group or company performance.

inchoate note A document issued in incomplete form, leaving the recipient to complete the details within a reasonable time, thereby establishing a valid legal document. This applies particularly to bills of exchange.

incidental expenses or **incidentals** Small sums of money spent at various times which are additional to larger budgeted amounts.

inclusive charge A charge which includes all costs.

Income 1 The remuneration or gains received for the use of services rendered by labour (wages and salaries, etc.), land (rent) and capital (interest and profits). 2 The revenue or gains earned by a business during an accounting period in the form of sales, rent, etc. 3 In economics, the evaluation of goods and services produced within an economy in a given period. See also **national income**.

income and expenditure account A statement of the revenues and expenses of an accounting period, produced by organizations which are not profit-orientated business concerns, e.g. sports clubs. The principles of the statements, format and compilation are basically identical to those employed in the business trading and profit and loss account.

income effect The extent of a reaction to a price change resulting from the fact that real income is affected by this action. This, plus the substitution effect, constitute the total reaction to a change in price.

income redistribution The sharing of wealth within a community in an attempt to reduce inequality. The main means of redistribution available to a government are a system of progressive taxation (with proportionately higher rates of tax at high income levels) and expenditure on social services (which benefit the poor more than the rich).

incomes policy A government policy that attempts to curb increases in wages and salaries either by restricting them to a stated maximum increase (in either percentage or monetary terms) or by banning them totally for a certain period. Incomes policies are usually accompanied by restrictions on price increases. Incomes policies have been criticized on the grounds that they disrupt the working of the market system and that incomes tend to surge ahead once a particular policy ends, so negating any advantages gained.

income statement 1 A statement of income received during a specified period. 2 See **profit and loss account**.

income tax A tax which is levied on personal income. The bases of assessment and collection vary for different types of income and are detailed in the various tax schedules.

income tax allowance A specific relief given against income for the purpose of assessment to income tax, being based upon marital status, number of dependants, certain disabilities, age, etc.

income tax return A completed form which officially declares income to the tax authorities.

incomplete records A term used to describe a bookkeeping system maintained for a business in which full documentation and recording of transactions have not been maintained. The profit and loss account and balance sheet are therefore constructed from the existing accounting records and any other details which can be determined, e.g. examination of debtors in order to determine sales for the period in question.

inconvertible note issue The note issue of a central bank which cannot be exchanged for gold but must be exchanged and accepted at the face value printed on the note.

incorporated company A company registered with the Registrar of Companies, having completed formalities associated with registration. Incorporation secures the privileges and imposes the obligations which are specified in the Company Acts, such as the privilege of limited liability, the obligation to present annual accounts, etc.

increasing returns A term used to describe the situation which arises in manufacturing activity when output expands at a proportionately greater rate than the increase in inputs of the factors of production. This happens where production facilities are being more fully and efficiently utilized. This may occur, for instance, if the whole of a factory floor is being utilized as a result of increased demand whereas before it was only half-used. Since the factory rent would be unaltered, there is greater productivity. Also called **returns to scale**. Compare **constant returns; diminishing returns**.

increment A regular automatic increase in salary.

incremental cost The cost of making one single extra unit above the quantity already planned.

incremental scale A salary scale with regular annual increases as an employee moves up the scale.

Indemnity An undertaking to make good costs or losses incurred by another person. The undertaking takes the form of a contract with a third party, the indemnifier assuming primary liability on the contract. Compare **guarantee**.

indemnity insurance A form of insurance whereby the insurers agree to cover the losses sustained by an insured person arising from, for instance, fire or accident.

indemnity, letter of see **letter of indemnity**

indent Originally, an order for goods prepared by an overseas agent of a merchant with details of price, etc. The word is currently used to describe any order of goods, especially from an agent to a principal, or the process of requesting goods from a store.

independent retailers or **the independents** Shops which are owned by individuals and are not part of a large national chain.

index A tabulation of index numbers designed to demonstrate the extent of the change in the data, e.g. prices, production, etc. over a time period. The compilation of an index requires: the selection of a base year from which movements are begun; the composition of the elements of the data and determination of their movements from the base year; weighting the elements according to the relative significance of each in relation to the complete tabulation; averaging the weighted movements for each element; and determination of the overall movement of the data from the base period. See also **Dow Jones Industrial Average, Hang Seng Index, Financial Times Ordinary Share Index**.

indexation The action of linking a figure to an annual index, such as the indexation of wage increases to the annual percentage rise in the cost-of-living index.

index-linked Rising automatically by the same percentage as the increase in the cost of living.

index number A single figure which quantifies the extent of change in the price, value or quantity of one or more items over a given period (usually one or more years).

Index of Industrial Production A tabulation, published by the Department of Trade and Industry, which measures the monthly changes in the level of industrial production, measured mainly in physical units. The tabulation incorporates data provided from the manufacturing, mining, construction, gas and electricity industries, but excludes agricultural and trade and transport activities. The index shows the growth or decline in production for each major industry and for the country as a whole.

Index of Retail Prices A tabulation, published by the Department of Trade and Industry, which measures the monthly changes in retail prices of a range of consumer goods and services. Consumer surveys are undertaken to establish the most significant types of expenditure, thereby assisting the process of determining the weighting of the goods and services.

Indices of Wholesale Prices A series of tabulations prepared by the Department of Trade and Industry which measure the monthly changes in wholesale prices of goods relating both to all industrial activities and to particular categories of industrial goods. Separate indices are prepared for: basic materials, e.g. brass, copper and fuel used in manufacturing; the output of certain industrial sectors, e.g. steel; and the output of specific industrial commodities, e.g. coal, soap.

indifference analysis A graphical technique for analysing consumer demand based on the use of a curve, from which it is possible to estimate the relative strengths of the income and substitution effects inherent in any price change.

indirect assistance A term used when the Bank of England, operating through the Special Buyer, provides assistance to the money market through the purchase of bills from the commercial banks. Funds are thereby provided to the banks for advancement to the discount houses, forestalling a rise in interest rates which might otherwise occur if the discount house remained short of funds. Compare **direct assistance**.

indirect costs see **fixed costs**

indirect exchange A term used to describe the process of conducting a transaction for the purchase and remittance of a foreign currency using the money market of an intermediary country because of the relatively advantageous rates of exchange quoted there. Compare **direct exchange**.

indirect expenses see **fixed costs**

indirect labour costs The costs of paying workers who are not actively involved in the manufacturing process, such as accounts staff or cleaners.

indirect taxation A form of taxation which is levied and collected from someone other than the final recipients of the goods in question. The tax is legally passed on by the payer to the final consumer by way of an inflated sales price. An example is value added tax. Compare **direct taxation**.

Individual Retirement Account In the United States, a private pension scheme to which individuals can make contributions separate from a company pension plan. Also called **IRA**.

indivisible plant Machinery or buildings which, for technical reasons, can operate only as large-scale units. Steel mills and power stations are both indivisible plant since they must both operate on a very large scale or not at all.

induction course A course for new employees, to train them in their jobs and at the same time introduce them to the company.

industrial accident An accident which occurs at a place of work.

Industrial and Commercial Finance Corporation A subsidiary of Finance for Industry Limited established to provide medium-term finance for small and medium-sized businesses. Now called **Investors in Industry**.

industrial arbitration tribunal A court which decides in industrial disputes, especially disputes between management and the workforce.

industrial capacity The amount of work which can be done in a factory, by a company or in a whole industry.

industrial design The design of products which are manufactured by machines, such as cars, domestic appliances, etc.

industrial espionage The action of trying to find out secrets concerning a competitor's work or products, usually by illegal means such as bugging offices, bribing employees, etc.

industrial estate An area of land near a large town, which is especially set aside for factories, warehouses and other businesses. Also called **trading estate**.

industrial goods Products bought by companies to use in the manufacture of other goods. Such products may be raw materials, semi-finished products or machinery used in manufacture.

industrial relations The relations and working practices between management and employees.

industrials Shares in manufacturing companies.

Industrial Training Board An organization established for each of a variety of industries by the Industrial Training Act, 1964, comprising representatives of the firms and trade unions within an industry, and educational representatives. The duties of a board relate to all aspects of training, e.g. assessing training requirements and recommending appropriate courses. A board is empowered to impose a levy on member firms to cover the costs of its operations, and grants are made to firms who provide approved training.

industry 1 A particular branch of trade which encompasses many companies or firms supplying similar or related products or services. **2** Manufacturing or trade as a whole.

inertia selling The selling of goods, where items are sent to prospective customers who have not ordered them, and then are charged to the customer if they are not returned within a stated period.

infant A person who at law has a limited capacity as he or she is under 18 years of age. The nature of the legal capacity of an infant varies. An infant's criminal responsibility is restricted: an infant is unable to commit a crime if under 10 years of age. Only contracts made by an infant for necessities or contracts of apprenticeship are enforceable against an infant. An infant may own shares but cannot be sued for arrears in calls. An infant may generally act as an agent or be a partner in a business.

infant industry A new industry which may not yet be able to compete on equal terms with established competitors from abroad. If this is the case, temporary protection from competition (perhaps through import controls or tariffs) may eventually lead to increased efficiency. In theory, protectionism should end once the infant industry is healthy. In practice this does not always happen.

inferior goods Goods of which consumers will buy less as their incomes increase even though they can, of course, afford to buy the same amount or more, for example, substitute or inferior quality foodstuffs.

inflation A general and sustained increase in the prices of goods and services thereby occasioning a fall in the real value of money, represented by its declining purchasing power. A single price increase is not enough in itself. The price of oil may rise, but this is not by itself inflation. It is, however, inflationary if this triggers a general and sustained increase in prices as people attempt to maintain their standards of living. See also **galloping inflation**.

inflationary spiral Any inflation that is self-sustaining. Typically, price increases lead to compensatory wage increases which raise labour costs and in turn cause a fresh round of price increases and so on. An inflationary spiral can become self-sustaining if people begin to expect and allow for future inflation when determining current prices and wages.

info quote A quotation given for information only without any commitment to deal at that price.

information agreement An undertaking made between firms in a particular industry to advise each other of their product prices, scale of charges, etc. in an attempt to prevent or restrict competition. It may thus be a strong indication that a cartel exists in that industry.

information technology The technology of acquiring, storing, processing and distributing information by electronic means, such as radio, TV, telephone, computer networks, etc.

infrastructure The capital which has been invested within an economy, which is peripheral to economic activity but facilitates such activity, e.g. a transport network, or which contributes to the social well-being of the community, e.g. health and education services.

infringement of patent The act of illegally using or making or selling a patented invention without the permission of the holder of the patent.

inherent vice The tendency for certain goods to deteriorate, leak, etc. For example, fruit are damaged easily, occasioning losses to the goods concerned and other goods with which they are in contact. If the carrier and insurer have not been informed of this, then they are not liable for damage arising solely from inherent vice.

initial capital Capital which is used to start up a business.

injunction A court order forbidding a person from performing a particular action (prohibitory injunction), or ordering the performance of a particular action (mandatory injunction).

injured party The party in a court case which has been harmed by the other party.

inland bill of exchange A bill which is drawn and payable in the British Isles. Unlike a foreign bill of exchange, an inland bill is drawn as a single document.

Inland Revenue The British government department which deals with income tax.

input tax VAT which is paid on goods or services which a company buys.

Input-output analysis The examination of the inter-relationships of the production situations for individual industries within an economy from the position that the output of one industry is the input of another. The final quantity and nature of goods available for consumption can be determined from such analysis and give reliable demand data. This economic technique can also be used to identify possible bottlenecks in the economy.

insert A leaflet or other piece of publicity material, put loose into the pages of a magazine and distributed with it.

insider dealing Trading in shares of a company using confidential details about the state of the company or about future developments, such as imminent announcement of a takeover bid. Insider dealing has been strongly condemned by the London Stock Exchange and legislation now exists declaring many aspects of it to be illegal.

insolvency The state of being unable to pay debts or meet financial obligations when they become due.

inspecting order A document, prepared by the owner of goods or his agent, requesting an official to allow the bearer of the document to examine the goods. This document is especially used when goods are stored at a dock in circumstances where a sample of the goods is

inspector of factories
insufficient to show the condition of the whole or where the goods are too bulky for a sample to be taken.

inspector of factories A government official who inspects factories and other places of work to see if they are safely managed.

inspector of taxes An official of the Inland Revenue who examines tax returns and decides how much tax is payable.

instalment Part of a payment which is to be paid regularly until the total has been cleared.

instalment plan see **hire purchase**

institute cargo clauses The clauses adopted by the Institute of London Underwriters and included in policies provided to cover for exceptional risks.

institutional investors Organizations which invest in stocks and shares, etc. the major proportion of funds deposited with them. They include the insurance companies, investment trusts, trade unions and unit trusts. They have grown steadily in significance and are now much more important than private investors.

insurable interest The monetary interest in a matter (especially the risk of financial loss), which is an essential prerequisite for the completion of a valid insurance contract. The interest must exist at the time of contracting for a life insurance policy. A marine insurance policy requires that the interest must exist at the time of the loss. Fire and other general forms of insurance require that the insurable interest exists both at the time of contracting and at the time of loss. See also **honour policy**.

insurance A contract whereby one party, the insurer, in consideration of a certain sum, the premium, undertakes to indemnify the other party, the insured, against loss resulting from the occurrence of certain events. The contract is always for a determinable period, either of fixed duration or on the occurrence of some specified event. Compare **assurance**.

insurance cover The provision of insurance by an insurance company or underwriter in accordance with the terms of a policy.

intangible assets Assets which have a value, but which cannot be seen, such as goodwill, patents, brand names, etc.

interbourse security A bond representing a loan which is raised in the security markets of several countries overseas. The bond carries a fixed rate of exchange.

interest Payment made by a borrower for the use of a lender's money. The percentage rate of interest is normally expressed as the amount of money a borrower would have to pay at the end of one year for each £100 of a loan. See also **minimum lending rate**.

interest coupon A slip of paper attached to a government bond certificate which can be detached and cashed to provide the interest.

interest-free credit   An arrangement to lend money to someone without charging interest on the loan.

interest or no interest   A form of insurance policy contracted with a person who may not have an insurable interest in the subject matter of the policy. The contract is, however, binding in honour.

interim accounts   A provisional statement of a company's financial affairs produced during the financial year to which it refers. Although they cannot be completely accurate, interim accounts are a valuable indicator of a company's health and are used for the estimation of liability to tax, the level of profitability, etc., with any inaccuracy being corrected at the end of the year.

interim dividend   A dividend paid at the end of a half-year.

inter-firm comparison; intra-firm comparison   Analysis of the performance and financial stability of units/departments within a business (intra-firm comparison) or between firms (inter-firm comparison). The analysis is usually conducted through the compilation of financial ratios and may be arranged by separate collaboration between firms or through a central agency.

interlocking directorship   A situation in which a company's representative is on the board of directors of various companies within a group of companies in which that company has a substantial interest. In this way, co-ordination as well as adequate representation of the major company's interests are made easier.

internal audit   The periodic examination of a business's accounting records, procedures and documentation, which is undertaken by a department within the organization reporting principally to officers within the company. Compare **external audit**.

internal check   A term used to describe control and checking procedures which are built into accounting systems in order to provide accuracy in the recording of data and the detection or minimizing of fraud.

internal rate of return   A means of evaluating the value of future projects by calculating the rate of return which the project earns on the capital invested. If this is a positive figure and greater than the market rate of interest then the project would provide an acceptable return.

Internal Revenue Service   (In the United States) the government department which deals with income tax.

International Bank for Reconstruction and Development   see **World Bank**

international commodity agreements   A series of agreements between producing countries of primary products setting minimum prices, to be achieved if necessary by restricting supply.

International Development Association   An organization which was established in 1960 as a complement to the International Bank for

International Finance Corporation

Reconstruction and Development in order to provide finance to developing nations for a variety of projects in circumstances where loans from the IBRD were not obtainable.

International Finance Corporation A United Nations organization which was established in 1956, as a complement to the International Bank for Reconstruction and Development, in order to provide finance for private industrial undertakings, especially in the less developed countries. The corporation does not provide total finance for a project.

International Labour Organization An affiliated agency of the United Nations which seeks to promote uniform principles of justice in matters relating to the employment of labour, e.g. dismissal procedures, and seeks to improve the general conditions of employment.

International Monetary Fund An organization established as a result of the Bretton Woods Agreement, 1945, creating a fund of gold and domestic currencies subscribed by member countries. The general objectives of the Fund are to promote international monetary co-operation and thereby to encourage international trade.

Member countries may purchase currencies from the fund in order to finance a short-term balance of payments deficit. However, if a country borrows deeply from the IMF, the loan may be conditional on the country following the Fund's advice.

intestate Denoting a person who has died without making a valid will.

in the black Showing a credit balance or profit.

in the red Showing a debit or loss.

in transit A description of goods, documents, money, etc. in the course of being conveyed from one place to another.

intra vires ('within the powers') A term used to describe an action, especially a contract, made by an official on behalf of a business which falls within the powers granted to the business as laid down in its memorandum of articles of association. The company is legally liable on any actions which are performed within its specified power. Compare **ultra vires act**.

introduction see **Stock Exchange introduction**

introductory offer The selling of a new product at a specially low price, to encourage customers to buy it. Such an offer is normally discontinued after a period such as one or two months.

inventory 1 A detailed listing and evaluation of a business's stock – raw materials, work in process and finished goods. 2 The value of total stocks. 3 A listing of all plant, equipment, furniture, etc.

inventory theory The operations research technique which studies the costs involved in holding and ordering stocks of material, seeking to minimize these costs and to determine an economic quantity to order each time replenishment is required.

inventory turnover The rate of consumption of a business's stocks of materials, usually expressed as a ratio of the costs of goods consumed or sold in a period and the average stock balance held.

investment 1 The purchase of securities, property, etc. or the deposit of money with a financial institution with a view to securing an income by way of interest, rent, dividend, and possibly a capital gain on disposal. 2 In economics, expenditure on factors of production in order to create physical assets which are themselves used to produce goods or other physical assets.

investment grant A grant allocated by the government to a company to allow it to invest in new machinery.

Investment Management Regulatory Organization An association of pension fund, unit trust and other investment managers who come together in order to regulate their members' dealings.

investment, negative The situation which occurs when accumulated stocks of capital are depleted rather than expanded.

investment opportunity The possibility of making a profitable investment.

investment trust A company whose capital is subscribed by the public as shareholders, and who funds are invested in securities issued by a number of other companies. Income and capital gains are sought from the investments, the spreading of risks through diverse investments being a special feature of the trust form of operation.

investor protection A series of measures designed to protect investors in securities from fraudulent company promotion and management. The measures include: company legislation which requires the disclosure of accounting reports and related information; legislation designed to eliminate misleading statements when promoting a company; and the Stock Exchange requirements and examination of applicant companies before a quotation of a company's shares on the Stock Exchange is permitted.

Investors in Industry A venture capital group, owned by the main clearing banks, formerly the Industrial and Commercial Finance Corporation. It is primarily concerned with businesses which are too small to warrant a public flotation and share issue. Finance is provided in the form of loans and share stocks.

invisible earnings Foreign currency earnings from services provided such as insurance, banking or tourism, and not in selling product.

invisible export Any service such as insurance, banking, or shipping, which is purchased by foreigners. The value of these services contributes to the balance of payments. See also **invisibles**.

invisibles Exports and imports which are services rather than goods. They include payments for tourism, insurance and shipping.

invitation to treat The action of sellers of goods in displaying goods with price tags, e.g. in a shop window or in a catalogue. Legally this action amounts to an invitation to the public to make an offer for the goods. However, the seller need not accept the offer and is not bound by the price which he has indicated.

invoice A statement showing particulars of goods sold, including quantity, price, quality, and packing details.

inward bill A bill of lading for goods arriving in a port.

inward mission A trade delegation which is visiting a company's home country.

IOU An acknowledgement of a debt, dated and signed by the debtor.

IRA see **Individual Retirement Account**

irredeemable (Of a stock or debenture) having no redemption date.

irrecoverable (Of a debt) which will never be paid.

irredeemable debenture A debenture loan which is issued by a company without specifying any provision for the loan's redemption. Its value lies in the interest payments due on it.

irrevocable credit see **documentary credit**

IRS see **Internal Revenue Service**

isoquant A graphical representation linking all the combinations of labour and capital which are just sufficient to produce a given output.

issue 1 The offer and allotment of shares in a company to applicants. 2 The shares so issued.

issued capital That part of the authorized stock or share capital of a company which has been subscribed for by the public and exchanged by the company, in the form of stock or share certificates, for full or part-payment of the issue price. In the United Kingdom the issued capital is evaluated for balance sheet purposes at nominal (par) value, any discount or premium on issue being separately evaluated.

issue price The price of shares when they are offered for sale for the first time. New shares are usually offered at a higher price than par value, and the difference between the two is the premium.

issuing bank or house Any financial institution that assists companies contemplating a share or loan issue. Its services may include: advising on the times and terms of the issue; arranging for the promotion of the issue; and securing from underwriters a guarantee that the issue will be fully subscribed. An issuing house may also advise on long-term financial matters.

IT see **information technology**

J

Jason clause A clause in a marine insurance policy under which the insurer undertakes to cover risks arising from latent undetected defects in the insured vessel if these defects were not discoverable by proper diligence.

J-curve A graphical representation of one reaction of the balance of payments to a devaluation. After a devaluation exports will become cheaper and imports more expensive. Through inertia, however, the same quantity of exports and imports is liable to be bought and sold and the balance of payments will worsen (represented by the downward stroke of the J). Eventually, the devaluation will cause exports to increase and imports to fall so that the balance of payments will improve (the upward curve of the J).

jerque note A certificate issued by a customs or waterguard officer to a ship's master, showing that the cargo is in order and agrees with the customs' cargo list. After it has been issued, outward-going cargo may be taken on board.

jerquer A customs officer who examines a ship's cargo, prior to issuing a jerque note.

jetsam 1 Goods cast into the sea from a ship in distress in order to lighten the load. 2 Such goods when washed ashore. Compare **flotsam**.

jettison To throw goods overboard in order to lighten a vessel in danger. The loss of goods is normally borne by all shippers under a general average insurance clause in marine insurance policies.

jingle A short, easily remembered tune which is used to advertise a product and becomes identified with the product in the mind of the public.

job 1 An individual piece of work. 2 A task. 3 A post, occupation or employment. 4 A piece of work undertaken for a fixed price. 5 Any material being worked upon in the performance of a task. 6 To work at various pieces of work; to work on a casual basis. 7 To let out work, or pieces of work, to contractors. 8 A cost unit consisting of a single order or contract.

job analysis The detailed analysis of a job, breaking it down into its component parts and assessing requirements. Job analysis is the first stage in any programme of job evaluation and salary administration. Also called **position analysis**.

jobber see **stockjobber**

jobber's turn

jobber's turn Formerly, a stockjobber's profit, being the difference between the buying and selling price of shares or securities.

job card A card on which details of a job are recorded. It shows time spent on each operation undertaken, and may show the actual operation details. The job card frequently follows the item of work through to completion and can then be used as a basis for costing the job. Compare **job ticket**.

job centre An office maintained by a central government department in all centres of population in the United Kingdom. The office seeks to bring together employers who notify the office of labour requirements, and people seeking employment. The office also provides the basic statistics of unemployment which are used by the government.

job costing The costing of individual pieces of work or contracts.

job creation scheme A scheme which is funded by the government to make new worthwhile jobs which can be filled by the unemployed.

job description A detailed description of a particular job, defining its responsibilities and duties, how it is to be performed and specifying the skills required of the job holder. Also called **job specification**.

job evaluation The systematic assessment of a work task by reference to the physical, mental and other requirements necessary for its performance. A points rating may be established for each job by means of this assessment, and the rating then forms the basis for relating the work task to a scale of remuneration for employees.

job factors The main headings under which a job is analysed, such as education needed, experience required, nature of decisions to be undertaken, etc.

job grades 1 Levels at which jobs having similar job characteristics, as ascertained by job evaluation, may be grouped. 2 Groups of jobs for which the same basic rate is paid.

job lot A quantity of miscellaneous goods, often of inferior quality.

job mix The composition of an order, production run, stockholding, etc. in terms of different specifications.

job number The identification number given to each job, product or contract.

job rate The prearranged basis of payment for the performance of all aspects of a specified task.

job satisfaction A feeling on the part of a worker that he is happy in his place of work and pleased with the work he is doing.

job security The situation where a worker feels he has a right to keep his job and that his job is likely to continue for the foreseeable future.

job sharing see **work sharing**.

job specification see **job description**

job ticket A card on which the details of an individual operation are recorded, including time taken, scrap produced, etc. It may often act as an instruction to an employee to perform the operation stated and provides an efficient way of booking productive time. Compare **job card**.

joint account 1 A bank account owned jointly by two or more people. It is a common arrangement for husbands and wives. 2 Any trading in a particular item or line by two or more separate companies where profits or losses arising from such trade are shared by the participating companies.

joint adventure see **joint venture**

joint and several liability The collective responsibility which an individual bears for an action or debt committed or assumed by other members of a group to which they all belong, for example, a partner's responsibility.

joint consultation The meeting and deliberation of representatives of management and of employees in order to settle disputes, exchange information and discuss mutual problems. A group constituted to participate in joint consultation is known as a joint consultative committee.

joint costs Costs of two or more goods that use the same raw materials, facilities, etc., even though they themselves are quite distinct. For example, wool and mutton are to a large extent subjected to joint costs.

joint demand The inter-related patterns of demand and supply which exist for products required to satisfy a single demand. For example, demand for housing results in a joint demand for bricks and tiles.

joint products Separate products which are produced or yielded during one process. Thus gas and coke are both produced during the carbonization of coal. Compare **by-product**.

joint stock bank A banking institution which has a public company, limited liability status. A principal distinguishing feature of this type of bank is the handling of current account transactions for depositors. See also **bank** (def. 1).

joint stock company A public company whose shares are held by many shareholders.

joint venture A partnership formed for a particular purpose, as a specific adventure, speculation, etc. Also called **joint adventure; joint trade**.

journal 1 (Formerly) a book of prime entry in which routine transactions were entered before being posted to a ledger and now supplanted by day books. 2 A book of prime entry in which are recorded miscellaneous transactions or adjustments for which no other book of prime entry is suited.

journal entry A record of a transaction or adjustment entered in a journal and showing the accounts and values to be debited and credited.

judgement creditor A person who has obtained a court order for payment by a debtor of an outstanding claim. The creditor, failing repayment, may sue the debtor or obtain an execution for seizure of the debtor's property. See also **judgement debtor**.

judgement debtor A person ordered by the court to pay a creditor in settlement of an outstanding claim. Failure to settle may result in an action to sue or in an execution ordering the seizure of the debtor's property.

junior partner A partner who holds a small number of the shares in a partnership.

junk bonds High-interest bonds raised as debentures on the security of a company which is the subject of a takeover bid.

junk mail Advertising material which is sent indiscriminately through the post to a large number of addressees, most of whom will throw it away without looking at it.

K

K Abbreviation for one thousand.

kaffir Nickname for any South African mining share and for most other South African mining shares dealt in on the Stock Exchange.

keen prices Prices which are kept low so as to be competitive.

Kennedy round A series of tariff negotiations, conducted under GATT auspices, which replaced negotiations relating to individual tariffs by negotiations relating to general reductions on most commodity tariffs. They lasted from 1964 to 1967.

key job see **bench mark** (def. 2)

Keynesian economics A branch of macroeconomics developed by John Maynard Keynes in the 1930s which was concerned with the determinants of the level of national income (and hence of employment). Keynes argued that national income is dependent upon the rate of investment, which was then at inadequately low levels.

Investment could not be encouraged by manipulating the interest rate (the monetarist solution), since the rate of interest could never be forced low enough. Instead, the state had to make investment more profitable by letting its expenditure exceed its revenue (by increasing public spending, cutting taxation or both). This would increase consumer demand, which would in turn encourage greater investment and hence production.

Keynesian economics was instrumental in ending the Depression and abolishing mass unemployment, and provided three decades of unparalleled growth. However, monetarists argue that this was achieved only by encouraging an ever-greater degree of inflation, which Keynesian economics cannot combat effectively.

kickback An illegal secret commission paid to someone, such as a government official, who helps in a business deal.

kilobyte A unit of storage in a computer, equivalent to 1,024 bytes.

kite An accommodation bill of exchange, i.e. one issued to obtain short-term credit for the financial convenience of the drawer.

kite mark In the United Kingdom, a mark put on goods to show they meet the quality standards of the British Standards Institution.

kruggerrands Coins containing one ounce of pure gold, produced by South Africa.

kurtic Humped, as in humpbacked curve.

L

labor union (In the United States) an organization of workers within an industry or a particular type of employment. The labor unions represent the interests of their members in negotiations relating to wages and conditions of work.

labour 1 Any work done for the sake of gain. 2 Those who engage in such work, particularly heavy or manual work. 3 A factor of production, including all aspects of human effort engaged in such production. 4 The human resources of an enterprise.

labour costs The costs of workers, especially hourly paid workers, involved in making a product.

labour force see **workforce**

labour-intensive Denoting any operating process, firm or industry which has a heavy proportion of labour input relative to capital input.

labour, mobility of The movement of workers between areas seeking similar employment (lateral mobility) or seeking different employment (vertical mobility).

labour productivity An expression of the input-output relationship achieved by an individual worker, group or labour force. The expression may be quantified in terms of units of output per hour of input, value added to products per pound of labour, etc.

labour relations The relations between management and workers.

labour shortage A situation where there are not enough workers available to fill vacant jobs.

labour turnover 1 The aggregate of employee replacements in a given period for a given business or industry. 2 The ratio of employee replacements in a given business or industry to the average number of employees during the relevant period. The term applies only to replacements and not to engagements related to expansion.

laches The delay in exercising a right, which deprives a party to the contract of his right to specific performance or to an injunction. A court of law must decide whether the delay has been reasonable or not.

laissez-faire (*French*, 'free to do') An economic doctrine, developed in the 18th century, which advocates no government interference in the performance of economic activities, whether pursued by individuals or by businesses. It contends that any government interference will actually hinder the best use of reserves.

lame duck 1 A member of the London Stock Exchange who is unable to meet his debts. 2 A firm or business in financial difficulties.

land agent A person who manages a farm or a large country property on behalf of the owner.

landing charges The payment for putting goods on land and the customs duties which are payable once they are landed.

landing officer see **land waiter**

landing order An authorization issued by customs authorities which permits a ship's officer to land goods. The fact of unloading is certified on the order by a land waiter.

land register A register of all land in the country, showing who owns it and what buildings are on it.

land registry The government office where land is registered.

land waiter The customs official who records and examines unloaded imported goods and who supervises the loading of exported goods certifying that they are shipped in the manner documented.

Laspeyres index An index constructed to measure price changes over a period, using base period data as weight factors. The index is derived from

$$1 = \frac{\Sigma Pu\ Qo}{\Sigma Po\ Qo}$$

Where Σ = sum of

Pu = price at current period

Po = price at base period

Qo = base period quantity

In periods of rising prices the index tends to overestimate the increases because, using base period weights, the tendency to buy less of those goods subject to increasing prices is ignored. Compare **Paasche index**.

last in, first out **1** A method of evaluating material issued to production and material stocks at the price which is chronologically the last price paid for material from which the issued material could be drawn. This is set out in the following table:

	received			issued	
date	units	price per unit	date	units	price per unit
1 Jan 1980	100	£1.00			
2 Jan 1980	150	£1.10	3 Jan 1980	80	£1.10

2 A redundancy policy where those employees who have been most recently appointed are made redundant first.

lateral filing A means of storing documents by suspension of files from parallel rails. This system makes greater use of height and saves more floor space than vertical filing.

lateral mobility see **labour, mobility of**

launch

launch The act of putting a new product on the market, including the promotion involved, special discounts to retailers, etc.

launder To pass illegal profits (such as from arms smuggling or selling drugs) into the normal banking system by using banks which accept cash deposits without questioning where the money has come from.

law of supply and demand The general rule that the amount of a product which is available is regulated by the needs of potential customers.

lay days The days allowed by custom, or specified in a contract, for the loading or unloading of a vessel. The days may be counted in working days, running days, or weather working days. Beyond the permitted lay days, a fine, known as demurrage, is imposed for loading or unloading.

layoff The temporary dismissal of a worker because there is no work to be done.

layout The arrangement of materials, items, etc. within an area. Such items may include plant, equipment, furniture, facilities, etc.

LBO see **leveraged buyout**

L/C see **letter of credit**

leading and lagging A term used to describe activities, in response to anticipated changes in the value of currency, of those engaged in international trade. Leading refers to the process of bringing forward transactions (purchases, sales, payment), lagging to the process of delaying transactions. This occurs when importing into or exporting from the United Kingdom (transactions being denominated in some currency other than sterling). If the value of sterling is expected to decline an exporter lags, i.e. delays sales, so that foreign currency receipts, when they arrive, are worth more in sterling terms. On the other hand an importer leads, i.e. brings forward purchases and payments before the sterling cost rises. If a rise in sterling is expected importers lag and exporters lead.

lead time The period of delay before a particular goal, such as the delivery of an item of stock, can be achieved: the time-span between ordering and receiving goods.

leapfrogging pay demands A series of pay demands where each section of the workforce asks for higher pay in order to overtake another section, which in turn asks for higher pay in order to retain differentials.

lease A contractual arrangement whereby one party uses an asset – land, buildings, etc. – which is owned by another, for a stated period and in return for a regular payment.

A lease may take various forms: a building lease, which confers the right to develop the land leased; an occupational lease, which confers the right to use land and buildings; a sub-lease, whereby the rights contracted for by the lessee may be conferred by him on another party, subject to the condition that the sub-lease extends for a shorter period than the main lease.

leaseback The leasing of property, machinery or other assets which were previously owned by the lessee but subsequently sold. The advantage of this procedure is that cash is generated from the sale of the asset, while the leasing rentals are permitted business expenses for taxation purposes.

leasehold Denoting a right to land and property. The right is held for a period of time on payment of rentals, etc. At the end of the agreed period the land or property reverts to the owner. See also **freehold**.

least square method A means of drawing a regression line in statistics. The line of best fit is drawn in such a way that the sum of the squared deviations from each observed point to the line is a minimum.

legacy Money or personal property (but not land) left by one person to another in a will.

legal claim Statement that someone owns something legally.

legal tender The forms of money – note or coin – which by law must be accepted in payment of a debt or in exchange for a good or service. Money must be offered in appropriate lots, i.e. notes to any value, but coins only up to a specified maximum value according to their denomination. For example, cupro-nickel coins worth up to ten pence are legal tender in lots up to £5 only.

legatee A person who receives a legacy from someone who has died.

lender of last resort The Bank of England in its position of providing assistance to financial institutions – especially the discount houses – in situations of funds shortage. For its aid, which usually takes the form of rediscounting bills of exchange, the Bank charges its minimum lending rate of interest, thereby securing the adherence of the money market to the interest rate structure operated by the Bank.

lending limit A limit on the amount of money which a bank can lend to individuals.

lessee A person or company holding a lease on a property.

lessor A person who grants a lease to a lessee.

letterhead The printed heading on the official notepaper of a company, with the company's name, registered address, VAT number and company registration number.

letter of administration A document issued by a court which authorizes a person to administer the estate of someone who has died intestate or who has died failing to name an executor.

letter of allotment A document issued by a company, detailing the number of shares which have been allocated to a subscriber at a share issue. The letter also indicates the money which is payable upon the allotment of the shares to the subscriber.

letter of comfort A letter supporting someone who is trying to obtain a loan or which helps someone in some way.

letter of credit 1 A document issued by a bank, merchant banker, etc. by which credit facilities up to a stated maximum amount are extended to a customer. The customer may obtain payment at various locations – including abroad – from branches of the bank or of its associated banks. The letter is not negotiable; payment can only be demanded by the person named in the letter. 2 A document issued by a bank, at a customer's request, by which credit facilities are extended to a third person – normally a foreign seller of goods. The letter enables the seller to obtain payment for his goods from an associated bank abroad on presentation of the letter and relevant shipping documents.

letter of hypothecation A document issued by the owner of goods, by which a lien on the goods is conferred on a banker from whom the owner has obtained a loan. The letter acts as security for the loan, giving the banker an interest in the goods should the owner default on the repayment of the loan.

letter of indemnity 1 A document in which the signatory agrees to bear the loss or damage caused to another named person arising from an event or the performance or non-performance of an action. 2 A document in which an exporting manufacturer agrees to make good losses arising through faulty packing, etc.

letter of intent A letter which states what a company intends to do if a certain event takes place.

letter of licence A document issued by creditors in which, they allow the debtor a stated period of time before they press their claims against him.

letter of reference A letter in which an employer or teacher recommends a person for a job.

letter of regret A document issued by a company in notification that applicants for a share issue have been unsuccessful. The letter is generally accompanied by the return of any money payable on application.

letter of renunciation A pro-forma document issued to a member of a company by means of which the member may renounce his rights to shares either totally or in favour of a specified person. The document is used when the company declares a rights issue or when shares are to be allotted to subscribers of a share issue.

letters patent A document issued by a government department which confers patent rights on a person or business or which confers a special privilege to be exercised for a period of years.

levelled time The average time taken for the performance of a given task, after adjustment for differences in skill, effort, conditions, etc. between workers.

leveraged buyout The purchase of a company with money which is borrowed against the security of the shares in the company being bought.

lex mercatorem Those trade customs and usages which, having been notified by the courts in a particular action, have become incorporated into the framework of the law. Also called **merchant law.**

liability An obligation to pay a third party incurred by an individual, or business, e.g. in respect of goods or services received, taxes, etc.

libel An untrue written statement which damages a person's character.

LIBID see **London Inter-Bank Bid Rate**

LIBOR see **London Inter-Bank Offered Rate**

licence An official document allowing someone to do something or use something, which would otherwise be illegal.

license To give someone permission to do something which would otherwise be illegal, such as the exploitation of a patented invention or the use of a trademark. Such licensing is usually made against the payment of a fee or royalty.

licensee A person who receives a licence to do something.

licensor A person (such as a patent holder) who grants someone a licence.

lien The legal right to take possession of another's goods in the event of the non-payment of a debt. A particular lien exists where the debt is related to the goods; for example, a carrier may retain goods pending payment by the seller. A general lien exists where the debt is unrelated to the goods, possession being taken as settlement of an outstanding balance. A lien may be voluntarily given by the owner of goods, for example, by depositing documents of title as security for a loan.

life interest The situation where someone benefits from a property as long as he is alive.

l.i.f.o. see **last in, first out**

light pen A pen that contains a light-sensitive device which can read computer-readable characters, such as a bar code.

limit The fixed price at which a broker is instructed to buy or sell securities or commodities.

limitation of actions A time restriction placed on the ability to bring a legal action, e.g. an action for damages relating to personal injury must be begun within three years of the cause. General actions in contract or tort must be begun within six years. Actions relating to mortgages and other sealed contracts must be begun within 12 years.

limited A word incorporated into the name of a limited company on all documents, etc., signifying a restriction of the liability of the members of the company for that company's debts. Such liability may be limited by guarantee as in the case of professional bodies, or by shares, in which case the members' liability is limited to the nominal value of the shares. Holders of fully paid shares have no further liability.

limited and reduced Words incorporated into the name of a limited

limited liability company

company on all documents, etc., signifying that, in addition to the restriction on members' liability for the company's debts, a court has approved a reduction of the company's capital. The incorporation of the words 'and reduced' into the company name extends for the period specified by the court.

limited liability company A company whose members bear a liability which is limited to the extent of the nominal value of the shares which they hold. Compare **unlimited company**.

limited partner see **sleeping partner**

limited partnership see **partnership, limited**

limiting factor Any element which constrains business activity and whose influence must first be assessed in order to incorporate other factors of production into a planned course of action, such as total sales potential, material availability, labour supply, and finance.

line management The organization of a business where each manager is responsible for a group of workers and takes instruction from superiors.

line of balance A graphical representation showing the relationship between actual progress and delivery commitments against a time scale. It is effective for pinpointing bottlenecks.

line printer A printing machine which prints information from a computer, one line at a time.

line production Any production flow where the product moves from one operation to another in a predetermined sequence.

liquid assets Assets that can be converted into cash comparatively quickly. They are widely regarded as comprising shares, short-term bills of exchange, bank deposits and cash itself.

liquidated damages Damages that a contract stipulates will be paid in compensation if a party to the contract fails to carry out his obligations. The amount of liquidated damages is set out before the contract is signed and, although not linked contractually to the amount of damage incurred, it must be a fair estimate of it.

liquidation 1 The conversion of assets, e.g. stock, debtors, into cash. 2 The settlement of a debt. 3 The bankruptcy proceedings of a limited company. See also **winding-up**.

liquidator The official who manages the winding up of a company or who settles the affairs of an estate. His duties include producing a list of assets and liabilities, arranging for calls on unpaid shares, disposing of assets, settling claims and distributing any residue to members/ beneficiaries. Where a winding-up is compulsory the Official Receiver acts as liquidator until one is appointed by the creditors. The liquidator's operation is subject both to supervision by the courts and by the creditor's committee of inspection. Where the liquidation is voluntary, the liquidator is appointed by the company, possibly together with creditors, and is less subject to supervision.

liquidity A state of having sufficient cash resources and assets easily convertible into cash in order to meet debts as they fall due.

liquidity preference The desire to hold money rather than other forms of wealth. The motives for this include the following: to provide a fund with which to pay for transactions or to meet unforeseen events, and to provide a fund for investment when price movements are advantageous. The degree of liquidity preference influences the pattern of consumption, saving and investment, and thereby affects the whole pace and nature of economic activity.

liquidity ratio – banks An expression of the relationship between the short-term investments held by a commercial bank and its total deposits. Short-term investments include cash, loans at call and short notice, and bills of exchange but exclude special deposits held at the Bank of England. The ratio is maintained at about 28% and limits the extent to which a bank may invest its funds in long-term investments or provide credit facilities.

liquidity ratios – financial The relationship between the current assets and current liabilities of a business. The ratio reflects the ability of the business to meet its obligations as they fall due.

A 1:1 ratio usually indicates some liquidity stability, although circumstances in particular businesses may make a higher or lower ratio more acceptable. See also **acid-test ratio**.

liquidity trap A situation in a period of economic depression when the real rate of interest is so low that investors prefer to hold cash instead of bonds or other interest-bearing securities. In such a state of affairs monetary policies are powerless. The liquidity trap was first deeply analysed by John Maynard Keynes.

listed company A company whose shares can be bought and sold on the Stock Exchange, which publishes the share price.

listed securities Shares which appear on the official Stock Exchange list, and which may be bought or sold on the Stock Exchange.

list price The official price of a good/service as quoted in a firm's catalogue or literature.

livery companies Companies whose origin derives from the medieval craft guilds and from incorporation by Royal Charter and who exercise a particular trade or craft. Such companies nowadays retain mainly their social and charitable functions. Some, however, still regulate the conduct of the business of the trade or craft.

Lloyd's A corporate organization of London underwriters whose members undertake a wide range of insurance activities including marine, aviation, fire and accident. The members usually operate in syndicates, the Corporation of Lloyds not being liable for its members' activities, but providing for them a range of standardized documents, shipping and intelligence services.

Lloyd's agent An agent employed by Lloyd's to supply shipping or aviation intelligence for the area of his agency. Frequently the agent may appoint on a member's behalf a surveyor to report on damage or loss arising from an accident.

Lloyd's list A daily publication issued by Lloyd's, which details the movement of seagoing vessels.

Lloyd's Register of Shipping A record of shipping maintained by Lloyd's and classified according to standard of construction and ships' fittings. The register is compiled from surveys made by authorized surveyors and is used by Lloyd's members in assessing insurance policies and claims.

load line The line painted on the side of a ship to show where the water should reach if the ship is fully loaded and maximum safety is to be observed.

loan capital That part of the finance of a business which is subscribed by way of a loan, e.g. a debenture, for a number of years, bearing a specified rate of interest. Loan capital is normally secured against business assets. Failure to repay the loan or to pay interest due may result in winding-up proceedings. Subscribers of loan capital are not thereby members of the business.

loan conversion The replacement of a loan, which is due for repayment, by the issue of a further loan in lieu of repayment. The interest rate may vary between the two loans.

loan shark A person who lends money at a very high interest rate.

loan stock Money which is lent to a company at a fixed rate of interest.

local acceptance see **qualified acceptance**

local authority The body of people responsible for the administration of local government.

local bond A form of short-term loan offered for public subscription by local authorities. Such bond issues are subject to government regulation and Treasury approval.

lock-out The withdrawal of working facilities by an employer through the prevention of access to work premises. It is equivalent to a strike by employees.

lock-up premises Business premises, such as a shop, which have no living accommodation, and which the proprietor locks up each evening.

loco Denoting that the price quoted for goods includes packing and transport costs from the present location to the customer.

locum tenens A person who acts as a substitute for another.

locus sigilli The position on a document where a seal is to be placed. Its location is often indicated on copies of the document by the initials 'l.s.'.

logo A symbol or series of letters used by a company to identify itself, usually an adaptation of the company name.

Lombard Street The London location of many of the financial institutions which collectively form the money market, the street being synonymous with the money market.

London Bankers Clearing House An institution, maintained by the commercial banks, which processes daily the cheque transactions to which member banks have been a party. The net balance arising to or from each bank is determined for settlement.

London Commodity Exchange The institution where commodities such as coffee and sugar are traded.

London gold fixing An arrangement where the world price of gold is fixed by dealers each day at the London Gold Market.

London Inter-Bank Bid Rate The interest rate at which banks will borrow money on the international market.

London Inter-Bank Offered Rate The interest rate at which banks will lend money on the international market.

London Metal Exchange The institution where dealing is done in metals such as copper, nickel and silver, but not gold.

long A bull operator on the US Stock Exchange.

long credit Credit terms which allow the purchaser a long time (usually over six months) in which to pay.

long-dated bill A bill of exchange which has from six to nine months to run before reaching maturity.

longs A Stock Exchange term used to describe the loan stocks which are repayable in the long-term, i.e. dated 25 years ahead. Compare **shorts**.

long term forecast A forecast for a period of three years or more.

loophole A way of avoiding something, especially in a law or contract which has been written without sufficient care.

loose time An allowed time for a given job which is greater than that required by a qualified worker performing his job with normal skill and effort.

loss in transport The amount of weight which is lost while goods are being transported.

loss leader A good sold at a low price (below cost) in order to attract customers into the shop on the expectation that they will make other purchases.

low-pressure salesman A salesman who does not promote sales very energetically, but concentrates on the needs of the customer and the suitability of the product to those needs.

Ltd see **limited**

lump, the A system of labour-only contracting used in the building and construction industries. Under the system an individual or group of workers contracts with a main contractor to perform a particular task in return for a lump payment. The individual or group then accounts privately for tax and statutory contributions covering health and accident insurance, etc.

lump sum An amount of money paid at one time, not in several instalments.

luncheon voucher A document issued to employees, which is exchangeable for meals but not cash at restaurants, etc. The voucher scheme is organized by a firm which sells vouchers to employers and which repurchases the issued vouchers from caterers. To the employee the voucher is a tax-free source of income up to a maximum daily value.

M

M1 A measure of money supply, including all coins and notes in circulation, and personal current accounts.

M2 A measure of money supply, including items covered by **M1**, plus personal deposit accounts.

M3 A measure of money supply, including items covered by **M2**, plus government deposits and deposits in currencies other than sterling.

M3 sterling A measure of money supply covering all **M3**, except deposits in currencies other than sterling, but including all current and deposit accounts of both public and private sectors.

machine-readable codes Sets of signs or letters which a computer can read, such as postcodes and bar codes.

Macmillan gap A gap in the range of financial facilities available to business through the capital market, as disclosed by the Macmillan Committee on Finance and Industry, 1931. Small to medium-sized businesses, which were too small to warrant a public share issue, had difficulty in obtaining long-term finance from the market. The Industrial and Commercial Finance Corporation was subsequently established in order to provide finance for these businesses and thus to close the gap.

macroeconomics The study of aggregate economic behaviour. Topics covered by it include the overall level of investment, the amount of consumption, taxation, etc. Compare **microeconomics**.

made bill A foreign bill of exchange which requires endorsement by a third party before the bill is fully valid and can be negotiated by the drawer. Compare **drawn bill**.

made money The additional cash made available to the commercial banks through the purchase of their bills of exchange by the Bank of England acting through the special buyer. The extra cash resources may be applied in advancing money to the discount houses. The transactions take place as part of the Bank's monetary policy in this case being designed to ease the money supply and perhaps also to encourage a fall in interest rates.

Madison Avenue The centre of the US advertising industry.

magnetic ink character reading A computer capacity similar to optical character reading except that the characters are written in magnetic ink. This is commonly used on cheques.

magnetic stripe A band of magnetized material which stores data which can be read by a special device. The data can then be collated, printed, or used as a basis for posting to ledger accounts.

magnetic tape Plastic sensitized tape used for recording information in large computers.

mailing The sending of publicity material to potential customers.

mailing list A list of the addresses of customers or potential customers, which is used for sending publicity material or circular letters.

mailing piece A single item of publicity material sent to an address on a mailing list.

mail order A method of selling which secures orders for goods through the circulation of catalogues to agents and potential customers. Ordering procedures and delivery of goods are conducted by post.

mail shot The sending of a publicity material to a series of addresses.

mail transfer A device used to remit the contracted purchase price in foreign trade, once the buyer has received the documents of title. The buyer's bank sends a letter of instruction to its local correspondent bank in order to arrange payment or the provision of credit to the seller.

majority interest A situation where an individual owns a majority of the shares in a company.

majority shareholder An individual shareholder who owns more than half the shares in a company.

maker A person who originates a promissory note.

making a market The quotation by a market maker of the buying and selling prices of a stock or share at which he is ready to trade.

making-up day One of the days in the Stock Exchange settlement period.

making-up price The price at which a transaction, which is to be carried forward to the next period, is recorded at the end of a Stock Exchange settlement period. The shares are not in fact taken up or delivered, the use of making-up prices being a convenience in order to close the books at each account period. At the start of the next period the transaction is reopened at the making-up price, less backwardation or contango charges.

managed cost A business expense, the extent of which is determined at the discretion of management in accordance with company policy. Compare **engineered cost**.

managed currency A currency which is regulated by the government's exercise of control over the note issue and over credit formation as well as by trading on the foreign exchange markets.

management 1 The carrying out of policies laid down by determining what results are to be accomplished, planning how these results are to be accomplished, building up the required organization, and controlling that organization. 2 The people responsible for carrying out these tasks.

management accounting The reporting of information to management, in monetary terms, in order to assist in the planning and control processes of a business, and as an aid to decision making.

management buyout The takeover of a company by a group of senior employees (usually managers and directors), supported by loans from banks.

management by objectives A method of managing a business by planning work for managers and testing regularly to see if it is completed correctly and within the planned time limits.

management shares Shares issued to managers of a business, or their nominees, and ranking for dividend or surplus profits after payment of dividends to ordinary shareholders.

manager One who is vested with the authority and accountability for directing the work of others in order to ensure the optimum use of resources at his disposal in the achievement of the objectives of the organization by which he is employed.

managerial capitalism A stage in political development when industry and trade are dominated by companies which are nominally owned by a shifting population of shareholders, but in fact run by salaried staff who make all the important decisions. The shareholders take little interest in the running of the firms – their roles resemble more that of rentiers rather than entrepreneurs.

managing director The director of a company with overall responsibility for the day-to-day running of its affairs.

mandate An authorization to a person or firm to manage a business or a transaction on behalf of the signatory.

man-hour The amount of work done by one employee in one hour.

manifest A detailed list of a ship's cargo issued by the shipowner or his broker, which is sent to agents overseas and to the customs authorities at the out-going port within six days of clearance.

man-machine chart A type of multiple activity chart in which the operations performed by the machine and its operator are shown against a common time scale.

manning levels The number of people required in each department of a company to ensure that work schedules are kept to efficiently.

manpower forecasting The calculation of the number of workers required in the future to satisfy anticipated needs, and the comparison with the number who will actually be available.

manufacturer's recommended price The price which a manufacturer suggests for his product in the retail market, though often reduced by the retailer.

manufacturing industries The industries which take raw materials and make them into finished products.

Maple Leaf Coin containing one ounce of gold, produced by Canada.

mare clausum (*Latin*, 'closed sea') The territorial waters over which bordering countries have sovereignty.

margin 1 See **gross profit**. 2 The price discretion on either side of a fixed price which is allowed by a client to his stockbroker when attempting to negotiate a transaction. 3 The excess of market value of an asset which has been given as collateral for a loan over the value of the loan. 4 See **margin dealing**.

marginal cost The amount, at any given volume of output, by which total costs are changed if the volume of output is increased or decreased by one unit. A unit may be a batch, a process, a department, an order or a single article. The total variable costs attributable to one unit equal its marginal cost. The marginal cost is composed of direct (variable) costs such as wages, power bills, etc. It is a condition of profit maximization that output takes place at that level where the marginal cost of production equals price.

marginal costing The ascertainment of marginal costs and of the effect on profit of changes in volume or type of output by distinguishing between fixed and variable (direct) costs. Compare **absorption costing**.

marginal pricing The pricing of a unit at the same level as the marginal cost.

marginal product The increase in output which results from adding one more unit of production, whether labour or capital.

marginal purchase A purchase which the buyer feels is only just worth buying.

marginal revenue The revenue from selling a single unit above the number which have already been sold.

marginal utility The increase in satisfaction which results from the consumption of the final unit of a good or service.

margin dealing The trading of securities or the forward purchase of commodities or currencies for a part-payment of the total price. The purchaser hopes to sell at a profit later, using the sale proceeds to complete payment of the original purchase.

margin of error 1 The number of mistakes which are acceptable in a document or a product. 2 The amount by which a forecast or budget may differ from the actual result.

margin of safety The difference between the planned sales level and the break-even level.

marine insurance The form of insurance which covers losses or damage arising to ships or cargo. A policy may be for a stated insured sum (a valued policy) or for a sum related to the loss as it occurs (an unvalued policy). The period of insurance may run for a single specific voyage (voyage policy) or may extend for a period covering all journeys made in that period (time policy). A policy may combine elements of voyage and time policies, e.g. covering a vessel on a particular route for a period of perhaps a year (a mixed policy).

markdown 1 The pricing of goods below that price originally shown. 2 The downward revaluation of stock or share prices following adverse market movements.

marked cheque see **certified cheque**

market 1 The demand for a good or service. 2 Any place where goods and services are bought and sold. It need not be an actual location – the advertisement columns of a local newspaper are one form of market.

market capitalization The value of a company calculated by multiplying the price of its shares on the Stock Exchange by the number of shares issued.

market economist A person specializing in the study of financial structures and the return on investments in the stock market.

market forces The influences which bear on the sale of a product or service (such as price, demand, availability, etc.).

marketing A business function whose responsibilities relate to: the assessment of potential sales for the businesses' products and services through market research; the conversion of the potential into effective demand through promotional and selling activities; the organization of the distribution of goods to customers via retailers and wholesalers or directly.

market leader The product which has the largest share of a market or the company which makes it.

market maker A person or securities house which buys or sells shares for clients on the Stock Exchange.

market opportunity The possibility of entering a market and taking a share of it.

market ouvert A market established by custom, charter or statute where goods are openly displayed for sale. A purchaser by law acquires a good title to the goods irrespective of any defect in the title possessed by the seller, provided that the goods are of a type normally dealt in by the seller and that the purchaser has acted in good faith.

market penetration The action of gaining a larger share of a market by promotion or other forms of marketing.

market rate of discount The fee charged by banks, bill brokers, etc. for cash purchasing, i.e. discounting bills of exchange. The fee is expressed as an annual rate of interest and is usually lower than the minimum lending rate.

market research The determination of the prospective demand for a product through the testing of consumer reactions to products, questions about preferences, etc. and the application of statistical techniques in order to evaluate the responses.

market share The percentage of a total market for a product or service which is represented by the sales of a one company's products.

market value The current price ruling in the market, at which price an article may be bought and sold.

marking names The financial firms (finance houses or brokers) whose names are recorded in a list of recognized names maintained by the Stock Exchange. The firms are used for the registration of ownership of American and Canadian share certificates which are endorsed in blank, thereby permitting a lawful transfer of ownership in a transaction. The firms receive dividends from the company and pay them to the owners of the shares.

markings The prices at which London Stock Exchange transactions have been made between the hours of 11 a.m. and 3 p.m. The prices are recorded in the Official List and published daily in the financial press.

mark-up The amount by which the retail price of an article is higher than the unit manufacturing cost or the wholesale price.

mass marketing Marketing which is aimed at reaching the widest audience possible.

mass media The means of communication with the widest audience possible, such as radio, TV and the national press.

mass production The manufacture of standardized or uniform articles in large quantities. Characteristically this type of production involves high capital investment and low unit costs of output.

materials control The process of ensuring the availability of the right materials at the required time and place in order to meet manufacturing requirements, while maintaining minimum investments in such materials. It also includes measures to prevent misappropriation and waste of materials.

materials cost variance The difference between the standard cost of materials specified for the actual output and the actual cost of materials used.

materials handling The movement of raw materials and semi-finished products from one place to another in an efficient way.

materials usage variance That part of a materials cost variance which is due to the difference between the standard quantity of material specified and the actual quantity used.

maternity leave Permission given to a female employee to be away from work to have a baby.

mate's receipt The receipt for goods shipped on board, signed by the mate and used by the ship's master in signing the bill of lading.

maturity The date on which a financial obligation, such as an insurance policy or gilt-edged security, can be exchanged for cash. The nearer to maturity such an item is, the nearer its value approaches its face value.

maximize To make a profit as large as possible.

MBO see **management buyout**

MD see **managing director**

mean see **arithmetic mean**

mean deviation A measure of the dispersion of a number of observations obtained by calculating the arithmetic mean of the absolute deviation of each observation from the mean of the group.

mean price The average of the selling and buying prices quoted by a dealer on the security or commodity markets. Also called **middle market price**.

means test An inquiry into how much a person or family earns, to see if they are eligible for government benefits.

measured daywork A payment system whereby standard performances are established for each job using work-study techniques. The rates applicable to each job are agreed by negotiation and thereafter the achievement of the standard performances depends upon the effectiveness of management.

media see **mass media**

median The middle value in a group of values that have been arranged in order of magnitude. In the case of an even number of observations, the median would be a calculated figure. It is one type of average, but is less commonly used than the arithmetic mean.

mediation An attempt by a third party to make the two sides in an industrial dispute come to an agreement.

medical certificate A signed certificate from a doctor to show that a worker is ill and cannot attend the place of work.

medium-dated Denoting a gilt-edged security that has more than five years but less than ten to run before its redemption date.

medium-term forecast A forecast covering two or three years.

megabyte A storage unit in a computer, equal to 1,048,576 bytes.

memorandum of satisfaction A document issued by a business which has borrowed money stating that any mortgage or other charge on assets used as security for the loan has been discharged by repayment of the loan. A copy of the memorandum is sent to the Registrar of Companies if the business is a company, provided that the mortgage or charge has previously been registered.

mercantilism An economic hypothesis that the acquisition of gold and silver bullion is by itself sufficient to create prosperity in a country. In fact, since this does nothing to increase the productive capacity of a country its sole effect is likely to be to increase inflation. Mercantilism was finally disproved by Adam Smith (1723–90).

merchandise Goods which are offered for sale.

merchandising The promotion of a product to the buying public, using special design techniques, or by producing manufactured spinoffs such as retail articles based on TV characters.

merchantable quality An implied condition in a contract for the sale of goods that the goods are fit for use. Failure of goods to be of merchantable quality renders the seller liable to an action for breach of contract.

merchant bank A financial institution which performs a wide range of activities: financing international trade; accepting bills of exchange; advising companies on takeovers, amalgamations, flotations and share issues; advising about pension funds, charities and companies' investment policies; and acting as trustee for unit trusts.

merchant law see **lex mercatorem**

merger The amalgamation of two or more businesses into a single entity. It is formally achieved: (**a**) by the dissolution of both companies and the creation of a new company with the combined assets of the previous companies; (**b**) by the formation of a holding company – the existing companies continue but with a controlling portion of the share capital being taken up by the holding company.

merit award The award of an increase in salary to a worker as a reward for good work performance.

merit rating The rating of an employee's performance, attitude and characteristics with a view to determining his potential for promotion, salary increase, etc.

methods study The systematic analysis of work, undertaken to eliminate unnecessary operations or movements and to establish the best layout of tools, work and workplace to ensure the best possible performance of the job being studied. Also called **methods engineering**.

methods-time measurement The analysis of the basic motions necessary to accomplish a given task and the establishment of standard times for the performance of each motion.

m.i.c.r. see **magnetic ink character reading**

microeconomics The study of the behaviour of individual economic units such as consumers, producers, and industries, and of the factors which determine the prices of products and the allocation of resources (e.g., labour, capital) among the available alternative uses. Compare **macroeconomics**.

micromotion study The study of work by filming the task being performed and by using a timing device to obtain times for each movement.

microprocessor A building block used in computer technology. Since they are small and cheap microprocessors have opened up new fields of computing applications.

middleman An intermediary between the producer/originator of a product or item and the final recipient. The middleman usually performs some form of service. For example, a wholesaler breaks bulk and distributes the item and brokers provide skilled advice and documentation services.

middle management The departmental managers who carry out the policy set by the directors and organize the work of sections of the workforce.

middle market price see **mean price**

minimize To make something very small or insignificant.

minimum dividend The smallest dividend which is legal and is accepted by the shareholders.

minimum lending rate The rate of interest charged by the Bank of England to discount approved bills of exchange or make short-term loans. It is this rate which indirectly determines the overall level of domestic interest rates charged by the banks and building societies. It replaced bank rate, which it closely resembles, in 1972.

minimum stock The lowest level to which stocks should normally be allowed to fall. It should permit some margin of safety in order that stock shortages do not disrupt production.

minimum subscription The value of share capital which a company's directors consider to be the minimum amount which must be raised for effective flotation of the company, i.e. providing for fixed and working capital, etc.

minimum wage The lowest hourly wage which is allowed by law.

minority interest The portion of the assets of a company which is attributable to minority shareholders, i.e. to members other than the controlling member. In company reporting it is frequent practice for a holding company to incorporate data of its subsidiary companies into its balance sheet, any minority interest in the subsidiaries being shown as a liability.

minority report The report of a single member or small group of a committee, commission, etc. representing a minority of the total membership.

minority shareholding The shares of a company which are not owned by the controlling member of the company (who may be another company). See also **minority interest**.

mint A place where coinage and notes of legal tender are produced.

minute book A record of meetings held by an organization. By law, a company must maintain a minute book, a signed minute book being regarded as evidence of the proceedings at a meeting.

minutes A written record of the proceedings at a meeting.

misappropriation of funds The illegal use of money by someone who is not the owner, but has been entrusted with it.

misfeasance summons An action brought during winding-up proceedings against a promoter, director, liquidator or company officer, relating to an alleged misappropriation of company money or property, or to an alleged breach of trust.

misrepresentation The action of making a wrong statement in order to persuade someone to buy a product or sign a contract.

Misrepresentation Act An Act of Parliament (1967) which provides for the recovery of damages for losses incurred by a party having entered into a contract based on a misrepresentation by the other party. The claimant need not prove that the misrepresentation was fraudulent.

mix The product composition of a business.

mixed economy An economy in which activity is organized by a combination of individual, business and state enterprises. Most countries have mixed economies, although the ratio of public to private industry differs greatly.

mixed policy see **marine insurance**

MLR see **minimum lending rate**

mobile workforce Workers who are willing to move from place to place to find work.

mobility of labour A situation where workers are prepared to move from place to place to find work.

mode The observation that occurs most frequently in a given group of observations.

modem A device which links a computer to a telephone line, allowing data to be sent from one computer to another over long distances.

monetarism The economic hypothesis that the money supply is the main determinant of the rate of inflation. The best-known proponents of monetarism are the Chicago School of Economists led by Professor Milton Friedman.

monetary unit The standard currency used in a country.

monetary working capital adjustment see **current cost accounting** (def. 1c)

money Any medium of exchange that allows trading to take place without the need for barter. In the past many exotic materials such as cowrie shells, ingots and beads have been used for money. The term applies to bank deposits as well as notes and coin.

money at call, money at short notice A bank loan which is repayable on demand (at call) or within 24 hours (short notice).

money market Financial institutions collectively, including discount houses, commercial banks and accepting houses, which transact business relating to short-term finance, e.g. bills of exchange, treasury bills, etc. The market also incorporates the foreign exchange market with transactions in international currencies.

money order A document which can be purchased, used for sending funds by post.

money supply The total quantity of money in circulation at a given moment. There are several definitions of it, of which the two most commonly found are **M1** and **M3**.

monitor 1 A computer screen. 2 To examine a process carefully to see what progress is being made.

monometallism A monetary system which is based on one metal – usually gold. Compare **bimetallism**.

Monopolies and Mergers Commission A commission appointed by the government to inquire and report on such matters as monopoly situations in relation to the supply of goods and services, unregistered trade practices, and protective mergers and takeovers. The commission is charged with reporting to the Department of Trade and Industry on a situation as it affects the public interest and making recommendations as to action to be taken.

monopoly An industry in which there is only one producer and many consumers. To maximize its profits, the monopoly will restrict its output so that marginal revenue equals average cost.

monopsony A situation in which a sole buyer exists, being able accordingly to exert pressure on suppliers in relation to prices and other terms of sale. Compare **monopoly**.

Monte Carlo method An operational research technique using a probability model to solve mathematical problems. The term, originally a code name used during the Second World War, has generally come to be applied to simulations of gaming methods.

month end The end of the month, when accounts for the month are completed.

moonlighting The practice of performing a second job, especially after the completion of one's main employment during the day.

moral suasion The influence which the Bank of England has over the commercial banks in order to persuade them to pursue a course of action voluntarily. The influence may be converted to actual authority through the use of monetary tools, e.g. the minimum lending rate, official directives, etc.

moratorium An extension of the time allowed to a debtor for repayment of a debt.

mortgage An interest in property which is transferred by the borrower of money (mortgagor) to the lender (mortgagee) as security for the loan. Failure to repay the loan may result in the mortgagee suing for repayment or foreclosing, subject to the mortgagor's equity of redemption. See also **equity of redemption; foreclose**.

mortgage bond A certificate showing that a mortgage exists and that a property is the security for it.

mortgage debenture A debenture where the lender can be repaid by selling property belonging to the company.

mortgage famine A situation where there are not enough funds available to provide mortgages to all house buyers who need them.

mortgage relief Tax relief, which allows no tax to be payable on interest on mortgages up to a certain total sum.

most-favoured nation clause A clause in a commercial treaty concluded by two countries whereby the signatories agree to extend to each other any benefits relating to customs duties which either signatory may negotiate with a third country.

motion study The study and analysis of all movements which occur in the performance of work in order that wasted movements may be eliminated and the performance of the task improved. It is thus a qualitative technique. Compare **time study**.

motivated workforce A workforce which has sufficient encouragement to work more efficiently and so achieve higher profits.

motivation The force which encourages a workman to work better, a salesman to make more sales, etc.

moving average An average of data compiled during a fixed period which is regularly updated by adding the data of the latest period, and removing the data of the oldest period.

multilateral trade Trade which is conducted between numerous countries with or without tariff barriers.

multinational (company) A company with controlling interests in numerous foreign countries, operating in similar or different activities to the parent company.

multiple activity chart A diagrammatic representation of work performed simultaneously by two or more machines, men or any combination of both, where the work of such men or machines is coordinated or interdependent. Such a chart shows idle operator or machine time and can indicate how a better balance of operations can be achieved.

multiple costing A hybrid form of costing system whereby costs of individual components, processes, operations, etc. are built up, using appropriate costing techniques and then combined to ascertain the total product cost.

multiple ownership The ownership of a property by several parties jointly.

multiplier The factor by which an initial capital investment expenditure generates a larger rise in income and employment because of the subsequent expansion of incomes which the initial expenditure creates. The multiplier effect was clearly seen in the effects on the Aberdeen local economy of the development of North Sea oilfields in the mid-1970s.

Murphy's Law The general rule that in commercial life if something can go wrong it will go wrong.

mutual funds (In the United States) organizations which accept money from the small investor and invest it in stocks and shares, the investment taking the form of shares in the fund.

mutual life assurance company   A company whose capital is contributed by policyholders in the form of premiums. Profits are distributed amongst policyholders by cash payment, reduction in premium or by revaluation of the policies.

N

name A member of a Lloyd's underwriting syndicate. Each name in a syndicate is responsible to the policyholder for his share of any loss. Names are not involved in the business of underwriting, but do have to possess substantial funds as backing.

name clause That part of the memorandum of association of a company which states the name by which a company shall be known. Although the choice of a name rests with the company's promoters it must be acceptable to the Registrar of Companies.

name day see **Stock Exchange settlement**

named policy A marine insurance policy in which the name of the ship carrying the issued goods is specified.

narration The explanation which should accompany an entry in a business journal, providing full information about any particular transaction.

NASDAQ (National Association of Securities Dealers Automated Quotations) The computerized service for dealing in securities in the United States.

national bank 1 A commercial bank chartered by the US government, as opposed to a state bank established by state charter. 2 A central bank.

National Debt The total debt owed by the government to the general public, comprising both long and short-term loans. It is composed of the internal debt, which is owed to UK citizens, and the external debt, which is owed to other countries or to foreign nationals. It is the external debt that is the more significant since interest payments on it adversely affect the balance of payments.

National Enterprise Board A government-backed organization created in 1975 to extend public ownership in manufacturing and to provide finance for investment.

national income The sum of the value of goods and services available to an economy through its economic activity in a given time period. The income may be evaluated: (a) by adding the incomes generated by economic activity, e.g. wages, salaries, dividends, profits and net income from abroad; (b) by adding the prices of goods and services, less indirect taxes plus subsidies, together with government expenditure.

Both methods produce similar totals and the movement in the total is indicative of economic progress over time, once allowance is made for price inflation, population growth, etc. Growth of national income need not be synonymous with improvement in living standards.

national insurance A group of insurance benefits provided by the government to ease unemployment, illness, retirement, etc. Since 1975 contributions to the scheme have been earnings-related and are paid partly by the employee and partly by the employer.

nationalization The acquisition by the state of the ownership and operation of a property, industry, or company.

nationalized industry An industry that is owned by the state. Examples in Britain are the coal industry and the railways.

National Savings A British savings scheme for small investors, which includes a savings bank, savings certificates and bonds, and premium bonds.

natural justice Those rules which must be followed by quasi-judicial bodies in arbitration, generally agreed as the provision of a fair opportunity to all parties to state their case and the understanding that the body conducting the hearing must be without interest in the outcome and must proceed in an unbiased manner.

natural person A human being as opposed to an artificial person recognized by law, such as a company.

natural wastage The reduction in the number of employees that takes place through resignation, retirement, or death.

near money Money not immediately realizable, e.g. money at call or short notice. It may be used to settle some debts but not others. As it is not universally negotiable, it is not included in the money supply.

NEB see **National Enterprise Board**

necessities Goods and services vital to an individual's existence and/or appropriate to the particular standard of living of the individual. Binding contracts for necessities can be made by infants and generally by wives acting as agents of necessity, if the infant or wife is not already adequately provided for.

neck chart A graphical method of indicating actual or potential bottlenecks in work flow by graphing quantities of work against a time scale.

negative cash flow A situation where a company is spending more money than it receives.

neglected 1 (Of shares) not bought or sold frequently. 2 (Of a company) not actively or efficiently managed.

negotiable instrument A document of title which can be transferred by its delivery, the transferee acquiring good title (providing he has given valuable consideration for it), regardless of the quality of the title of the transferer. The most important examples are cheques, promissory notes and bills of exchange, the latter requiring endorsement in addition to delivery. Normally, the assignment of a contractual right is subject to equities insofar as the assignee will not have any better title than the transferer. Instruments such as bills of lading, warehouse certificates, and some government bonds are in this category. Thus, negotiable instruments are said to be transferred free from equities.

negotiate 1 To discuss a problem formally with someone, so as to reach an agreement. 2 To transfer value by delivery or by endorsement and delivery.

net 1 Excluding any deductions; remaining after all appropriate deductions have been made. Compare **gross** (def. 1). 2 To gain a clear profit.

net assets Generally, fixed assets plus net current assets. It is a vague and loosely used term, generally equating with capital employed.

net book value The value of an asset representing the actual cost or revalued amount of the asset less any portion of that cost or value which has been charged against income during the asset's life.

net capital employed Fixed assets plus current assets, minus current liabilities.

net cash flow The amount by which receipts exceed payments.

net current assets Current assets less current liabilities.

net estate The disposable property of a deceased person after the deduction of funeral and administration expenses, liabilities, and any duties or taxes due.

net loss The actual loss suffered by a company after overheads and interest charges are deducted.

net output The gross output of an industry, firm, etc., less the value of inputs supplied to it. The net output is thus the value added by the industry's or firm's own activities. Compare **gross output**.

net present value The current, immediate value of sums of money payable or receivable in the future.

net price the amount paid by a buyer for goods or services after all discounts have been deducted.

net proceeds The balance due to a consignor after deducting expenses and commission from the gross proceeds of a sale or venture.

net profit The balance of a profit and loss account after taking into account all expenses and losses attributable to the business and revenue from all sources applicable to the relevant accounting period.

net receipts The total of receipts after deduction of commission, tax, discounts, etc.

net sales The total amount of sales, less damaged or returned items.

net weight The weight of goods, excluding the weight of all packing materials. Sometimes immediate packing is included, as when goods are in packs, which are in turn packed in boxes or crates. In this case, the weight of the goods alone, without any packing material, is net net weight. See also **gross weight; tare weight**.

network analysis The analysis of the activities required for the completion of a project in order to determine the sequence of jobs which optimizes time and costs. The optimum sequence is described as the critical path, completion of which in the allowed time ensures minimum duration and cost.

networking   A computer system where several microcomputers are linked together so that they can all draw on the same database.

net worth   The value of a business attributable to the ordinary shareholders. This value comprises the total assets of the business less liabilities to all those other than ordinary shareholders.

net yield   The yield of an investment after deduction of tax.

New Deal   A domestic recovery programme instituted by President Franklin D. Roosevelt in an attempt to pull the United States out of the Depression of the 1930s.

new issues department   The section of a bank which deals in the issuing of shares in new companies.

new technology   The introduction of electronic equipment, such as computers and modems, into a business.

night safe   A facility offered by many banks whereby customers can deposit cash, cheques, etc. in the strong room by insertion through a special opening in the outside wall of the bank. The customer collects the cash, cheques, etc. during normal banking hours and banks the contents in the usual way.

no-claims bonus   A percentage deducted from an insurance premium if no claim has been made in the previous insurance period. It is most common in motor insurance.

no funds   The notation placed on a cheque before it is returned to the payee, when the payer has insufficient funds in his bank account to meet the cheque.

nominal accounts   Those accounts in which the expenditure, revenue, profit and loss of a business are recorded.

nominal capital   see **authorized capital**

nominal ledger   The ledger recording a company's income and expenditure.

nominal partner   A person who, though having no real interest in a business, allows his name to be used by and associated with the business, generally for the purpose of maintaining the reputation or goodwill of the business.

nominal value   see **face value**

nominee   One who is named and participates in a transaction on behalf of some other person.

nominee account   An account held on behalf of another party.

nominee shareholder   A holder of shares in whose name the shares are registered, the beneficial interest in the shares being possessed by some other person.

non-acceptance A situation where the person who is to pay a bill of exchange does not accept it.

non-durables Goods which are used up after having been bought, such as food and drink, petrol, etc.

non-executive director A director who attends board meetings, and gives advice, but does not hold an executive position with the company. Non-executive directors can be seen as more impartial than working directors, and possibly more able to represent the interests of the shareholders.

non-feisance Not doing something which should be done by law.

non-negotiable instrument A document, such as a crossed cheque, which cannot be exchanged for cash.

non-profit-making organization An organization such as a club or charity which is not allowed by law to make a profit.

non-recurring items Special items in a set of accounts which appear only in the accounts for one year.

non-voting share A company share (especially a preference share) which does not carry any voting rights at company meetings or on company resolutions.

no par value (US) A share which has no nominal face value.

normal curve The frequency distribution curve which can be drawn by measurement of a population showing normal distribution. Also called **Gaussian curve** after the name of the man who used the theory of normal distribution to explain errors arising in the calculation of orbits of heavenly bodies.

normal distribution The most commonly encountered frequency distribution which, when plotted, shows a bell curve or normal curve. Frequency is greatest in the middle range of values observed, measurements lying at a greater distance from the average occurring less frequently. Most statistical techniques assume that the population being studied conforms to this distribution.

normal profit The amount of profit that makes it only just worthwhile for an individual or company to remain in an industry rather than transfer to the next most profitable activity.

nostro account A customer's account with a bank which is held abroad in a foreign currency.

notary public A public officer whose duties include certifying and attesting documents, and presenting and protesting dishonoured bills of exchange. The acts of a notary are recognized in many countries. See also **noting and protesting**.

note of hand see **promissory note**

notice 1 Knowledge or information. It may be either express notice, by being given in plain words, or implied notice, knowledge presumed from the particular circumstances. **2** A note or placard giving information in writing. **3** A notification of termination of an agreement (as for rent or employment) given by one party to the agreement to the other.

noting a bill The recording on a bill of exchange the fact that the bill has been refused acceptance or payment when presented. Noting is performed by a notary public who re-presents the bill and records the reasons for refusal. The procedure is required in order that the holder preserves his legal position in relation to the bill and to all parties to the bill. See also **noting and protesting**.

noting and protesting The action taken by a notary public when a bill of exchange has been presented, but dishonoured. On the day of dishonour or the next succeeding business day the notary notes relevant particulars on the bill. This acts as proof that the holder of the bill has complied with rules regarding presentment. In the case of a foreign bill, the notary also completes a protest, a document attesting that the bill has not been paid. Thereafter proceedings may be taken to recover the amounts due.

notional income The invisible benefit which a person receives, which is not money, goods or services.

notional rent A sum put into accounts as rent in a case where the company itself owns the property, and so does not pay an actual rent.

not negotiable A phrase added to a general crossing of a bill or cheque indicating that the party taking the bill cannot possess a better title than the title held by the person from whom the holder received the cheque. See also **general crossing**.

novation The substitution of a new obligation for an old one, as the substituting of a new party to a contract in place of the original debtor or creditor. Replacement of a debtor generally requires the consent of all parties to the original contract, although such consent may be presumed by continuation of business (as in the case of a change in partnership).

n.p.v. see **net present value**

null and void Having no legal force or effect.

numbered account A bank account which is known only by a reference number, the name of the account holder being kept secret.

O

O and M see **organization and method**

obiter dictum An incidental opinion upon a matter of law expressed by a judge and not essential to the decision of the case in question. It is therefore not binding.

objects clause That essential clause in a company's memorandum of association which outlines the activities in which the company may engage. This clause serves to protect the shareholders of the company, by stating the purposes to which their money may be applied, and the company's creditors, by stating the limit of the company's powers.

obligation 1 A binding requirement, duty or promise. 2 An agreement enforceable at law. 3 A document containing such an agreement. 4 A bond, bill or certificate serving as a security for payment of indebtedness.

obsolescence The diminution in value of an asset for reasons other than wear and tear. Such reasons may include the invention or development of superior techniques or equipment or a change in demand.

occupancy cost Any cost associated with the occupation of premises.

occupational hazard A danger which is likely to occur in connection with a job.

occupational test A test designed to determine whether a person possesses the skills and abilities necessary in a particular occupation. Also called **trade test**.

o.c.r. see **optical character recognition**

OECD see **Organization for Economic Cooperation and Development**

offensive trade A trade which, by its very nature, is noxious or offensive, such as leather tanning or glue manufacture.

offer The act of presenting or putting forward for acceptance or rejection. In contract law an offer is not operative until communicated to the other party. An offer can be revoked before acceptance, but when unqualified acceptance is effected the contract is made. An offer may be expressed, or it may be implied by conduct. Compare **acceptance** (def. 1).

offer by tender An invitation to the public to subscribe for shares in a company, extended by the company by way of a prospectus. The company states that bids below a given price will not be accepted, and that above this price shares will be allotted to the highest bidders.

offer document The letter which a company making a takeover bid sends to the shareholders of the target company, with details of the offer being made.

offer for sale An invitation to the public to subscribe for shares in a company, the sale being made by an issuing house which has previously purchased the shares, or debentures, from the company. The offer must be in the form of a prospectus.

offer price The price at which goods, services or securities are offered.

Office of Fair Trading A government agency set up to protect the consumer against unfair or illegal business practices. It is the OFT which may recommend that a takeover bid be referred to the **Monopolies and Mergers Commission.**

official exchange rate An exchange rate which is imposed and maintained by a government.

official list The daily list of quotations of stocks and shares showing prices at which dealings have been made. It is published under the authority of the council of the Stock Exchange.

official receiver An official appointed by the Board of Trade to supervise the winding-up of a company's affairs or the realization of the assets of a bankrupt. In the absence of an appointed trustee in bankruptcy, the official receiver is trustee of the estate.

official support Activities of the Bank of England which are designed to maintain the exchange rate of sterling or raise it.

off-the-job training Training given to workers away from their place of work, such as a college or other training establishment.

OFT see **Office of Fair Trading**

oligopoly A market situation in which a few producers/suppliers are able to influence the market price. The producers are mutually dependant on one another and any action by one will lead to a reaction and counter-reaction by the others.

ombudsman An official who investigates complaints by members of the public against government departments and other official bodies.

omnibus agreement An agreement covering many different items.

on approval A sale where the purchaser pays for the goods only if they are satisfactory.

on cost see **overhead**

on demand (Of a bill of exchange or cheque) on presentation.

one-off production A method of manufacture in which a single item is produced according to customer specifications.

one-stop shopping Shopping which is done in one central place, such as a hypermarket or large shopping centre, where the shopper leaves the car in a central car park and walks round various retail outlets making purchases.

on-line Linked directly to a computer system.

o.n.o. see **or near offer**

on-pack premium An item attached to goods and given free, or at a reduced price, as an inducement to purchase.

on tap

on tap see **tap issue**

on-the-job training Training given to workers at their place of work.

OPEC see **Organization of Petroleum-Exporting Countries**

open account Unsecured credit, or an amount lent with no security.

open cheque An uncrossed cheque which may be presented for payment over the counter at the banker on whom the cheque was drawn. Compare **crossed cheque**.

open-ended (Of an agreement) with no fixed time limit or with some items not specified.

open indent The freedom for an agent to choose any suitable manufacturer or supplier for the supply of goods or services, usually to be exported.

opening bid The first bid at an auction.

opening price The price quoted for stocks or shares at the commencement of business on the Stock Exchange.

open market see **market ouvert**

open market operations Measures adopted by the Bank of England and other central banks in order to control the monetary system and secure the adherence of the system to the official interest rate structure and monetary policy. The operations are conducted by the special buyer in the discount market and by the government broker in the gilt-edge security market.

The sale of treasury bills or gilt-edge securities by the authorities reduces the cash balances of the commercial banks as money is withdrawn to pay for the purchases. The credit base of the banks – which is tied to their liquidity ratio – and the banks' ability to advance money to potential customers is thereby restricted while interest rates rise. The authorities can in this way curtail the supply of money and increase its cost and vice versa, in accordance with official monetary policy.

open-plan A large office with no internal walls, divided into working areas by low partitions.

open policy A form of marine insurance policy in which a provisional sum is insured in circumstances where the value of goods is unknown at the time of concluding the policy. The premium is adjusted upon determining the value of the goods.

open shop A business or firm which provides employment for workers whether they belong to a trade union or not.

operating budget A forecast of income and expenditure over a period of time.

operating costs The costs involved in the ordinary day-to-day organization of a company.

operating profit or loss The profit or loss made by a company in its normal trading, not including property or asset sales, etc.

operating ratio An expression of the relationships between various items of business expense and revenues used as indicators of operating efficiency.

operating statement see **profit and loss account**

operational research The application of scientific principles and methods to the problems of business strategy by the systematic study of all available resources. With the increasing complexity of business problems and the need to quantify diverse scientific approaches, applied mathematics has become an integral part of operational research.

operation process chart see **process chart**

opinion poll An attempt to find out the opinion of the general public on a matter by questioning a random sample of people.

opportunity cost The cost incurred in following an alternative course of action: the extent of this cost represents the real sacrifice incurred in pursuing a particular course of action. For instance, the cost of building a factory is the opportunity cost of other manufacturing plant which might have been purchased as an alternative.

optical character recognition The capacity possessed by some computer units which enables them to read and recognize documents without the need of an intermediate stage such as punched tape.

option An arrangement whereby, in return for the payment of a fee, a person acquires a right to buy or a right to sell goods, shares, etc. at an agreed price, at or within a specified future time. See also **call option; double option; put.**

optional extras Additional items which can be purchased to attach to a machine, such as a sheet feed mechanism to a printer.

option contract A contract which gives a person the right to buy or sell shares at a fixed price.

option dealing The buying and selling of share options.

option to double see **put of more**

or see **operational research**

ordinary share A type of company share generally making up the bulk of the company's capital and carrying no preference as to dividend or return of capital. The owners of such shares are said to own the equity of the company and are entitled to receive distribution of profits at the discretion of the directors. The number of ordinary shares in a company can be reduced only under special circumstances. Ordinary shares confer the right of voting at general meetings.

organization and method The activity of investigating and advising upon the structure of an organization, its management, control, methods and procedures.

organization chart A pictorial representation of the responsibilities and authority relationships within an organization.

organization expense The cost of getting a business into an operating position. It may include legal fees, the costs of raising initial capital, etc.

Organization for Economic Cooperation and Development A body founded in 1961 which has as its aims the encouragement of economic stability, economic development in the Third World and the expansion of world multilateral trade.

Organization of Petroleum-Exporting Countries An international cartel of oil-producing nations whose members include Algeria, Ecuador, Indonesia, Iran, Iraq, Kuwait, Libya, Nigeria, the Arabian Gulf states, Saudi Arabia and Venezuela.

organized labour A labour force which is represented by a union.

original bill A bill which has been drawn and sold before being endorsed.

or near offer Phrase indicating that a seller may accept an offer slightly below the asking price.

ostensible authority An implied authority of an agent to bind his principal contractually.

outage The quantity lost from a container, as by evaporation

outgoings Expenditure.

out-guide A card inserted into a filing system when a file is removed, generally showing the name or number of the file, the person or department borrowing it and the date. Also called **tracer**.

outlet 1 A market for goods or services. 2 A facility for marketing of goods or services, as a store, merchant or agent.

out-of-pocket expenses An amount of money which is paid to an employee to reimburse him for money he spent on behalf of the company.

output 1 The quantity or value of goods produced in a given time. 2 The production or yield from a mine. 3 The information produced by a computer. 4 The physical form in which such information is provided.

output bonus An extra payment for increased production.

output budgeting A quantitative statement of production for some stated future period. See also **functional costing**.

output tax VAT charged by a company on goods or services which it sells.

outright deal An exchange deal for the purchase or sale of currency for forward delivery.

outside broker A stockbroker who is not a member of the Stock Exchange.

outward mission A trade delegation which is visiting a foreign country.

outwork Jobs of work for a business which are performed outside the business premises, usually in a private home or institution.

outworker A worker who works at home for a company.

overcapacity The state of having greater productive facilities (in terms of men, space, machinery, etc.) than are required by the demanded output.

overcapitalized (Of a company) with more capital than is necessary.

overdraft An amount due to his bank by a customer, generally limited to a specific amount in excess of moneys deposited to the customer's account. Interest is calculated on the fluctuating daily levels. An overdraft may be with or without security. Compare **bank loan**.

overdraw To take more money out of a bank account than there is in it.

overdue 1 Denoting a debt outstanding beyond its due date of payment. 2 Denoting a bill of exchange for which the time of payment has passed.

overextend To spend more money than a company's financial situation will allow.

overhead An indirect cost, such as administration expenses, selling expenses, distribution expenses, etc. In Britain the word is usually used in the plural (**overheads**) referring to all such costs as they appear in a company's accounts. In the United States the word is used in the singular (**overhead**), even if it refers to several items of expenditure.

overhead variance The difference between the standard cost of overhead absorbed in actual output and the actual overhead cost.

over-insurance The insurance of property at a value above its worth. In the case of an open policy, the declaration of the short-interest (the difference between the value of goods and the sum insured) entitles the insured to a proportionate return of the premium.

overmanning The situation where a company has more workers than is necessary to carry out the normal volume of work.

overnight loan A loan repayable on the morning of the next business day. It generally refers to a bank loan granted to a bill broker, enabling bills of exchange to be taken up.

over-production The manufacturing of goods or supplying of services in excess of the current demand.

over-riding commission A commission payable to stockbrokers for finding underwriters willing to underwrite a share issue.

over-riding interests Interests in land which are not disclosed in title documents, such as rights of way, land charges, etc.

overseas companies Companies having a place of business in, but incorporated outside, the United Kingdom.

oversell To sell more than can be produced.

overspill A taxation relief granted to companies trading overseas, being the difference between the overseas tax payable and the corporation tax suffered.

oversubscribed Denoting a share issue in which the number of shares applied for exceeds the number to be issued. Applications may be refused or scaled down pro rata.

over-the-counter sales The legal market in shares which are not listed in the official Stock Exchange list.

overtime 1 Time during which work is done outside regular working hours; extra time. Such time is usually paid for at premium rates. 2 The payment made for such work.

overtrading A situation in which a business is operating at a level in excess of its working capital capabilities, characterized by the accumulation of large stocks, debtors and creditors. The position is a precarious one since cash is not available or being generated in sufficient volume to sustain the operations, while a creditor who presses might cause the business to fold.

own brand products; own label goods Products which are specially manufactured for a large retailer and clearly labelled with the retailer's name.

owner-occupier A person who owns a property and also lives in it.

P

Paasche index An index constructed in order to measure price changes over a period, using current period data as weight factors. The index is derived from:

$$\frac{\Sigma Pn\ Qn}{\Sigma Po\ Qn}$$

where Σ = sum of; Po = price in base year; Pn = price in current year under consideration; Qn = quantity (weight) in current year under consideration. Compare **Laspeyre's index.**

package deal **1** A transaction in which several different goods or services are bought for an inclusive price. **2** The outcome of negotiations in which all parties have made concessions on various issues decided together.

packaging The containing or wrapping of goods in order to protect and/or identify. Thus, it can fulfil the functions of protection against breakage, contamination or deterioration. It can also facilitate handling and storage, communication with the user/consumer, as in labelling. **Primary packaging** is the container in which a product is displayed for sale and sold. **Secondary packaging** is the container in which a product is enclosed during transit between the manufacturer and the retailer.

paid-up capital The value of a company's share capital which has been issued and on which all calls for payment requested by the company have been met. Compare **called-up capital.**

paid-up shares Shares which have been issued and completely paid for.

pallet A wooden or metal platform used to convey or stack goods. It is generally designed so that it can be moved, complete with its load, by a fork-lift truck or similar equipment.

panel testing A sampling technique employed in market research in which responses are obtained from a group of selected individuals. In many cases the panel is semi-permanent and its responses to a wide range of products or product groups are recorded.

panic buying A rush to buy something at any price before stocks run out.

paper currency Bank notes which form part of a nation's legal tender. The notes have no intrinsic value, their value as a medium of exchange depending on their acceptability to the public.

paper loss A loss made when an asset falls in value but has not been realized.

paper money All forms of obligation to pay money, issued by banks, government agencies, etc. Examples are bank notes, promissory notes, money orders and bills of exchange.

paper profit A profit made when an asset has increased in value, but has not been realized.

par 1 The official value of a currency expressed in terms of gold or another currency. 2 The face value of a share or stock as stated on the certificate of issue.

parameter A fixed limit set to an instruction.

parent company see **holding company**

Pareto principle The principle which states that a relatively small number of individuals have an influence which is greater than their proportionate number. This may be seen in a sales analysis, where a small number of customers may account for a large proportion of total sales.

Pareto's law The number of people (N) receiving a specified income (Y) declines at a constant rate (b) as the specified income is increased in increments of one per cent. This law may be expressed by the formula: $N = aY^{-b}$, where 'a' is a constant that differs for different societies. The higher the value of 'b', the more rapidly will the number of recipients decrease as the income level rises, and hence the greater the degree of equality of incomes. Pareto's law applies particularly to the highest 10% of incomes.

Paris Club An association of countries which forms the developed nations' pressure group, lending to the International Monetary Fund. The group comprises the United States, the United Kingdom, West Germany, France, Italy, Japan, Canada, the Netherlands, Belgium and Sweden.

parity The situation that occurs when the exchange value of a currency equals its official exchange value.

Parkinson's law 'Work expands to fill the time available for its completion.' A semi-serious proposition made by Professor C. Northcote Parkinson. A derivative of this is that expenditure rises to equal income.

par of exchange That amount of one country's currency which in metallic content is equal to a given sum in the currency of another country.

parquet 1 The area on the Paris Stock Exchange which is reserved for official brokers. 2 A collective term for the official brokers of the Paris Stock Exchange.

parri passu (*Latin*, 'with equal step') It describes the equal relationship which may exist between persons, articles, etc. of a similar nature. The most common example is that the holders of the same type of share have an equal right to dividend payments or to reimbursement if the company is wound up.

part exchange A purchase made when an old item is traded in as part of the payment for a new one.

partial acceptance see **qualified acceptance**

partial equilibrium analysis The examination of one facet of the economy in isolation on the assumption that there is no interaction between that particular sector of the economy, perhaps an industry, and the rest.

partial loss Loss or damage (other than total loss) suffered by a vessel or cargo arising from an insured risk. The loss is borne by the insurance underwriters. Compare **total loss.**

participating preference share A unit of ownership of a company, with preferential rights to a fixed dividend (before claims of ordinary shareholders) and with the right to an additional share of profit after the ordinary shareholders have received a specified level of dividend.

particular agency A situation in which the authority of an agent extends only to one particular act or to one particular occasion. Compare **general agency.**

particular average loss A loss caused by damage to a particular cargo and borne by the insurers of that cargo instead of being shared by the insurers of all the cargo on board the lost or damaged ship. Compare **general average.**

partly secured creditor A creditor whose debt is not fully covered by the value of the security given.

partner A person undertaking some task or directing some business enterprise in combination with one or more others.

partnership A form of business organization which is conducted by two or more partners. The relationship between the partners in terms of respective profit shares, responsibilities, etc. is normally expressed in a partnership agreement.

Certain common features of partnerships are: **a** Each partner binds all other partners to any contract entered into in the ordinary course of business. **b** Each partner is fully liable for the firm's debts, to the extent of his private assets, except where a partner has limited liability. **c** The partnership ceases when the existing relationship between the partners ends through death, bankruptcy, etc.

partnership, limited A partnership in which at least one member has limited liability for the firm's debts, i.e. is liable only to the extent of his capital in the firm. Such a partner cannot participate in the management of the business and cannot withdraw his capital.

A limited partnership must be registered, with details of the partnership's name, nature of business and terms of the partnership.

part ownership A situation where two or more people own a property.

part-time Not working for a full working day.

party selling The selling of items of domestic hardware and clothing by individual agents who organize parties where the goods are shown and orders taken.

par value see **face value**

pass book A book given by a bank or building society in which transactions such as deposits, withdrawals and credit of interest are recorded.

passing a dividend Not paying a dividend because the company is in financial difficulties.

passing a name 1 A London Stock Exchange term for the procedure of naming the buyer of a share or stock on the account day of the settlement period to enable documentation to be made out. 2 The guaranteeing by a broker of a buyer's solvency to the seller of a commodity on an international commodity market.

passing off The practice of operating a business using a name or trademark which is likely or intended to mislead consumers into believing that they are dealing with another (more substantial) business.

At law the aggrieved business may claim damages or obtain an injunction to prevent further misrepresentation by the offender. Also called **holding out.**

passive bond A security which does not currently bear interest but which entitles the holder to some future benefit or claim. Compare **active bond.**

passive trade balance An unfavourable balance of trade where the value of imports exceeds exports. Compare **active trade balance.**

patent 1 A legal property right granted by the state, giving the creator of an invention the sole right to make, use or dispose of his invention for a limited number of years, usually 16. 2 An invention or process which has been patented.

patent agent One who acts as an agent for a person applying for a patent.

patent infringement The action of illegally making or selling a patented product without the permission of the patent holder.

Patent Office An office of the Department of Trade and Industry which is responsible for the granting of patents and the registration of trade marks. It operates according to the Patent Acts, Registered Designs Act and the Trade Marks Act.

patent rights The rights which a patent holder holds under a registered patent.

paternity leave Permission given to a male worker to be away from work when his wife is having a baby.

pawnbroker A person who is licensed to lend money on the security of articles deposited with him. Interest charges and procedures relating to the disposal of unclaimed articles are prescribed by law.

payable A claim of creditors against a business for services rendered or goods supplied, for which payment has not yet been made. See also **accounts payable.**

payable on demand (Of a bill) which must be paid when payment is asked for.

payback clause A clause in a contract which states the terms under which a loan is to be repaid.

payback method A technique used in the appraisal of capital investment proposals, which seeks to determine the pay backperiod for each proposed investment. This is the simplest appraisal method in common use, but it takes no account of the distribution of expenditure and income over a period of time, particularly after the payback period. Discounting techniques overcome this disadvantage.

payback period The time period within which the additional income generated by an investment offsets the initial capital expenditure of the investment.

pay day see **settling day**

PAYE (pay as you earn) The system used to collect income tax from employed people in the United Kingdom. The employer deducts the tax payable, calculated by reference to earnings and the employee's code number, and remits the tax so deducted to the Inland Revenue. The employee thus receives his wage or salary net of income tax.

payee One to whom a note or cheque is made payable.

paying-in slip A document on which details of notes, coins and cheques are entered by a firm or individual when depositing money into a bank account. Also called **deposit slip.**

payment by results Wages or fees paid, which increase with the amount of work done or goods produced.

payment for honour supra protest The discharge of a bill of exchange by any person acting on behalf of someone who is a party to the bill, where the bill has previously reached maturity, payment has been refused and the bill protested.

payment in kind A form of payment, where goods or services are provided in settlement of a debt, but no money is involved.

payment-in-lieu Money paid by an employer to an employee whose employment has been terminated before the expiration of the period of notice contained in the employee's contract of employment. The payment is instead of all or part of the notice period.

payroll 1 A list of employees to be paid, giving wage or salary payable, detailing deductions and showing the net amounts payable. 2 The aggregate expenditure on wages and/or salaries incurred by a business for a given period.

payroll ledger The list of employees and their salaries and allowances.

payroll tax A tax levied on an employer which is directly related to the size of the wage and salary outlay.

pay slip A statement given to an individual showing his gross earnings for a given period, detailed deductions and the net pay due. The statement is either included with the cash payment of wages or passed to the employee as an advice of a payment into his bank account.

pay threshold The point at which pay increases under a threshold agreement.

peaceful picketing Non-violent attempts by strikers to dissuade colleagues from continuing to work during a strike.

peak period A period of high activity, such as the time of highest consumption of electricity, the highest volume of sales, the highest number of passengers using a transport system, etc.

pegging the exchanges Dealing on the foreign currency market by a government to stabilize the exchange rate of the domestic currency around the official rate of exchange. This is achieved through judicious buying and selling of the currency involved but can only be a temporary expedient.

penalty A payment made for failure to comply with the terms of a contract, especially with reference to the contracted completion date. Such a payment must be specified in the contract in a penalty clause.

penetration The degree to which a product is known or bought by potential customers. See also **market penetration**.

penny share or **penny stock** A very cheap share, sold for less than 50p.

pension 1 A weekly or monthly sum paid by the state to men and women attaining the ages of 65 and 60 respectively and who have made National Insurance contributions during their working lives. 2 A weekly or monthly sum remitted by a company to its retired employees, the pension being paid either from contributions made during employment by both the employer and employee or paid exclusively from employer contributions.

pension fund A fund maintained by a company, trade union or other organization to provide pensions for employees or members upon retirement. Contributions from the organization and the employee/member are invested, with interest accumulated, into the fund. The fund may be self-administered by the organization as a trust or managed by outside experts, such as a life assurance company. Pension funds are now one of the main purchasers of stocks and shares. With other institutional investors, they greatly overshadow in importance the private investor. Also called **pension plan; pension scheme**.

peppercorn rent 1 A nominal rent on property which is designed to establish the fact that the property occupied is leasehold rather than freehold. 2 Any regular payment of a nominal sum in exchange for a right.

P/E ratio The ratio of a share's price to its earnings. It is the most widely accepted guide to determine whether or not to buy or sell shares. Firms with good growth rates will often have high profits (and earnings), and hence a high P/E ratio but probably a low yield on shares.

per annum In each year; in a single year.

per capita For each single person.

per capita income The income earned per individual, calculated by taking the total income of a group and dividing it by the number of individuals in the group.

percentile One of a series of 99 figures below which a certain percentage of a total falls.

per contra (In bookkeeping) On the other side.

perfect competition A market in which no single individual or unit can influence the market price of the goods. For this to occur there must be a very large number of producers and consumers, a totally homogeneous product and no barriers to entry. Few industries can satisfy even one of these conditions, but one example could be the international cultivation and marketing of grain.

performance The execution of a contract according to its terms.

performance bond An undertaking given by one party to another which guarantees the work of a third party.

performance unit trust A unit trust which specializes in shares which may rise in value more than the average shares.

periodical A magazine or other publication which is published regularly every month or every quarter.

periodic reordering system The system of reviewing stock levels at fixed time intervals and of reordering such quantities as are necessary to bring stocks up to their required levels. Compare **base stock system**.

peripherals Items of hardware such as printers and monitors, which are attached to a main computer system.

perishable items Items of food which will become rotten if not eaten quickly.

perks Extra items given by a company to an employee in addition to a salary. Such items can include a company car, subscription to a sports club, private health insurance, etc.

perpetual inventory A system of ascertaining the current stock position of a business by the continuous recording of stock levels. Receipts and issues of stock items are recorded and the balance adjusted accordingly, so that at any one time the stock position is known. It should be operated with a system of continuous stocktaking though the two terms are not synonymous. Also called **continuous inventory**.

per pro

per pro ('by procuration') Appended to a signature it indicates that a person signing a document does so in a representative capacity and is acting on behalf of another. Also called **p.p.**

perquisites see **perks**

personal accounts The bookkeeping records which detail the transactions conducted by a business with other firms and individuals – a separate account being maintained for each firm, etc. Compare **impersonal accounts; real accounts.**

personal allowance A tax relief deductible from income for the purposes of income tax assessment. There are different rates, depending upon the marital circumstances of the taxpayer.

personal bank loan A loan made by a bank to a customer, the loan bearing interest at a fixed rate on the total loan, repayment of principal and interest being spread over a number of periods.

personal cost centre A person or group of people in a business with whom costs may be associated.

personal estate Moveable assets such as debts due, money, goods, furniture, stocks and shares, etc., and leasehold property. Compare **real estate.**

personal grade A salary grade which is determined for the holder of a particular job rather than for the job itself. Such a grade would frequently be higher than the job grade.

personality 1 An identity recognized by the law, possessing the right to initiate and defend legal actions. Limited liability companies have personality, being able to sue and be sued in the company's name. 2 Personal wealth in the form of moveable property – money, goods, etc.

personality inventory A list of questions which a candidate is required to answer about his own attitudes, tastes, etc. which is intended to provide a character profile.

personnel management The field of management primarily concerned with people at work and their relationships within the enterprise. Areas of concern include recruitment and selection, pay and conditions, and education and training.

PERT see **program evaluation and review technique**

Peter principle The principle, noted in many cases, that employees and directors are promoted until they occupy positions for which they are incompetent.

Petite Bourse An unofficial stock exchange which has connections with the official Paris Bourse (Stock Exchange), formed by the larger financial institutions.

petrodollars Funds belonging to members of OPEC in excess of their immediate needs and acquired as a result of the rapid increase in the price of oil in the 1970s. Most of these foreign currency surpluses are in dollars, hence their name. Since the OPEC states had no immediate need for them, the petrodollars were largely reinvested in the financial centres of the West, and this helped to offset partially the inflationary effects of the rise in oil prices.

petty cash Cash (notes and coin) held by a business, office or department in order to reimburse small expenses incurred, e.g. postage stamps, travelling expenses. See also **imprest system**.

Phillips curve A curve which can be graphed showing a relationship between unemployment and inflation. If it exists, and this has been doubted, it means that there is a possible trade-off between unemployment and inflation, and that one can be reduced at the expense of the other. It is named after an Australian economist, A. W. Phillips (1914–75).

picket A striking worker who stands at the gate of a factory or other place of work, and tries to dissuade other workers from entering the premises.

picking list A list of items which have been ordered, but shown according to the place where they are kept in a warehouse.

piece rate A method of employee renumeration whereby earnings are calculated by reference to the number of units of work produced and the rate paid for completion of each unit. Compare **time rate**.

piecework A method of remuneration based upon results, where payment is directly linked to the number of units produced. This encourages high output, but quality will often suffer unless rigorous quality control systems are enforced.

pie chart A diagrammatic representation of quantitative information, in which the data is shown as segments of a circle, like slices of a pie, the area of each segment (or slice) being proportional to the data frequency.

piggy-back export schemes Government-assisted programmes which encourage the setting-up of piggy-back selling arrangements between exporting and would-be exporting businesses.

piggy-back selling An arrangement whereby a business having a well-established trading organization offers its facilities to smaller businesses, especially for contacting overseas markets. The smaller company is said to be 'piggy-backing'.

Pigou effect The theoretical effect on the real value of wealth as a consequence of changes in the level of prices, which by themselves would be sufficient to return an economy to full employment in the long run. This effect exists, but it has never been indisputably identified in action.

pilfering The stealing of small amounts of money or small items for sale, from a shop.

pilot scheme A scheme which is introduced in a small area or to a small group of individuals as a test, which may be extended to cover a larger area or group if successful.

pink form see **preferential form**

pirate To make an illegal copy of copyright material, such as a book a tape or a computer program.

placing A method of arranging a share issue for a company, whereby a broker is employed to introduce clients who will subscribe for the shares. Details of the shares must be advertised and, following the issue, permission to deal on the Stock Exchange may be obtained. Compare **offer by tender; offer for sale.**

planned economy An economy in which the government sets production output targets, prices, wages, etc. rather than allowing them to be determined through the operation of the price mechanism. The best examples of planned economies are those of Eastern Europe and the USSR.

planned maintenance The systematic checking and repairing of plant or vehicles in order to prevent breakdown, as opposed to the carrying out of repairs after faults have disrupted production, etc.

planned obsolescence The deliberate creation in a product of features which will encourage the consumer to replace it before the end of its expected useful life.

planning permission An official document issued by a local authority or ministry, which allows someone to construct new buildings or to build extensions to existing property.

planning-programming-budgeting-system A method of cost control and project evaluation in which long-term projects are analysed and compared by function rather than by department of origin. This system was instituted in the US Defense Department in the 1960s and is still most commonly used in governmental decision making.

plant 1 The equipment such as machinery, tools and instruments necessary to carry on a business. 2 The complete equipment for a particular process or operation, e.g. heating plant. In this context it may also include buildings and fixtures. The scope of the term is being extended to include buildings and general premises.

plant engineer The individual in a business generally responsible for inspection, maintenance, repair and replacement of the fixed assets. His duties also include maintenance of services such as electricity, gas and water.

plant register A detailed list of all plant owned or leased by a business, showing details of cost, description, location, and supplier of each asset or groups of assets. It may also contain details of depreciation charges, maintenance costs and disposal details. It thus provides valuable information regarding the assets of a business as well as being used as a subsidiary book of account – a detailed breakdown of the fixed asset accounts.

PLC see **public limited company**

pledge An object given to a pawnbroker as security for a loan.

plough back To retain and employ earnings in a business as distinct from distributing the earnings to shareholders in the form of dividends. These ploughed-back or undistributed profits are subject to corporation tax.

point of sale The precise location at which a sale is effected, such as the shelves on which the goods are displayed.

point-of-sale material Promotional material, such as posters, special displays or counter packs, which are used to promote products at the place where goods are offered for sale.

points assessment A technique of job evaluation in which every factor is assigned a scale of points, against which each job is assessed.

policy A document which details the terms of a contract of insurance or assurance concluded between the two respective parties: insurer and insured.

policy holder A person who is covered by an insurance.

policy proof of interest A clause in an insurance contract by means of which the insured may recover from the insurers in the event of loss without necessarily having an insurable interest in the subject matter, the policy being binding in honour only.

political levy Part of the subscription of a member of a trade union which is paid to support a political party.

poll A vote taken at a shareholders' meeting, members having votes in proportion to the number of shares held. See also **opinion poll**.

pollster A person who conducts an opinion poll and analyses the results.

pool 1 An association of firms within an industry who determine and allocate total industry output to member firms. 2 A group of employees with similar skills used to service the requirements of a number of different departments of a business, e.g. fitters and typists. 3 A group of people collectively dealing on the Stock Exchange by agreeing not to sell below a specified price or before a specified date.

population In statistics, the total number of units sharing a common characteristic. Normally, the population is too large to be examined thoroughly and so a sample is taken from it, the samplers being careful to ensure that the sample is absolutely typical.

port authority An organization which manages a port.

portable pension A pension entitlement which can be moved from one pension scheme to another without loss as a worker changes jobs.

portfolio A list of investments in stocks, shares, etc. that a person or institution has made.

portfolio management The buying and selling of shares by a person or by a specialist on behalf of a client.

port of call A port at which a ship calls to load or unload cargo.

port of registry The port where a ship is registered.

POS see **point of sale**. Compare **EPOS**.

position analysis see **job analysis**

position statement see **balance sheet**

positive cash flow A situation where more money comes into a company than is paid out.

postal order A voucher bought at a post office as a method of paying small amounts of money by post.

postcode A code forming part of an address, in the form of a series of letters and numbers, which allows electronic sorting of mail. In the United States known as the **zip code**.

postdate To date (a document) later than the date on which it is issued. Generally the document is effective from the time it is dated. Compare **antedate**.

poste restante A term written on letters, parcels, etc., to indicate that the item is to remain at a post office until called for. This is a facility extended to travellers and is available in many countries.

posting The transferring of entries in subsidiary books of account to their appropriate ledger accounts.

posting run A series of postings made by an accounting machine, at the end of which the totals stored in the machine are printed out for the purposes of exercising control.

post obit bond An undertaking to repay a loan (plus interest) after the death of a third person named in the bond and from whose estate the borrower expects to benefit.

post war credits Additional taxes levied in the United Kingdom between 1941 and 1946 which are repayable in certain circumstances, e.g. to a male holder over 60, to a female over 55, to successors of holders who have died, etc.

potential market A market in which a company may achieve new sales.

power of attorney A legal document which gives a person the right to act on behalf of someone in legal matters.

p.p. see **per pro**

PR see **public relations**

preacquisition profits The profits earned by a business which has been taken over before its formal incorporation within the parent company. The profits cannot be distributed by the parent company as dividends but must be added to reserves.

preceding-year basis A method of assessment of income for income tax whereby, under normal circumstances, the profits of the accounting period ending in the preceding year of assessment are taken as the basis for the assessment for the current tax year.

pre-emptive right 1 The right of a government or a local authority to buy a property before anyone else. 2 (In the United States) the right of an existing shareholder to be first to buy a new issue of stock.

pre-emptive strike Swift action to prevent something happening, such as the rapid buying of shares to prevent a possible takeover.

preference share A unit of ownership in a company which gives the holder the right to a fixed dividend each year before ordinary shareholders receive a share of profit and also confers the right to repayment of capital before the ordinary shareholder.

Various classes of preference share may be created, each having a ranking order in the receipt of dividend. Voting rights vary as between companies but are set out in the Articles of Association.

preferential creditor One who, in the event of the winding-up of the debtor company or the insolvency of the debtor, is entitled to repayment before other creditors.

preferential debt A claim against a company which takes precedence in the event of a winding-up. The order of settlement of debts is laid down by law and follows the pattern: secured creditors, such as debenture holders; unsecured creditors including those organizations or individuals to whom rates, taxes, wages, holiday pay and the like are owed; trade and other creditors; and finally shareholders – first preference shareholders and then ordinary shareholders.

preferential duty An import duty levied at a lesser rate on the imports of certain countries. Countries that have most-favoured-nation status conferred on them by the United States pay lower import duties than countries without this designation. The EEC levies preferential duties on the produce of many developing countries.

preferential form A document which invites existing shareholders to subscribe for new shares being issued by a company. The document is coloured pink to ensure that existing shareholders receive special consideration when the allotment of the new issue is being made. Also called **pink form**.

preferential terms Terms which are specially favourable to a certain customer.

preferred ordinary share A unit of the ordinary share capital of a company which carries the right to payment of a fixed dividend after preference shareholders but before the body of the ordinary shareholders receive a share of earnings. Also called **preferred stock**.

prefinancing The arranging of financial backing in advance of a deal.

preliminary and formation expenses Those expenses incurred in the creation and flotation of a company and arising as a result of the meeting of statutory requirements before business begins. They include costs of preparing the prospectus, stamp duties on the nominal capital and registration of the company, printing costs, etc.

premium 1 The periodic payment for an insurance policy. 2 A sum in excess of nominal value paid in order to secure a share, asset, etc. 3 A lump sum payable on the acquisition of a lease. 4 The difference between the spot price paid for a currency or commodity and the price for forward settlement.

premium bond A government security bearing no interest but participating in a lottery. Units must be retained for a short period before becoming eligible for the lottery, prizes from which are free of tax. The bond serial numbers are selected by Ernie (an acronym for *E*lectronic *R*andom *N*umber *I*ndicator *E*quipment).

premium offer An offer of a cash refund or goods at a reduced price on the surrender of a coupon detached from a packet or from an advertisement in a newspaper, etc.

prepaid expense see **deferred expense**

preparation allowance A time allowance included in assessing job times, which reflects the time spent on preparing for an operation. This may include obtaining tools, setting up a machine and restoring the machine to normal after the operation is complete.

presentation A formal meeting organized to show something to a group, such as the plans for a new industrial development, the season's new product line, etc.

presentment The act of taking a bill of exchange to the drawee (the person liable on the bill) for his formal acceptance of liability or for his payment.

Presentment for acceptance is required where the bill is drawn payable 'after sight', in order to fix the date of maturity; where the bill states that it must be presented; and where the bill is drawn payable at other than the normal place of business. Presentment for payment is required so that in the event of dishonour formal proceedings may be undertaken, thereby preserving the holder's claim against the parties to the bill.

press conference A meeting organized to give detailed information to the press, allowing journalists to ask questions after a presentation has been made.

press release A document in which information about a new activity is sent to the press and TV.

pressure group A group of people who try to influence the central government or a local authority to take decisions in the group's favour.

present value An assessment of the worth of investing in a project or security, based on discounting at the current interest rate the value of all future benefits, less future outlays, to arrive at the equivalent current value of the proposed project. The project or the security is worth investing in if its present value is a positive figure. This concept is used in cost accounting and cost-benefit analysis.

prestige advertising 1 Advertising intended to enhance a company's image rather than promote an individual product. A frequent example is the publicizing of contributions to scientific or technological achievements. 2 Advertising which is aimed at promoting sales by appealing to the consumer's desire for status.

pretax profit The net profit, after overhead and other deductions, but before tax is paid.

price The monetary value at which an article is offered for sale.

price cutting The business strategy of reducing prices of goods or services in an attempt to increase total sales or to weaken or eliminate competition. Although prices may be cut, the effect on volume may be such that total revenue increases.

price differential The difference in price between products in a range.

price discrimination The setting of different prices for a product in separate markets, the differential being possible because of the geographical separation of markets, because of product differential in the same geographical location (i.e., a basic product is marketed with various modifications thereby facilitating separate markets and price structures for a single product), or because the two classes of consumers cannot trade between themselves. Cases of this include setting different prices for electricity to domestic and industrial users and different railfares for businessmen and senior citizens. Price discrimination assists in the maximization of profits.

price/earnings ratio see **P/E ratio**

price effect The total change in the demand for a good resulting from a change in its price. It is made up of the income effect and the substitution effect.

price fixing A business strategy whereby a group of manufacturers, wholesalers or retailers set mutually agreed prices for their products, or specific products. Such arrangements are frequently illegal unless they an be proved to be in the general interest.

price leadership The action of a major firm in a particular industry in setting prices which it knows its competitors will follow.

price mechanism The system of resource allocation based on an unhindered movement of prices. Through the working of the price mechanism output of goods is increased or decreased without the need for a single central authority.

price range The difference between the highest and lowest prices for similar products from different suppliers.

price ring An association of manufacturers who exchange information relating to their product or tender prices and, by manipulation of quotations, distribute contracts among member firms.

prices and incomes policy see **incomes policy**

price-sensitive (Of a product) liable not to sell if the price is increased.

price war Price-cutting by two or more competitors in an attempt by each to gain a larger share of the market and/or eliminate its rival.

primage A charge for the use of loading and unloading gear, which is normally included in total freight charges.

primary industry An industry dealing with the production of basic raw materials, such as coal, metals, farm produce, etc.

primary packaging see **packaging**

primary production The production of commodities used in the manufacture of consumer and capital goods. The exports of most developing nations consist of primary products. Compare **secondary production**.

prime bills Bills of exchange which do not involve risk.

prime cost The cost involved in creating a product, excluding overheads.

prime rate The best rate of interest at which a US bank will lend money to its best customers.

prime time The time when most people watch a TV programme, which is therefore the most expensive time for advertisements.

primogeniture The legal principle of inheritance by which an estate passes to the eldest child, specifically the eldest son.

principal 1 The head of a firm, particularly a partnership. 2 One who employs an agent to represent him in business transactions. 3 A sum of money on which interest is paid: a capital sum invested at interest.

prior charge A security, such as preference shares, which is repaid before other securities when a company goes into liquidation.

private enterprise All businesses which are in the private sector.

private income An income received by an individual which comes from shares and deposits, not from paid employment.

private limited company A company whose shares cannot be bought and sold on the Stock Exchange. Its membership is restricted to a maximum of 50, the members having limited liability for the company's debts. The rights of members to transfer their shares is restricted and the company is prohibited from inviting the public to subscribe for shares.

A private limited company must be registered and is required to file annual accounts with the Registrar of Companies.

private means see **private income**

private placing The issue of shares or raising of a debenture by a company through a direct approach to a financial institution such as an issue house, inviting its subscription for the whole issue.

private sector The areas of economic activity conducted by companies, firms and individuals on their own behalf and outside government control. Compare **public sector**.

privatization The action of changing the status of a nationalized industry by selling shares in it to new private shareholders.

privilege money Loan facilities which are granted by the commercial banks to the discount houses under special arrangements.

PRO see **public relations officer**

probability The likelihood of an event occurring. When tossing a coin, the probability of its falling 'heads' is $\frac{1}{2}$, as is the probability of its falling 'tails'. Together these two values equal 1, and any event with a value of 1 is a certainty. In contrast any event with a probability of 0 will never occur. Naturally, most probabilities lie between these two figures. Probability theory is an important branch of mathematics.

probate 1 The formal procedure initiated by an executor to ensure the validation of a will. In undisputed cases the procedure is conducted through a local registry office, but reference must be made to the courts in disputed cases. 2 The official copy of a will, sealed to indicate that it has been verified.

procedure flow chart A process chart applied to the flow of paperwork.

process 1 A systematic series of actions directed to some specific end, particularly in a manufacturing activity. 2 A summons or writ by which a defendant is brought before a court.

process chart A graphic representation of the points at which materials are introduced into a process. Operations and inspections are shown but not material handling details. Also called **operation process chart**.

process cost centre A cost centre consisting of a specific process or a continuous sequence of operations.

process costing A method of determining product costs in which all the costs associated with each process cost centre are averaged over the production of each cost centre. The method is suitable for industries employing continuous operations, the output of one operation or process being charged as the input of the subsequent process.

process flow chart A graphic representation of the sequence of all operations occurring during a process or procedure, providing information relating to the events within the process or the activities of the operator.

procuration 1 The authority given by one person to another to enter contractual agreements, sign documents, etc. on his behalf. The term 'p.p.' or 'per pro' is used to signify the relationship. 2 The commission charged for arranging a contract for the loan of money.

produce broker An intermediary who operates in commodity markets on behalf of either seller or buyer in a transaction. The broker also undertakes the administrative functions involved in the import of goods.

producer goods Assets which are manufactured in order to produce goods for final consumption. All factory equipment is classed as producer goods. Also called **capital goods**. Compare **consumer goods**.

product Anything produced by an action or an operation.

product advertising Advertising a particular named product or brand, not referring to the company which manufactures it.

product analysis The examination of each separate product in a company's range to see why it sells, who the customers are, etc.

product centre A physical location, machine, or process through which a product passes and with which costs may be associated for the purposes of cost control.

product design The design of consumer products.

product development The improvement of an existing product line to meet the needs of the market by adding new products or updating old ones.

product differentiation A marketing process which establishes a separate identity and thus a separate market demand for a firm's product which has several competitors. Differentiation may be achieved through the use of brand names, special packaging and extensive advertising. Compare **homogeneous product**.

product diversification The introduction of products of a kind different from those hitherto marketed by a company. Diversification usually arises from the need to utilize or expand the business resources during, or in anticipation of, a decline in demand for the original product.

production control That function of a business responsible for the direction of production activity and the procurement of materials to ensure that the production plan of the business is achieved. The areas of responsibility vary from business to business but generally include material control, tooling control, control of quality and quantity of output, and scheduling.

production cost The cost, or any element of such cost, associated with the manufacture of an article from the raw material to the finished state, in its primary packaging.

production cycle The entire phase of a manufacturing process, starting at the raw materials stage and finishing with the output of finished goods.

production line A system of manufacture, where each item, such as a car, moves slowly through the factory, new sections being added to it as it goes along.

productive capital Capital which is invested to give interest or dividends.

productivity The efficiency with which factors of production are utilized, frequently measured in terms of output per factor of input, e.g. output per man hour. Productivity depends on a variety of factors including use of modern equipment, availability of a skilled workforce, and efficiency of methods and processes.

productivity bargaining Negotiations between employers and employees which seek to relate increases in earnings to increase in efficiency through improvements or changes in existing manning arrangements.

productivity bonus Extra payment made to workers because of increased productivity.

productivity drive An extra effort made to increase productivity.

product line A series of products which are marketed by a company as a related group.

product management Directing the manufacture and selling of a product or brand as an independent item.

product manager A manager who is responsible for the design, manufacture and selling of a single product, such as a brand.

product mix The range of different products which a company makes and sells.

profit 1 The excess of the relevant revenue over the relevant expenses during a period of time. 2 The amount of money needed to reward an entrepreneur for his enterprise and activity. 3 The excess of the proceeds from the sale of an article over its purchase cost.

profit and loss account An accounting statement of a business's performance over a stated period of time, scheduling the revenue and expenses attributed to that period. Also called **income statement; operating statement.**

profit centre A person or department which is considered separately in management accounts for the purpose of calculating a profit.

profit margin The percentage difference between sales income and cost of sales.

profit motive The desire to earn profits through the investment of capital in a business. This desire is held to be the major motivating force in encouraging private economic activity, although various behavioural and social motives are also regarded as significant elements in the development of economic activity.

profit sharing The distribution by a firm of a defined proportion of each year's business profits to employees on an agreed basis such as length of service, wages and salaries, etc. It thus provides an extra remuneration beyond the normal wage or salary, and is generally given as a cash bonus.

profit taking The selling of commodities, stocks and shares, etc. in order to obtain a profit on the purchase price paid. Frequently, profit taking occurs during a period of rising prices, the action of selling causing a temporary check to the rise in prices.

pro-forma customer A customer from whom payment is required before delivery of goods or services, as in the case of one with a bad credit rating, a bad payments record, etc.

pro-forma invoice A preliminary invoice normally submitted before goods are dispatched, stating their value. Such invoices are often sent when the value of a consignment is known, but not its exact weight or quantity.

program The sequence of coded instructions which cause a computer to operate in accordance with a pre-arranged system.

program evaluation and review technique A technique which is used in critical path analysis to determine the critical times for completion of the individual operations within a project if the whole project is to remain on schedule.

programme budget A financial or quantitative statement of a policy to be pursued in a future period in a particular section of a business's operations.

programmed costs Expenses incurred in operating a business which have no scientifically determinable relationship with the level of production and whose extent may therefore be determined only by the subjective decisions of the management.

programmed dealing Dealing on the Stock Exchange which is done automatically on the instructions of computers, which are suitably programmed to take investment decisions.

progress chaser A person who is responsible for checking that a job is being carried out on schedule, that orders are being fulfilled on time, etc.

progressive matrix An element of an intelligence test in which the candidate is required to complete various patterns. It is intended to remove educational and cultural influences from the test and to assess intelligence alone.

progressive taxation Taxation in which the rate of tax increases in relation to the size of income or property on which tax is to be assessed. Also called **graduated taxation**. Compare **proportional taxation; regressive taxation**.

progress payments Payments which are made as each step of contracted work is completed.

project evaluation The process of determining the financial results arising from a proposed investment. The evaluation covers the establishing of criteria against which the investment may be judged, the relevant data for the project(s) and the calculation of the results.

projection A forecast of future trends.

projective technique An interviewing technique which eliminates inaccurate responses and personal bias from market research surveys by disguising the true nature of the research undertaken.

promissory note An unconditional written promise to pay a certain sum of money on demand or at a specified future date to or to the order of a specified person or to the bearer of the note. The note is negotiable and can be exchanged except where the note specifies a particular person as payee.

The promissory note differs from a bill of exchange in that a note is a promise of payment by the originator. A bill is a request by the originator to some other person to pay.

promotion 1 Any form of sales publicity, especially a particular effort to sell a specific product or line, such as a joint effort by the manufacturer and retailer by cutting prices and setting up large displays. 2 The upgrading of an individual in his employment. 3 The formation of a limited company.

promotion ladder The series of steps by which an employee progresses to more responsible jobs.

promotion money Money paid to the first board of directors of a company or its promoters as reward for securing the formation of the company. The money is derived from the capital subscribed by shareholders and details must be disclosed in the prospectus.

prompt cash payment A term on an invoice requiring payment within a few days of receipt without receiving a discount.

prompt day The day in international commodity markets when settlement for purchase of goods must be made.

propensity to consume The desire to consume expressed as the proportion of income spent on goods and services to that saved. The poorest have the highest propensities to consume since they can afford to save very little if anything.

propensity to save The desire to save expressed as the fraction of income saved rather than spent.

property 1 Anything which is owned. 2 A piece of land or real estate. 3 The right of ownership as 'property in the goods', i.e. ownership of the goods. All property other than land and things affixed to land (fences, houses, etc.) is classified as personal property or personalty.

property bond A unit of ownership in a fund which is used to invest in property. The unit value is linked to property values, while rental income from the property is distributed or reinvested. The fund is managed by specialist investment firms.

property developer A company which buys property to renovate or to demolish in order to construct new buildings on the site.

proportional taxation Tax levied at the same rate at all income levels. Compare **progressive taxation; regressive taxation**.

proprietary see **Pty**

proprietary goods Goods (especially medicines) which are manufactured

pro rata

and sold by one company, which owns them and markets them under a special brand name.

pro rata ('at a certain rate; in proportion to') A term used when expenses, income, etc. are apportioned on an inferred equitable basis.

prospectus A document issued by a newly formed company inviting public subscription for a share or debenture issue.

The prospectus must comply with the Companies Acts as to the subject matter of its contents, providing details of the minimum subscription considered necessary to be raised by the issue and a report by the auditors of past profits and losses, dividends, future prospects, etc. The prospectus must be registered by the company with the Registrar of Companies.

protected bear   see **covered bear**

protectionism A policy that protects domestic producers from foreign competition by the imposition of tariffs, quotas, etc.

protective tariff A tariff imposed on imports to try to restrict their sale in order to protect locally made products.

protest The formal act before a notary public signifying that a foreign bill of exchange has been unpaid or unaccepted. This act enables proceedings to be initiated against drawers or endorsers of the bill.

provision 1 An amount charged by a business against the profits of an accounting period to meet a specific requirement or contingency. It is any amount so retained as a means of providing for depreciation, renewals or diminution in value of assets, or for known liabilities, the amount of which cannot be determined with substantial accuracy. Provisions are generally shown in the balance sheet as a deduction from the assets against which they are made. Compare **reserves** (def. 1). 2 A clause in a legal document.

proviso A condition laid down in a contract.

proximo (In a document) The next month or the month following that named.

proxy 1 A person acting in place of another with the latter's permission, e.g. voting for him at a shareholders' meeting. Normally the proxy votes in accordance with the principal's instructions, but he may have the freedom to vote as he thinks fit. 2 A document in which a member of a company or other organization can register his vote upon a resolution to be presented to a meeting which the member cannot attend.

PSBR   see **Public Sector Borrowing Requirement**

Pty A term used as part of the name of a private limited company in Australia and South Africa.

public company A limited liability company whose membership is unlimited and whose shares are freely transferable and can be bought by the public.

public corporation A form of business organization established by central or local government in order to manage a state-owned activity. The constitution, functions and powers of the corporation are defined by the instrument which establishes the organization. The government exercises overall responsibility, the corporation being responsible for its own management.

public expenditure The money spent by central or local government.

public finance The theory and practices associated with the raising of government revenue and the distribution of government expenditure, with examination of their resultant economic, social and political implications.

public good Any good or service provided for the public, generally by central or local government. It must be a good that, if supplied to one person, can be supplied to others at no extra cost. For example, television broadcasts do not need a greater output of power if more people are watching. It must be a good that cannot be denied to a person even if he does not pay for it. For example, litter removal. It must be a good that cannot be denied to a person even if he does not want it, for example, the provision of education.

public issue The raising of share capital by a company through the invitation to the public to subscribe for shares. Notification of the issue and the invitation to subscribe are normally made through newspaper advertisements.

publicity The action of making the general public aware of a product or service.

publicity slogan A group of words which can be easily remembered and which are used to promote a product.

public limited company A company whose shares can be bought on the Stock Exchange by members of the public.

public ownership The ownership of the capital of an undertaking by the state or by a municipal authority.

public relations The creation and maintenance of goodwill between a company and the public by the promotion of a favourable image of the company.

public relations officer An official who is responsible for the public relations activities of an organization.

public sector The areas of economic activity which are controlled by central or local government authorities or their agencies and by the public corporations and nationalized industries. Compare **private sector**.

Public Sector Borrowing Requirement The difference between public expenditure on goods and services and public revenue from taxation, etc. The difference has to be met by borrowing.

public trustee A government official appointed to administer estates and act as trustee.

public utilities Those industries which provide essential public services and which because of their strongly monopolistic positions have been brought under public ownership in Britain, e.g. the production and distribution of electricity, gas and water.

puff 1 Exaggerated praise or recommendation of one's own goods for the purpose of advertisement but without misrepresentation or fraudulent intent. 2 To bid up prices at a sale by auction.

puisine mortgage A mortgage on land where the title deeds are not deposited as security when the mortgage is established. The mortgage can be protected by registration on the Land Charges Register.

pull strategy A marketing policy whereby vigorous advertising of products stimulates demand by the final consumer, which forces the distributive network to supply the product and hence in turn to increase demand from the manufacturer. Compare **push strategy.**

pump priming Investment by government agencies in new projects which it is hoped will bring benefit to the economy of the country in general.

punched card A card designed to carry information in a computer input system. Information is recorded by means of holes punched in specific patterns, the positioning of the holes representing sets of data. Such cards are generally standard dimensions to enable processing by a wide variety of equipment.

punched tape A means of storing information for computer processing, whereby data is recorded at specific locations in the form of punched holes. Each set of holes across the width of the tape represents a character and can be read rapidly by a tape reader either mechanically or by a photoelectric cell.

punter A small speculator who holds stock or shares for very short periods, seeking to earn profit from a rapid regular turnover of his investments.

purchase 1 The annual return or rent from land. 2 The annual return accruing from an investment.

purchase requisition A request to the purchasing department of a company to buy a stated quantity of specified goods.

purchase tax A tax formerly levied (generally on the wholesale value) on certain goods when they passed from a registered person (generally a wholesaler) to an unregistered person (generally a retailer). The tax did not apply to goods exported, but it could apply to imports.

purchasing That area of a business activity devoted to procuring all materials, equipment and services required to operate successfully all aspects of the business.

purchasing power The money available to a group or sector of the population for the purchase of goods.

push strategy A marketing policy which uses the normal promotional efforts of efficient display, advertising and salesmanship to sell the whole range of a firm's products through the distributive network. Compare **pull strategy.**

put A right to sell stock, shares or commodities at an agreed price at or within a certain specified time. The right is acquired in return for the payment of a charge, which is a proportion of the value of the subject matter. If price movements are favourable the option will be exercised and a profit earned. If price movements are adverse the option is not taken up and the potential seller merely loses the option-purchase price. Also called **put option.** Compare **put of more.**

put and call The right either to buy or sell a quantity of stock, shares or a commodity at an agreed price at or within a specified period.

put of more The right to sell double the amount of a commodity or shares which have been previously sold at a specified time at an agreed price. Also called **option to double; seller's option to double.** Compare **call option.**

pyramiding The snowballing effect which derives from a shareholding in a business and the acquisition and control of other companies. For example, a share holding of 50,000 shares in a company may acquire control of a company with 100,000 shares, which may control a company with 200,000 shares, etc.

pyramid selling An illegal method of selling goods to the public through an organization with a network of agents who must each pay a fee to join. Each agent is paid to recruit other agents and the fees paid by new entrants (which may be disguised by inflating payments for stocks) often greatly exceed their likely future commissions on sales. The activity of selling to the public may be almost incidental, the main source of the organization's revenue being the agents' joining fees.

Q

qualified acceptance A condition specified on a bill of exchange by the person on whom the bill has been drawn (drawee) and who is acknowledging liability on the bill by the acceptance procedure.

The qualified acceptance may take three forms: a conditional acceptance, by which the drawee accepts liability provided that a condition specified on the bill is fulfilled; partial acceptance, whereby liability is accepted for part of the sum stated on the bill; and local acceptance, whereby payment is to be made at a place specified by the drawee.

qualified accounts A company's annual accounts which have a qualified report from the auditors.

qualified report A statement by the external auditors of a company's finances, which details any reservations which the auditors have concerning the manner in which the books of account are maintained or any reservations as to the trading and financial positions disclosed by the company in its financial statements. A breach of certain accounting rules or conventions will frequently give rise to a qualification of the accounts.

qualifying period A period of time which has to elapse before someone or something qualifies.

qualifying shares The fully paid shareholding which the articles of a company specify as a qualifying requirement for its directors.

qualitative analysis The analysis of material, processes, information, etc. in order to ascertain the nature of the constituent parts.

quality control The functions of, and procedures relating to, the testing and acceptance of all materials and components at all stages of manufacture from raw materials to finished product.

quality control chart A graph which plots the fluctuations of a variable within prescribed limits. Time is plotted on the horizontal axis, while the central vertical axis plots the average value of the variable. Accompanying it on either side are the prescribed upper and lower limits of the variable (usually +/- three standard B deviations from the average). If these limits are exceeded then the variable is out of control. Also called **control chart**.

quality control, statistical The application of statistical techniques based on probability theory to establish standards of quality and to maintain adherence to such standards in an economical manner.

quality gauging The use of instruments to determine whether pre-quality requirements are being met.

quality report A report on the condition of materials received from suppliers prepared by the inspection function of a business.

quango An official agency set up by the government to deal with or supervise a special section of government responsibility. Abbreviated from **quasi-autonomous non-governmental organization**.

quantity discount, quantity rebate A discount made for a high volume of purchases. See **aggregated rebate scheme**.

quantity theory of money A theory which seeks to express the relationship between the supply of money in circulation and the level of prices. It is commonly expressed as: $MU = PT$, where M = quantity of money, U = velocity of circulation of money, P = the level of prices, and T = quantity of goods.

More recent expressions of the relationship between money and prices regard the desire to hold money rather than spend it as an equally significant factor in determining price level as the quantity of money. Thus $M = kPT$ where k = desire to hold money as a proportion of expenditure.

quarter day The last day of each quarter of the year on which traditionally payment of rents, interest and other quarterly charges become due. In England and Wales these are 25 March (Lady Day), 24 June (Midsummer Day), 29 September (Michaelmas) and 25 December (Christmas Day). In Scotland they are: 25 February (Candlemas Day), 15 May (Whitsuntide), 1 August (Lammas) and 11 November (Martinmas).

quartile A statistical term applied to each of the four groups of events or variables within a frequency distribution having equal frequencies. The event in the series at the quarter stage of the distribution is the lower quartile, the half-way stage is the median and the three-quarter stage the upper quartile.

quasi-rent A temporary form of profit accrued only because of some short-lived advantage, such as control of a patent. See also **rent**.

Queen's Award for Industry An award presented annually by the monarch on the advice of the government in recognition of a firm's outstanding achievements in industry, especially in export performance and technical innovation. The award takes the form of a plaque and an emblem which may be displayed in the firm's literature and on its products for five years.

questionnaire A printed list of questions used to elicit responses from respondents in a market survey.

queuing theory A branch of probability theory based on the study of queues at a servicing facility. The capacity and characteristics of the servicing facility are studied in relation to the demands for service. Also called **delay theory**.

quick assets ratio The relationship between the value of debtors and

quid pro quo

cash and the value of current liabilities. The ratio is used to indicate the ability of a business to obtain cash quickly in order to meet its liabilities.

quid pro quo A concession made by one party to a business transaction in response to a concession made by the other party.

quorum A minimum number required to be present at the beginning of a meeting of a board of directors, etc. in order for the meeting to be able to conduct business. The number is specified in the organization's constitution or articles of association.

quota A maximum quantity, specially that specified by a government for the importation of a product, or that specified by an industry for the production of goods by individual member firms. See also **import quota.**

quota sampling A statistical technique employed in market surveys, which permits the interviewer to select the individuals to be questioned within each characteristic group.

quota system A system where imports or other supplies are regulated by a government-fixed maximum amount.

quotation 1 A written or verbal statement of the price and terms on which an article or service is offered for sale. Also called **quote.** 2 The privilege of having one's company shares, etc. dealt in on a Stock Exchange and the current market price listed in the official publication. In return for this privilege the Stock Exchange requires various conditions to be met with regard to the disclosure of information about the company.

quotations committee A committee of the London Stock Exchange that vets the applications of private companies for quotation on the Stock Exchange.

quote see **quotation** (def. 1)

quoted company see **listed company**

quoted investment A stock or share having a quotation on a recognized stock exchange. Generally, only shares having a quotation may be dealt in, although permission may be granted to deal in unquoted shares.

R

rack rent The rent which a property might command on the open market, being the full annual value of the property. It is generally calculated on the basis of the landlord being responsible for repairs, maintenance and insurance.

raider A company which suddenly buys shares in another company before making a takeover bid.

rally A recovery in the price of a commodity, security or currency following a downward movement in its price.

r and d see **research and development**

random access A facility of some computers which permits the rapid retrieval of data from the computer store without the need for input data to be presented in any particular sequence.

random sample A sample taken from a population in which each unit has an equal chance of being selected.

range A measure of the dispersion of a number of observations: it is the difference between the largest and smallest observation. It thus considers only the two extreme observations and has limited statistical use. The median is an average calculated by taking the mid-point of the range.

rank and file The ordinary members of a trade union or political party.

ranking method The placing of jobs in order of importance, as determined by crude subjective criteria. This is a rough and ready method of job evaluation.

rateable value The notional gross rental value of property, less a percentage or allowance to cover the costs of repairs, insurance, etc. The valuation is assessed on domestic, commercial and industrial property, forming the basis on which rates are levied. See also **rates**.

rate card A card or sheet giving the prices for advertisements of different dimensions in a newspaper or magazine.

rate for age scale A scale of remuneration in which rates of pay are based upon the employee's age. Also called **time progression scale**.

rate of interest An expression of the price charged for the facility of borrowing money. The rate is determined by expressing the charge as a percentage of the sum borrowed and related to a time period of one year. For example, interest charges of £10 on £100 borrowed and repayable in one year are expressed as a rate of interest of 10/100 = 10% a year.

rate of return 1 The profit arising out of an investment, expressed as a percentage of the sum invested. 2 The annual profit of an enterprise, expressed as a percentage of capital employed during the year.

rates Taxation levied by local authorities to finance in part the services which they provide for the community. The tax is assessed on the rateable value of the property at a determined rate in the pound. The tax is the rateable value multiplied by the taxable rate in the pound.

rate support grant A form of financial assistance to local authorities provided by the central government. The grant is for general purposes and is designed to supplement the finance raised locally by rates, etc. The grant comprises three elements. Firstly, there is a needs element, which is related to population size, etc. Secondly, there is a resources element, which is designed to equalize the differences in financial resources of authorities by bringing the rateable resources of the authorities with below-average resources up to the average. Thirdly, there is a domestic element which is designed to relieve part of the burden on domestic ratepayers of increasing rates.

ratification The action of a principal in formally binding himself to the terms of a contract arranged by his agent who, in concluding the contract, has gone beyond the authority conferred by the principal.

rating 1 An evaluation of the creditworthiness of an individual or business. 2 An evaluation of the general value of a share. 3 An assessment of workers' performance used to establish the standard time allowed for performance of the job.

ratio decidendi A judicial decision based upon the facts of a case and creating a binding precedent for the future.

rationalization 1 The process or result of reviewing total industry or company operations with a view to improving efficiency and effecting extensive economies. 2 The employment of scientific techniques with the aim of optimizing the use of the resources of a business.

ratio scale graph see **semi-logarithmic chart**

rat race The intense competition which exists for success in business or in a personal career.

raw data Data in its original state, as it is put into a computer, before being processed.

raw materials 1 All minerals, metal, ores, or vegetable matter in a natural and unprocessed state prior to manufacture. 2 Any materials or products which are converted into a different form during processing or manufacturing.

R/D see **refer to drawer**

re In the matter of, relating to.

readership analysis A market research technique which tests the impact of press advertising by assessing the relationship between given advertisements and buying habits.

ready cash Money which is immediately available for payment.

real accounts A bookkeeping record of the assets acquired by a business, such as cash, buildings and capital introduced by the proprietors. Compare **impersonal accounts; personal accounts**.

real estate Immovable property such as land held on a freehold. Compare **personal estate**.

real income The amount which is available for spending from income, after tax and social security contributions have been deducted.

realizable assets Assets which can be sold for cash.

realization The process of disposing of the assets of a business, the business itself or an estate, etc.

realization account A bookkeeping record of the transactions relating to the dissolution of a partnership. The cost of assets acquired is compared with their disposal values and other expenses incurred in the realization. The balance on the account represents a profit or loss to be attributed to the partners before the final bookkeeping entries winding up the business are made.

realization, piecemeal The distribution of the proceeds of disposed assets to partners engaged in a dissolution of their business.

real time Time for processing data in a computer which is the same as the time of the problem being solved, with the result that the action of the computer can affect the source of the problem.

real time control The control of activities as each event occurs, so that any corrective action necessary may be taken without delay. This is commonly applied to some information systems where computerized processing of information allows the control of current activities.

realtor (US) a real estate agent.

rebate An allowance or deduction from the invoice price of an article given in return for prompt payment or as a price concession for large volumes of sales.

receipt 1 A written acknowledgement that a sum of money has been received. Certain transactions do not require a receipt as evidence of the transfer of value, one such example being the cheque. Since it is an acknowledgement of the payment of an outstanding debt a receipt does not form part of the contracted arrangement. 2 The acquisition of cash by an individual or business.

receipts and payments account A bookkeeping record of all cash transactions occurring during a period.

receivables Sums of money due to a business from persons or businesses to whom it has supplied goods or services in the normal course of trade.

receiver A person appointed to safeguard property or to protect the rights of persons entitled to it. If a receiver is appointed by a court he becomes an officer of the court (as when a company is being wound up). Debenture holders may appoint a receiver in order to protect charged assets. A receiver may act as supervisor of the affairs of a business and he may in addition act as manager.

receiving order A court order which authorizes the Official Receiver to take charge of a debtor's property or business for the benefit of his creditors. The order is made where the debtor has committed an act of bankruptcy and where either the debtor or a creditor has petitioned for a winding-up.

recession A reduction in the level and volume of economic activity occasioned by loss of business confidence, lack of investment, etc. The size and duration of the cut-back depends on the efficiency of government fiscal and monetary measures designed to arrest the downward movement.

reciprocal demand Mutual demand for one another's products, especially between different countries. Such demand may determine the feasibility of home manufacture as opposed to importing.

reciprocal holdings A situation where two companies each own shares in the other, in order to prevent takeover bids.

recision A legal right to abandon or rescind a contract upon the occurrence of certain events or conditions.

recognized marking names see **marking names**

recommended retail price see **manufacturer's recommended price**

reconciliation statement A record which seeks to produce agreement between the balances of two related accounts such as a firm's cash book and its balance as shown on its bank statement. See also **bank reconciliation**.

red clause A clause contained in a credit arrangement between purchaser and seller which authorizes the seller to obtain an advance from the purchaser's bankers to cover the transport costs before the goods are delivered.

redeemable preference share A preference share which is to be repurchased by the issuing company on a specified date and in a specified manner, e.g. for cash or by a further issue of shares. Where the share is redeemed for cash an equivalent value must be set aside from distributable profits/reserves in order to establish a fund which may be used only for a limited number of purposes.

redemption The repayment of a mortgage or repurchase by a company of issued shares or debentures, etc. in exchange for the related document of title. The company may pay cash or exchange the issued shares/debentures for a bond issue.

redemption date The date on which a company purchases redeemable preference shares which it had previously issued or repays a debenture loan. The date of redemption is indicated when the shares or debenture are originally offered.

redemption value The value of a security when redeemed.

redemption yield The average annual yield a redeemable bond will pay out until it reaches maturity.

redeployment The action of moving personnel from one workplace to another or from one job to another.

redevelopment The action of demolishing existing buildings on a site and replacing with new buildings.

redistribution of wealth The proposal to share out the wealth of a country among the population (as by taxing the rich and increasing government benefits to the poor).

red tape Excessive official paperwork which delays business development.

reducing balance depreciation A method of determining that portion of the cost of an asset to be charged to each accounting period in which the asset is expected to contribute value. The period charge is a fixed percentage of the total net asset cost, allowing for anticipated disposal value, the cost being reduced by accumulated depreciation charges. The charge will thus alter every period and, in theory, the asset will never be fully written off.

redundancy The disappearance of a job generally as a result of a reduction in demand or the introduction of equipment which reduces manpower needs.

redundancy payment A lump sum payment made to an employee who is declared redundant. Under the Redundancy Payments Act, 1965, such payments are determined by the length of service and annual pay of the particular employee.

re-exchange The charge made by the holder of a dishonoured bill of exchange and levied on the drawer on redrawing a new bill, the charge including any losses or expenses incurred through dishonour.

referee 1 A person appointed to arbitrate in a dispute between two parties. 2 A person who is asked to give a confidential report on the character or ability of a candidate for a job.

reference 1 A testimonial, usually written, indicating the character, abilities, conduct, etc. of an individual. 2 Proceedings brought before an arbitrator in order to settle a dispute.

reference, trade A testimonial given by a company indicating the credit record of a firm with which it deals. It is common practice to request a new customer to provide such references, so that the length and amount of credit taken can be assessed.

refer to drawer A note put on a cheque by the bank on which the cheque is drawn signifying that the bank is refusing to accept the transaction because the account does not have sufficient funds to cover the cheque.

refinancing

refinancing (Of a loan) the action of floating a new loan to pay back a previous loan.

reflation An expansion of the economy brought about by government activity. It is characterized by rising employment and increased production.

reflationary measures Actions taken by the government which are likely to stimulate the economy.

refund 1 To give back money; to make a repayment. 2 To fund anew, especially in order to meet an old debt by new borrowings, such as the issue of bonds.

regional employment premium A governmental labour subsidy designed to encourage companies to operate in areas of high unemployment or areas requiring economic stimulation. It was ended in 1974.

registered business name A partnership name which is registered with the Registrar of Companies. A partnership name requires registration when the name does not consist solely of the names of the partners.

The Registrar may refuse registration if the name might prove misleading or too similar to that of an existing business.

registered capital   see **authorized capital**

registered office The official business home of a limited company. Certain company records are required to be maintained for public inspection at the office, which is also the address to which legal notices, etc. may be delivered. The Registrar of Companies must be notified of the address of the office.

registered shares or stock Shares or stock whose issue is recorded in a company's registers. The stock is not issued with a coupon sheet (whereby interest/dividends may be claimed), the dividend being paid directly by the company by means of a dividend warrant. The transfer of ownership is possible only through the holder signing the register to this effect.

registered trademark   see **trademark**

register of charges A record maintained at the registered office of a company showing details of all mortgages and charges on the property of the company.

registers, company Records which a limited company must maintain by law. They comprise: a share register which gives details of members and their shareholdings; a register of directors which details names and addresses; registers of directors' shareholdings and debenture holdings; and registers of charges which detail the mortgages and debentures of the company.

registrar of companies A government official with whom limited companies and partnerships must file certain particulars and documents in accordance with legal requirements. These are: a company's memorandum and articles; a company's annual return (balance sheet, profit and loss, directors' report); charges on company property by way of mortgages and debentures; and the name and details of a partnership whose name differs from that of the names of the individual partners.

regression analysis   A statistical technique for examining and estimating the relationship between two or more variables. See also **correlation**.

regressive taxation   A tax paid at a lower rate the higher the income of the taxpayer. Compare **progressive taxation; proportional taxation**.

regulator   A discretionary government economic device by which the Chancellor of the Exchequer could adjust the rate of purchase tax within fixed limits without needing to obtain Parliamentary approval.

reimburse   To pay back money, especially money which someone has spent on behalf of a company.

reinsurance   The business activity related to the passing on of all or part of a contractual insurance risk to another insurer. In the event of a claim the liability initially exists between the insured and the first insurer, who may subsequently claim from the reinsurers.

reinvestment   1 The action of investing again in the same securities. 2 Investment by a company in its own business, by ploughing back its earnings in new product development.

related products   Two or more products which, although different, are connected either by common basic components or, more usually, by an interrelationship of demands. Thus, solid fuel and suitable grates may both be supplied by the same company.

relating back   The dating of the powers and position of trustees or liquidators retrospectively from the procedures initiating the bankruptcy. Assets fraudulently disposed of since this date may be recovered. The trustee is entitled to all property, etc. in existence from the commencement of the bankruptcy proceedings, except subsequent transactions entered into in good faith.

remainder   1 A future interest of an estate, as when property is conveyed to X for life, and on his death, to Y, who is called the remainderman. 2 The stock of a book remaining after sales have virtually ceased. Such stock is frequently sold at a reduced price.

remainderman   One who takes over the residue of an state following the death of a life tenant of the estate.

remainder merchant   A book dealer who buys stock very cheaply from a publisher and sells it at a much lower price than the original published price.

remainder value   see **net book value**

reminder   A communication to a customer indicating that payment of a debt for goods supplied or services rendered is outstanding and due.

remission of taxes   The repayment of tax which has been overpaid.

remit 1 To send money. 2 To refrain from claiming a debt. 3 To send back a case to a lower court for further action.

remittance Money sent as payment for goods or services.

remittance advice A statement detailing a payment for goods or services. It may accompany the payment or may be sent separately, as when money is being remitted by bank transfer.

remittance basis The basis on which taxation may be assessed on income arising from outside but remitted to within the United Kingdom.

remittance, constructive Income which would be subject to taxation if remitted to the United Kingdom but which is applied by a person ordinarily a UK resident towards the payment of a debt for money lent in the United Kingdom.

remuneration system The various components which go to make up a gross wage. They may comprise basic pay, bonus payments, and allowances such as for dirty work, etc.

rent 1 A periodic payment by a tenant to the owner of land or buildings in return for their use. 2 The surplus paid to any economic factor of production above the sum of money necessary to prevent its transfer to another occupation.

rentes French government bonds bearing interest.

rentier A person whose income is derived from the ownership of capital in any form, e.g. interest on securities, dividends, rent from property.

reorder level The level to which stocks may be allowed to fall before an order for further supplies is placed. It is the sum of the minimum stock level and the expected usage during the reorder period.

reorder quantity see **economic order quantity**

rep see **sales representative**

repayments mortgage A form of mortgage where the borrower repays the capital borrowed at the same time as he pays interest on it.

repeat order An order for further stock of an item which was ordered previously.

repetition factor An expression for the type of production operated by a business (e.g., one-off, batch, mass production). The rate of recovery of set-up costs, such as tooling up, pattern making, etc., is a function of the repetition factor.

replacement cost The current market price required for the replacement of an asset. Business assets may be valued in this manner and the valuation taken into a company's financial records provided that the fact of adjustment and the basis of the valuation are set out in financial statements.

reply paid card A card used in mailings, on which an interested potential customer can place an order or ask for further information, without paying the postage.

repossess To take back a property which someone is purchasing under a mortgage or an item which is being bought under a hire-purchase agreement, when the purchaser is incapable of paying the interest.

represent To act on someone's behalf; to visit clients to sell a company's products or services.

representative see **sales representative**

representative firm A notional average company within an industry, used as a yardstick for comparative purposes.

reproductive debt The proportion of National Debt that is backed by real assets. Compare **deadweight debt**.

repudiate To refuse to acknowledge, as a debt, or to declare an intention not to be bound by a contract.

reputed ownership A legal doctrine which states that the estate of an insolvent debtor includes goods in his possession of which he is not the owner but which have been left with him in the normal course of business.

required earnings An estimate of the level of earnings which a company's management considers desirable in providing a reasonable return on assets employed, such as to satisfy shareholders and other interested parties. When expressed as a percentage of assets employed, it may be used in evaluating investment projects.

requisition A document which requests articles to be issued to the presenter, such as a request for goods from a works stores.

resale price maintenance The fixing of prices by suppliers, ensuring that branded goods are sold to the public at prices at or above a fixed minimum level. This is considered a restrictive practice hampering competition and has been made illegal under the Resale Prices Act 1964 unless it can be shown to be in the public interest. It still applies to books, newspapers and some drugs.

rescind To cancel an agreement or law.

research and development The scientific analysis of materials, processes, etc. and the application of findings to the formulation of new products, processes, equipment, etc., including preparation for the translation into production. Also called **r and d**.

reserve Money from profits not paid as dividend, which is retained by a company to be used for a special purpose later.

reserve capital That part of a company's issued share capital which by special resolution is not to be called up except in the event of a winding-up. Also called **capital reserves; reserve liability**.

reserve currency A strong currency which is held by foreign countries to support their own weaker currencies.

reserve fund Undistributed profits represented by investments outside the business.

reserve liability

reserve liability see **reserve capital**

reserve price The price of an article offered for sale, especially at an auction, below which the seller refuses to accept any offer. The price need not be specified but there must be a reference in any literature mentioning the article and at the sale itself to the fact that a reserve price has been placed on the article.

reserves 1 Sums set aside from company profits or surpluses which are retained within the business without any specific intention as to their use. Reserves derived from profits may be used as the directors think fit. Share premium reserve (arising from the issue of shares above par) and preference share redemption reserve may be applied by the directors in a limited number of ways, including the issue of bonus shares. Asset revaluation reserves may not be utilized. 2 The funds of gold and foreign currencies held by a nation in order to settle international debts and to stabilize exchange rates. 3 Cash held by the commercial banks in their tills and on deposit with the Bank of England.

residual value The value of an asset at the end of its useful or economic life.

residuary estate That part of an estate of a deceased person remaining after setting aside property allocated in the will of the deceased.

residue The surplus of an estate after all legal claims such as debts, funeral expenses, etc. have been met.

resolution A proposal which is put before the shareholders at an AGM, and on which they have to vote.

respondent A person who answers questions in a questionnaire, or in a market research survey.

respondentia A loan negotiated by a ship's master to provide funds for the completion of a voyage. The cargo is usually pledged as security and repayment of the loan with interest is conditional upon the safe arrival of the vessel. See also **bottomry bond**.

responsibility accounting A concept of control whereby executives are regarded as performance centres with which costs, etc. can be associated, the executives being accountable for the financial results produced by the centre. Only those costs which the executives can control should be associated with their respective cost centres.

restitution 1 The action of giving back property to its owner. 2 Compensation paid for damage or loss suffered.

restraint of trade 1 The prevention of a person from exercising his trade or profession or restriction of such exercise. A restraint of this kind, which may, for example, seek to prevent an employee from joining a competitor company is prima facie against public interest and therefore void. However, it may be enforceable if it is considered reasonable to the restricted party and to the public. It may not be wider than is necessary to protect the party imposing the limitation. 2 An attempt by companies to fix prices or create monopolies or reduce competition in a way which can affect freedom of trade.

restrictive covenant A clause in a contract which prohibits the performance of certain specified actions on or about a property or prevents the performance of certain specified activities during and/or after the contractual period. Such a clause may be inserted in a contract of employment in order to prevent the employee from competing with the employer.

restrictive endorsement A form of endorsement written on a bill of exchange by someone who transfers ownership to a person from whom he has received value. The endorsement may restrict the ability of the holder to negotiate the bill to the extent specified or may prohibit negotiation of the bill.

restrictive practice An action which curtails competition, e.g. agreed prices, production quotes, allotment of markets, scale of fees, demarcation of skills and jobs.

restrictive practices court A court established to consider cases relating to restrictive arrangements between traders and producers referred to it by the Registrar of Restrictive Practices. The court may impose a fine or order the discontinuance of practices which are held to be contrary to the public interest.

restrictive trade agreement Any agreement, written or oral, whereby two or more manufacturers or suppliers agree to restrict the manufacture, distribution, conditions of sale, etc. of goods. Such practice is presumed to be contrary to public interest and may be prohibited by the court unless the parties can justify the restrictions. All such agreements must be registered with the Registrar of Restrictive Trade Agreements.

restructure To reorganize the financial basis of a company.

résumé US usage for **curriculum vitae**.

retail The sale of commodities, generally in small quantities, to the ultimate consumer, the general public.

retailer A shopkeeper who sells goods to the general public.

retail prices index The index which shows the change (usually an increase) in the retail price of a number of frequently purchased domestic goods and appliances. See also **cost-of-living index**.

retained earnings The part of net income generated from the transactions of a company in an accounting period that is not distributed to shareholders.

retainer 1 A sum paid on a regular basis in order to secure the services of a firm or individual as and when required. 2 The right of an executor

retention

to hold back property of the estate which he is administering to the value of his claim for services rendered.

retention That part of the price of a contract which is kept back for a certain period after completion of the contract in order to give the purchaser time to ensure that work has been correctly carried out. This is especially common in contracts for the erection of, or work done on, plant or buildings.

retention money Part of a contracted value which is retained by the customer for an agreed period after completion of the contract. The money is handed over when the customer has satisfied himself as to the competence with which the contract has been performed.

retire 1 To withdraw a bill of exchange from circulation, e.g. by purchase at or before maturity by the person liable on it. Also called **take up a bill**. 2 To withdraw an asset from its service within a business. 3 To cancel shares previously issued by a company and now repurchased. 4 To terminate an employee's employment upon attainment of the legally pensionable age, or the pensionable age established by a company's pension scheme.

retrenchment A reduction in expenditure or in new product development.

retrieval The action of getting back information which is stored in a computer.

retroactive Which takes effect from some time in the past.

return 1 Any statement or report made to meet statutory requirements. 2 A regular statement of facts and figures. 3 The extent of the reward for the employment of capital by a business or individual, generally expressed as a percentage of earnings to investment. 4 (plural) Goods rejected by a customer and sent back to the supplier. 5 The value of sales during a given period.

return on capital The profit earned by an investment, often expressed as a percentage of the investment. There is little consistency in the application of the term, in view of the many alternative ways of assessing both profit and capital. The criteria for measuring the return on capital may depend upon whether the ratio is to be used as a guide to potential investors, creditors, management, etc.

return on investment Profit expressed as a percentage of money invested.

returns to scale see **increasing returns**

revaluation A valuation of one or all of the fixed assets of a business in terms of current market values – either disposal values or replacement values. The new valuation may be taken into the accounts of the business and the basis of evaluation and its extent must be stated on any financial statements on which the revalued assets appear. The excess of revaluation over purchase cost must be taken to an asset revaluation reserve.

revenue 1 The money a company receives from selling its products. Also called **sales revenue**. 2 The proceeds of taxation to a government. Also called **tax revenue**.

revenue account The bookkeeping statement used by statutory companies which records the revenue and expenses attributable to normal business operations during an accounting period.

revenue expenditure Expenditure by a business on purchases of goods or services which, except to the extent of any unsold stocks or prepayments, are wholly exhausted during the accounting period in which such expenditure is incurred. Thus, expenditure on the day-to-day purchase of goods, services and running of the business is of a revenue nature. Compare **capital expenditure**.

reverse takeover 1 The result of an amalgamation between two companies, whereby the acquired company comes to control the new business instead of the acquiring company. 2 The acquisition of company B by company A following a previous bid by company B to acquire company A.

reverse yield gap The negative difference between the yield, i.e. return on shares, and the yield on fixed interest stock. This circumstance arises in inflationary periods as ordinary share prices rise, because investors are buying shares as a hedge against inflation, while the return is below that obtained from fixed interest stock.

reversion A right to property which will be taken up by the grantor after the expiration of a grant of the property to some other person.

reversionary annuity An annuity which is paid to someone on the death of another person.

revision variance The evaluation of the difference between the original standard cost and the revised standard cost.

revocable credit Credit facilities extended by a bank which may be withdrawn without notice.

revolving credit A credit facility extended by a bank to cover a number of successive transactions. The limit of unused credit is reduced from a maximum as a part of the facility is taken up by the customer, but the facility reverts to the maximum when the credit taken up is repaid.

rider An addition to a document, clause or resolution after its initial completion.

rigging the market 1 Operations which are designed to secure an artificial market for a security or commodity in order for the operator to secure a profit, e.g. a bear transaction – selling in order to induce a fall in price at which point the operator repurchases. 2 The announcement of a high dividend prior to a new share issue. The market price of the company's shares is thereby raised, which permits the issue of the new shares at a higher price.

rights issue An invitation to existing shareholders to subscribe at a favourable price for new shares being issued by the company. The number of shares which may be purchased is related to the current shareholding.

ring trading A form of market trading, especially the futures market in commodities, whereby a group of dealers negotiate to buy and sell. The prices established by the group determine the market price in the futures market.

risk 1 A chance of loss which may be insurable, such as risk of loss through fire, or uninsurable, such as loss arising from adverse price movements. 2 The legal liability on goods. Normally liability passes with legal title and possession, but may be independent of possession, as, for example, goods carried at owner's risk.

risk capital see **venture capital**

risk yield The additional return required on an investment to make allowance for any inherent risk.

rock-bottom prices The lowest prices possible.

rogue event An individual occurrence in a (statistical) series of events which varies markedly from the norm.

ROI see **return on investment**

role playing A management training technique in which members of a group assume the parts of managers in a (generally) fictional or imaginary company in order to test and assess their reactions in business situations, or in which members of a group of managers assume the role of different managers in order to facilitate the understanding of business problems from the viewpoint of others.

rolling budget A financial or quantitative budget which is constantly revised and extended to cover the period following the existing budget period, as each period elapses. Thus, the total period covered by the budget is constant in length but changing in content.

roll over 1 To make a credit facility continue to be available for a further period of time. 2 To allow a debt to stand after the repayment date has passed.

root of title Documentary evidence of ownership of land. A valid ownership is evidenced by documents going back at least 30 years and starting with a good root of title, for example, a mortgage or conveyance which details the whole legal and equitable interest in the land and which leaves no doubt as to the title.

rotary card index A filing system whereby information is recorded on cards fixed to a horizontal spindle, so that it can be quickly retrieved.

rotation of directors The retirement of a number or proportion of the total number of directors of a company each year and their submission for re-election by the members. The law requires some provision to be made for rotation but the detail is left for the company to determine and record in its articles.

roundabout   see **filing wheel**

route sheet   A record which moves with an item being manufactured showing how much time is spent on the work in various departments.

routine diagram   A diagrammatic representation of the operation of a process or the movement of a document through various departments, drawn with a view to analysis and improvement of procedures.

Rowan system   A method of incentive remuneration for production employees providing a bonus which is evaluated by applying a rate of pay to bonus hours which represent a percentage of the time taken to complete the job. The percentage is derived from the relationship between time saved and time allowed.

royalty   The sum paid for the right to exploit the property rights held by another. Thus, royalties may be payable for exploitation of mines, the use of patents or the publication of books. The royalty is generally based upon the extent of such exploitation, e.g. the quantitative use, or the income yielded from such use.

RPI   see **retail prices index**

RPM   see **resale price maintenance**

RRP   see **recommended retail price**

rubber check   (In the United States) a cheque which cannot be cashed because there is not enough money in the account to pay it.

rundown   1 To reduce a quantity of stocks gradually. 2 To slow down the business activity of a company before it is closed.

running costs   Those expenses associated with the operation or activity of a machine, equipment, or a department of a company.

running down clause   see **collision clause**

run on a bank   A heavy demand for withdrawal of money deposited with a bank. The run is the cause of, or is caused by, a financial panic and may result in the bank being unable to meet its liabilities in cash.

S

s.a.e. see **stamped addressed envelope**

safe deposit A safe in a bank, where private individuals can keep jewels, documents and other valuable possessions safely.

safety precautions Actions taken to try to make sure that there is no danger to the workforce in their current working practices or environment.

salary A fixed payment, usually expressed as a yearly sum but payable monthly or weekly, being the reward for services rendered by an employee or the holder of an office. Salaries are paid to white-collar workers rather than manual workers and are not directly related to output or hours worked.

salary curve A graph which shows salary plotted against age, the slope indicating the rate of salary increase at varying age levels.

salary eview An examination of employees' salaries in a company to decide on possible increases.

salary structuring The concept of ensuring that salaries are consistent within a company and competitive with salaries elsewhere in the same industry or in the same geographical location.

sale 1 A contract or business transaction whereby the seller transfers the property in goods or services, or agrees to such transfer, in exchange for a money consideration. 2 A term used in retailing to denote that goods are being offered for sale at specially reduced prices in order to clear stocks.

sale and leaseback A situation where a company sells a property to raise cash, and then leases it back from the purchaser. See also **leaseback**.

Sale of Goods Act An Act of Parliament passed in 1893 but consolidated in 1979 which relates to contracts for the sale of goods. The Act covers such points as how a contract of sale is made and how price is ascertained. The Act is particularly noteworthy for the implied conditions on which a sale is made, e.g. that the seller has a right to sell and that the goods supplied are of merchantable quality.

sale or return A form of trading where the transfer of property rights and exchange of monetary consideration follow only when acceptance of the goods is expressly signified by the recipient or implicitly signified by failure to return the goods within a specified or a reasonable time.

sales conference A meeting of all sales representatives and managers, at which past performance is reviewed and new products are presented.

sales coverage The extent in terms of market, consumer, geographical area, etc. to which goods or services are, or could be, available.

sales force The sales personnel employed by a company.

sales forecasting The estimating of future sales, by value or volume, using a variety of statistical predictive techniques or projective techniques.

sales inventory ratio The relationship between the value of sales for a given period and the average value of finished stocks held during that period.

sales ledger The records of sales in a company.

salesmanship The art of persuading customers to buy a product or service.

sales mix The actual or expected composition by product type of total sales value or total sales quantity. The term is sometimes used to describe the variety of different markets or customers.

sales pitch The words used by a salesman to persuade a customer to buy.

sales progress chart A graph showing the level of sales for each business period, and cumulatively, so that the sales trend may be observed.

sales representative A salesman working for a company, whose job is to explain and demonstrate the goods or services offered by the company and to persuade customers to buy.

sales revenue see **revenue** (def. 1)

sale warrant A document issued to the purchaser of imported goods when a deposit is paid to secure the goods. The document is exchanged for the documents of title when the balance of the purchase price is paid.

salvage 1 The reward paid for the voluntary service of saving a ship or its goods from danger or loss at sea. 2 The goods so saved. 3 The scrap value of a good.

sample 1 A small part of a material or one of a number of items intended to show the qualitative characteristics of the whole. If a sample is used to effect a sale, the buyer is entitled to rely upon the fact that such a sample is representative of the bulk. 2 A number of units chosen at random in order to determine and express characteristics of the whole population.

sampling error The degree of imprecision existing in the relationship between sample results and the characteristics of the whole population. It is usually expressed as the standard deviation of the sample distribution. Also called **standard error**.

sampling theory The calculation of the statistical error of estimates based upon samples; the determination of the validity of sample results, and their application to the population being studied.

sans recours (*French*, 'without recourse'.) A phrase added to a note or bill of exchange by the endorser, freeing himself from any liability.

saturation The situation where a market has taken as much of a product as it can, and further sales are likely to be small.

save as you earn A scheme introduced by the British government to attract savings by providing for the deduction of savings from earnings. The scheme has been extended to allow any regular contribution, up to a maximum limit, to the savings scheme.

saving That portion of income not spent on goods and services.

savings account An account where a depositor deposits a certain sum regularly, and which pays an interest, often at a higher rate than a deposit account.

savings and loan association (In the United States) a financial association which accepts and pays interest on the deposits of small investors and lends money to people who are buying property.

savings bank A bank controlled by the government or a non-profit organization whose purpose is to safeguard the deposits of small savers. Examples are the Post Office Savings Bank and local Trustee Savings Banks. See also **bank** (def. 1).

SAYE see **save as you earn**

scalar principle The theory that there must be a clearly defined line of formal authority running throughout an organization.

scam (US) A case of fraud.

scatter chart A graph obtained by plotting a series of points, each expressing a relationship between two variable sets of data. The resultant chart can assist in determining a relationship between the two sets of variables. Correlation may exist if the plotted points form a regular pattern, such as a straight line.

schedule 1 A detailed statement, commonly affixed to a legal or financial document. 2 Those categories in which income is classified for the purpose of assessing tax liability. For instance, Schedule E applies to earned income.

schedule slippage The occurrence of events (or the non-occurrence of expected events) during the implementation of a capital project which thereby modify the original evaluation of the project.

scheduling theory A branch of operational research which seeks to determine the most efficient order of processing a range of products through several combinations of machines or processes.

science park An area near a town set aside for technological industries.

scrap value The estimated or actual price at which an asset can be disposed of at the end of its useful life or at which defective goods can be disposed of.

scrip certificate A provisional document issued to subscribers of a company's share or debenture issue. The certificate details the number of shares allotted, the amount paid up, and the dates and amounts of further payments. The certificate is exchanged for the share certificate or debenture instrument when all instalments have been paid up. Frequently the letter of allotment, which notifies successful subscribers of an issue, acts as a scrip certificate.

scrip dividend A distribution to a company's shareholders in the form of shares or debentures of other companies held by the company.

scrip issue see **bonus issue**

scrip, piece of A certificate of a holding of shares or debentures, showing the number taken up by the subscriber, details of the amounts paid, and the amounts and due dates of instalments which remain to be paid. When all payments have been made, it is exchanged for a bond or certificate.

seal A distinctive mark produced by the impression of wax or embossing on a document. By law the seal must be marked on certain documents including conveyances. Sealed deeds are valid even in the absence of a consideration. Limited companies are required to have a seal in order to authenticate documents issued in their name.

seal book A record showing the occasions on which a company's seal has been used.

sealed tenders Tenders for a contract which have to be sent in sealed envelopes and which are all opened and evaluated together.

SEAQ see **Stock Exchange Automated Quotation**

search An inspection of a record or register which is legally maintained in order to protect the public and inform interested parties.

seasonal adjustments Changes made to official statistics, such as the rate of unemployment, to take account of seasonal variations.

seasonal variation The fluctuations in demand or output of a business or industry which occur within the cycle of one year.

second To lend a member of staff to another employer, such as a government department, for a fixed period of time.

secondary industry An industry which uses basic raw materials to produce manufactured goods.

secondary packaging see **packaging**

secondary picketing The picketing of a factory which is not directly involved in a strike in order to prevent it from supplying a striking factory or receiving supplies from it.

secondary production The production of manufactured goods. Compare **primary production**.

second mortgage A mortgage on property on which a first mortgage has been taken out. A certificate of second charge must be issued by the Land Registry in order to validate it.

seconds Items which have been rejected by a quality controller and are sold at a low price in a sale.

second via A copy of a bill of exchange or bill of lading which is forwarded by a different route from that taken by the original document as a precaution against loss or delay.

secretary 1 The chief administrative officer of a business, whose appointment is required by law for incorporated companies and who performs certain statutory duties in addition to normal administrative responsibilities. 2 An office-worker who types correspondence, maintains records, etc. for an individual or for a group of individuals.

secret reserve see **hidden reserve**

secured creditor A creditor whose claim is guaranteed by a pledge of assets by the debtor by way of mortgage, deed, bill of sale, stocks or shares, etc. In the event of bankruptcy or liquidation the creditor may obtain possession of the assets and dispose of them in satisfaction of his debt.

secured debt A debt which is guaranteed by assets.

secured loan A loan which is guaranteed by the borrower, who gives property or assets as security.

Securities and Investments Board An independent organization which supervises the self-regulatory organizations and draws up the rules under which financial services operate.

securities market A Stock Exchange, a place where stocks and shares and other securities can be bought or sold.

securities trader A person whose business is buying and selling securities.

security 1 Any document representing finance raised by companies or governments. Examples are ordinary shares, preference shares, debentures, treasury bills and consols. 2 Anything given or guaranteed by the borrower as a safeguard for a loan.

security of employment The right of a worker to remain in a job until he reaches retirement age.

security of tenure The right to keep a job or rented accommodation, provided always that certain conditions are met.

security printer A printing company which prints confidential or valuable documents, such as paper money, takeover bid documents, etc.

see-safe An agreement where a supplier will give credit for unsold goods at the end of a period.

self-employed person A person who works on his own account, either earning fees and commissions or receiving a salary from his own company.

self-financing ratio The relationship between the total cash required by a business for investment and daily operations, and the total cash generated through its operations.

self-liquidating advance 1 A loan made by a financial institution, especially a bank, to finance a project which will generate sufficient earnings to pay off the loan. 2 Any loan made to remedy a short-term funds shortage where there is a guaranteed future funds inflow sufficient to repay the advance.

self-liquidating asset An asset which creates sufficient earnings to repay its original cost.

self-liquidating offer An offer of goods at a price which covers only promotion costs, not the costs of production.

self-made man A person who is rich and successful because of his own efforts at work.

self mailer An advertisement or circular having a tear-off reply-paid section.

self-regulatory body An association, such as the Stock Exchange, which is regulated by its own members.

self-sufficient Producing enough food or raw materials to satisfy its own requirements.

sell at best An instruction to a broker to sell shares at the best price possible.

sell-by date The date stamped on a container, showing the date after which the product should not be sold. Compare **'best-before' date**.

seller's market A market where a seller can ask a high price for goods or services because there is a large demand and supply is limited.

seller's option to double see **put of more**

seller's over A situation occurring on the Stock Exchange, commodity markets, etc. where the number of sellers of a particular item exceeds that of potential buyers, with a depressing effect on prices. Compare **buyer's over**.

selling 1 The distribution of the products and/or services of a business to the consumer and the ensuring of customer satisfaction. 2 The creation and stimulation of demand as well as securing orders for goods or services.

selling agency A business which performs part or all of the marketing function of one or more products on behalf of a manufacturer.

selling costs The total expenses or part of such expenses incurred by a business in stimulating demand, securing orders and retaining custom.

selling out The process of selling securities which have already been contracted for by a person, where failure to complete the contract entitles the seller to sell the securities elsewhere and also to recover any expenses incurred thereby from the original intended purchaser. Compare **buying in**.

sell out The situation where all the stock of an item has been sold.

semi-fixed cost A cost which is partly fixed and partly variable with variations in output. Thus, supervisory costs may be fixed until such increase in output has been achieved to necessitate one extra supervisor.

semi-logarithmic chart A graphical representation of data in which one scale is shown logarithmically so that equal distances represent equal proportional movements. The resulting graph indicates the rate of change of the variable rather than absolute changes in value. Also called **ratio scale graph**.

senior partner A person with a large number of shares in a partnership.

separation (In the United States) leaving a job, either by resignation, retirement or by being fired.

sequestration 1 The action by a third party of assuming title to disputed property, pending settlement of the dispute. 2 The act of assuming title to the estate of a bankrupt with a view to its disposal among creditors.

service charge An extra charge for services rendered, such as a charge for cleaning offices or the public areas of a block of flats.

service contract A contract by which a company keeps a piece of equipment in good working order.

service department Department in a company which keeps machinery belonging to customers in good working order.

service industry A section of the economy which produces a service rather than a manufactured end-product. Insurance, banking and tourism are all service industries.

service life The estimated useful life of an asset to a business, which may be less than its physical life.

set aside The use of farming land for other purposes (such as recreation).

setting up costs or setup costs The cost of getting a factory ready to make a new product after finishing work on a previous one.

settlement 1 The payment of a claim or account. 2 The regular clearing of accounts on the Stock Exchange. See also **Stock Exchange settlement**. 3 Agreement reached after a dispute.

settling day The final day of the Stock Exchange settlement period on which stocks and shares are delivered and paid for. Also called **pay day**.

set-up time The time required to prepare a machine for operation.

seven-point plan An early and widely used list of characteristics developed by the National Institute of Industrial Psychology and used in employee selection. The aspects, which in practice are often associated with a points system, are physique, attainments, general intelligence, special aptitudes, interests, disposition and circumstances.

seven sisters The world's seven largest oil companies. These are: British Petroleum, Exxon (also called Esso), Gulf, Mobil, Shell, SoCal (also called Chevron) and Texaco.

severance pay Money paid as compensation to a person who is being asked to leave his job.

share   A unit of ownership of a company conferring a right to participate in the profits earned by the company, a right to its assets after all other claims have been met, and a right to vote at company meetings (depending on the type of share). A share in a public company is freely transferable. See also **ordinary share; preference share**.

share at par   A share whose Stock Exchange quotation is the same as its face value.

share capital   The total value of shares issued or authorized to be issued by a company.

share certificate   A document issued by a company indicating the number and type of share units held and the amount paid up on the units. The certificate is not a document of title, although it acts as prima facie evidence of ownership, this being legally evidenced by entry in the company's share register.

shareholders' equity   The share capital, reserves and retained profits of a business which belong to the owners of the shares of the company.

share index   An index of the market price movements of selected company shares, taken as representing the market movement either for a selected sector grouping or for the whole market. There are many share indices: perhaps the most important British share index is the Financial Times Ordinary Index, whereas the most important American index is the Dow Jones Average.

share option   see **option**

share premium   The excess of market price of an issued share over its nominal value. When a company issues shares at a premium the excess value is recorded in a share premium account whose use is prescribed by law: thus an issue of fully paid bonus shares may be made from a share premium account.

share register   A record maintained by a limited company listing in respect of each member of the company name, address, number and nominal value of shares held, amounts paid up, and the dates of commencing and ceasing membership. Entry in the register is formal legal evidence of share ownership. The register must be available for public inspection.

share transfer   A transaction for the exchange of ownership in shares. A share transfer form is completed by the seller and sent with the share certificate to the company's registered office. The buyer's name is then entered in the share register. The company either retains or destroys the original share certificate and issues a new certificate to the buyer. The buyer bears the costs of registration, duty on the shares and brokerage commission.

share warrant   A form of share certificate which details the number and nominal value of a shareholding without specifying the name of the holder, being made out to bearer. The warrant and therefore ownership in the shares is transferable by delivery without special transfer procedures.

A share warrant is issued only when shares are fully paid, and upon issue of the warrant the member's name is deleted from the share register.

shelf life 1 The length of time a product remains in stock before sale. 2 The length of time during which a product retains its required qualities before deteriorating.

shell company A company which does not trade, but exists as a name only, to acquire shares in other companies or to be used as the vehicle for a takeover bid.

shift 1 The hours worked by a group of employees. A continuous 24-hour production period may comprise three such periods (each of 8 hours), typically 10 a.m.–6 p.m., 6 p.m.–2 a.m. and 2 a.m.–10 a.m. 2 The employees who work during such a period.

shift premium An additional element in an employee's gross earnings as a reward for participating in shift-working arrangements.

shipbroker An agent appointed by a shipowner to perform various functions relating to the operation of a ship, such as obtaining cargo and passengers, arranging insurance and freight charges, issuing bills of lading, etc.

ship laden in bulk A ship carrying a loose cargo, such as corn or gravel, not packed in containers.

shipping certificate of registry A document issued by the registrar of shipping which details a ship's name and tonnage and the names of the owner, master and country of origin.

shipping conference An association of shipowners whose vessels operate a particular route, which determines a rate structure for the carriage of passengers and cargo and establishes common policies among members.

ship's articles The terms and conditions of employment signed by merchant seaman.

ship's manifest A document giving details of a ship's cargo and listing ports to be called at during a voyage.

ship's papers Documents which must be carried on board ship – certificate of registry, manifest, charter agreement, bill of health, log-book, ship's articles and bills of lading.

ship's register see **certificate of registry**

shop floor The place of work in a factory or office, together with the employees who work there.

shoplifting The crime of stealing goods from shops.

shop-soiled Goods which are dirty as a result of having been on display in a shop.

shop steward An elected trade union representative who negotiates with management on behalf of the workers in his department.

shopping centre A large complex of shops and car parks, built outside a town for the purposes of one-stop shopping.

short 1 An unexplained cash deficit. 2 A delivered quantity which is less than that shown in a delivery note, invoice, etc. Also called **short order**. 3 Not possessing shares, etc. which one has sold as part of a bear transaction and whose delivery to the purchaser is imminent. Also called **short of stock** (US).

short bill A bill of exchange which is payable on demand, at sight (i.e., upon presentation) or within a short period – commonly ten days.

short credit Credit terms which allow the customer only a short time to pay.

short-dated bills Bills which are payable within a few days.

short-dated securities Government stocks which will mature in less than five years' time.

shortfall An amount which is missing and which should make up an expected total.

short-handed see **short-staffed**

short list 1 A list of some of the better candidates for a job who are asked to come to interview or to take a test. 2 To put a candidate's name on a list of people to be invited to take a test or to attend for an interview.

short order see **short** (def. 2)

short-period asset An asset which changes its form, e.g. into cash, within a time-span of a year. See also **circulating assets**.

short-range forecast A forecast which covers a period of months.

shorts British government and local authority stocks with less than five years to repayment. Compare **longs**.

short-staffed With too few employees to be able to provide a proper service.

short selling Arranging to sell in the future something which it is believed can be obtained for less than the agreed price.

short time A working period which is less than normal either in terms of hours per day or shift or days per week. Short time may be occasioned by a reduced demand for a product which causes a cutback in the rate of production.

showcard Point-of-sale display material advertising goods. It is generally placed on a counter.

show of hands A vote where people raise their hands to show their voting intentions.

shrinkage The loss of stock by pilfering, especially by members of staff.

shrink-wrapping The wrapping of goods in transparent plastic film which is heated under vacuum.

shunter A member of a provincial stock exchange who ties in local transactions with those made on the London Stock Exchange.

SIB see **Securities and Investments Board**

sick leave A period when a worker is away from work because of illness.

sickness benefit A payment made by the government or by a private insurance company to someone who cannot work because of illness.

sight bill A bill of exchange payable upon presentation without days of grace being allowed.

signatory A person who signs a contract or agreement.

silent partner see **sleeping partner**

simo chart (simultaneous motion cycle chart) A detailed representation of the method of work performed by the hands or other parts of the body. The chart shows the work performed against a time scale, and is thus a Therblig chart plotted against time. The basic data are frequently obtained by micromotion study.

simple interest Interest which is calculated on the original capital sum. For example, 100% simple interest on a capital sum of £100 means that interest of £10 will be due each year. Compare **compound interest**.

simulation The mathematical expression of business problems, and their solution by the application of mathematical methods.

single-entry bookkeeping A method of keeping books, where each deal is entered once. Compare **double entry**.

single premium policy An insurance policy where only one premium is paid, as opposed to one with regular annual premiums.

sinking fund A sum of money set aside by a firm for the purpose of paying off a specific debt which will arise in the future.

sister company One of several companies which are part of the same group.

sister-ship clause A clause in a marine insurance policy whereby the owner of two vessels is covered against losses arising from the collision of the two vessels. Without the clause no claim could succeed against the insurer since a person cannot sue himself for damages.

situations vacant A section in the classified advertisements section of a newspaper where companies with jobs vacant advertise.

skeleton staff A small number of staff left to carry on essential work while most of the workforce is away.

skewness The lack of symmetry sometimes apparent in the graphical representation of a frequency distribution.

skilled labour Employees who have special training and skills, and are employed in particularly specialized jobs.

slander An untrue spoken statement which damages a person's character.

sleeper A share which has not changed in value for some months, but which suddenly increases in price.

sleeping partner A member of a partnership who introduces finance but who does not participate in the management of the business. Unless otherwise stated he is fully liable with other partners for the debts of the business. Also called **dormant partner; limited partner; silent partner**. Compare **active partner**.

slip A piece of paper attached to an insurance policy on which underwriters indicate the share of the total insurance risk which they are prepared to accept.

slow payer A company which is known to delay payment of invoices beyond the normal credit terms.

slump A situation of depressed economic activity characterized by falling production or static production at a low level, little investment and high unemployment.

slush fund Money which is kept aside secretly to use as bribes.

small businesses Small companies with low turnover and few employees.

small investor A private individual who buys small numbers of shares.

small order surcharge An extra charge imposed by a supplier on orders of less than a certain amount, the object being to encourage customers to place large orders.

snake An agreement between certain European countries (mainly in the EEC) to keep the exchange rates of their currencies within certain fixed limits. It began in 1972, but by 1974, Britain, Ireland, France and Italy had withdrawn. In 1978 the snake was revived as the European Monetary System. See also **European Currency Unit**.

social accounting **1** The system of recording economic data for various sectors in the economy; the personal sector – data on incomes and consumption; the productive sector – production in private and public industries; government sector – central and local government expenditure; the international sector – data on the balance of payments. The data provide a framework of national economic statistics which is used both as a basis for future economic policy and as a means of assessing the effectiveness of past or present policies. **2** The relating of the activities of a business to its general environment, such as its impact upon employment, the local economy, physical conditions of the environment, etc.

social costs The ways in which an action will affect people, such as the influence of the redevelopment of part of a town on those living nearby.

social insurance The collective insurance of the community organized by the state through a system of compulsory contributions during the working lives of members of the community. Benefits provided include provision for old age and for periods of sickness, unemployment, etc.

social security Payments made by the government to people who need it, the payments being funded by social insurance.

socio-economic groupings The categories into which the population may be classified according to the criteria of occupation or income.

soft currency A currency which has an unstable value in international exchange, with a tendency to decline in value in the long run. This results from internal economic weakness and an externally adverse balance of payments. Compare **hard currency**.

soft loan A loan from a company to an employee or from one government to another with little or no interest being charged.

soft sell An approach used in advertising which seeks to promote a product through a subdued persuasive appeal to consumers. Compare **hard sell**.

software In computing, the programs and documentation as opposed to the machinery ('hardware') itself. Compare **hardware**.

sola A bill of exchange which has no copies in circulation.

sold note see **bought notes and sold notes**

sole agent A person or company who is the only representative of another company in an area.

sole trader An individual who operates a business independently, providing the capital and being personally liable for the debts which the business incurs.

solus advertisement An advertisement which does not appear near other advertisements for similar competing products.

solvency 1 The position of being able to meet one's debts as they fall due for payment. 2 The long-term financial viability of a business indicated by its ability to earn an adequate return on investors' capital and to repay long- and short-term liabilities as they become due.

span of control The number of subordinates who can be successfully controlled by one person. The number depends to some extent upon the level within the organization. Thus, the maximum number successfully controlled by a foreman might be 10 and by a managing director, 5.

special agent An agent who has authority to act outside his normal sphere of business, the scope of his authority to so act being limited by actual instructions.

special buyer An agent (a member of a discount house) of the Bank of England who operates in the money market buying and selling bills in order to secure the market's adherence to Bank monetary policy.

special crossing A mark added to a general crossing on a cheque which gives details of a banker's name or of a specific account. The additional mark indicates that the cheque must be paid into an account at the bank stated or must be paid into the account specified. See also **general crossing**.

special deposit Money belonging to a commercial bank which is placed with the Bank of England by government directive. Money thus deposited reduces the bank's credit-making base and can be used as an instrument of government policy.

special drawing rights Reserve assets held by the International Monetary Fund for the settlement of international debts incurred by its member-countries.

special endorsement An endorsement on a bill of exchange, naming the person to whom the bill has been transferred. The endorsement ensures that the bill can be paid only to the person named or can be negotiated further only by his endorsement.

specialist responsibility see **functional responsibility**

speciality contract A contract in the form of a deed – signed, sealed and delivered to the contracting parties.

speciality debt A debt which remains legally enforceable for a period of 12 years, e.g. a dividend or a call on shares.

specialization The reduction of a product range in order that productive resources may be used more economically.

special manager One with specialized knowledge applicable to a business which is in liquidation, and whose services are used by the Official Receiver in order to manage the business. A creditor may also request the Official Receiver to appoint a special manager to act in a bankruptcy.

special resolution A motion put before a shareholder's meeting requiring approval by 75% of the members for its acceptance: 21 days' notice of the resolution must be given to members. This form of resolution is required for certain matters, including alteration to the articles or objects of a company, changing the company's name and reducing its capital.

specie Coins.

specification A detailed statement of the constituent elements of a particular subject matter including: goods for sale; an estimate for a job; a description of a form of employment; a design for a product – with the material, labour and machine requirements; and the customs form used for the outward entry of duty free goods.

specific duty A tax or levy of a fixed amount. Compare **ad valorem**.

specific performance A legal remedy relating to a disputed contract whereby the court may order the offending party to complete the terms of a contract where such completion is reasonable and preferable to an award of damages.

specimen chart A collection of forms assembled in the sequence in which they are used to show the flow of paper required to achieve a particular objective.

speculation Dealing in stocks, shares, commodities or currencies, etc. with a view to earning profits through market price movements such as bull and bear transactions.

speculative share A share which is not a blue chip, and which may be bought as a gamble.

spending power The amount of money which an individual or group has available for the purchase of goods.

spending variance The difference between budgeted expenditure for a period and the actual expenditure, related to items of expense which are not directly variable with the level of production.

spin-off 1 (US) The transfer of a portion of the assets of a company to a newly formed company in exchange for its share capital which is distributed to the shareholders of the original company. 2 (US) The distribution by a parent company to its shareholders of the shares of an existing subsidiary. 3 A discovery or innovation made as a by-product of a research or development project.

spiralling inflation Inflation caused by an **inflationary spiral**.

split inventory method see **ABC method**

split-off point That stage in a single production process when separate end products become identifiable and costs can begin to be specifically assigned.

split platen A printing roller in two or more sections which permits forms to be used side by side for recording or posting of information while allowing independent vertical spacing.

split register The facility which enables two or more entries to be entered on a keyboard machine simultaneously, generally permitting the separate accumulation of several totals.

sponsor A company paying for an artistic or sporting activity, as a means of promotion, usually retaining the right to advertise the company's products at the event.

spot carbon Carbon placed selectively on a document so that only the specifically required parts are reproduced on the lower sheet of paper.

spot price The price for immediate delivery of a commodity paid for in cash.

spot transaction A deal made on the foreign exchange, commodity or stock markets which is for immediate cash payment and delivery.

spread 1 (US) A combined put and call option, giving the purchaser the right to sell or buy given quantities at specific prices within the option period. The put and call prices differ in a spread situation. Compare **straddle**. 2 The difference between the buying and selling prices of a currency, stock, commodity, etc., at a specific moment in time.

spreadsheet A computer printout showing a series of columns of figures.

squeeze A restriction on credit facilities and consumption by raising interest rates, imposing stiff purchase controls, etc. The object of a squeeze is to reduce inflationary pressures and to improve the balance of payments position by discouraging imports.

squeezed bear   see **bear squeeze**

staff   1 The group of people carrying out the work of an undertaking; a group of persons employed by an organization. 2 Personnel engaged in administrative or clerical duties. 3 An assistant to an executive, authorized to act on behalf of the executive. 4 An organizational relationship denoting that a specialist function is performed, sometimes in an advisory capacity.

staffing levels   The numbers of employees needed in various departments of a company in order for the company to operate efficiently.

staff inspection   The examination of work loads of a department or a business as a whole in order to determine the number and grade of employees required. Also called **staff survey**.

stag   A speculator who subscribes to an issue of new shares, anticipating a higher market price than the issue price.

stagflation   A phenomenon in which an economy shows signs of stagnation (high unemployment, slow or negative growth, etc.) but also has a high inflation rate.

stake   The money invested by one individual in a company.

stale bull   A person who has made a speculative purchase on the stock exchange in anticipation of a quick price rise, which, however, fails to materialize.

stale cheque   A cheque which has been in circulation for an excessive length of time, generally six months or more, which a bank may refuse to honour when presented.

stamp duty   A tax levied on the transfer of certain types of assets, e.g. land conveyances and on the issue of certain documents, such as company articles of association, insurance policies, etc., because of the requirement that these documents should be officially certified in order to render them legally valid. The tax may be a fixed charge or ad valorem.

stamped addressed envelope   An envelope with the return address and stamp on it, used when writing for information.

standard allowance   The accepted amount by which a normal time for an operation is increased within a particular industry or plant in order to compensate for fatigue, personal needs, etc.

standard cost   A predetermined estimate of what present or future costs should be under expected conditions of operation for an item of material, labour or overhead, or for part or the whole of a product.

standard costing   An accounting system using standard costs as the basis for recording transactions and reporting on performance, comparing standard with actual results and seeking explanations for the differences.

standard deviation The square root of the average of the squared deviations of each value from the average of the values. It provides the most useful statistical measure of the variability of a population.

standard error see **sampling error**

standard, expected A standard cost which can be attained during a specified period, based upon achievable efficient production.

standard hour A hypothetical hour which represents the amount of work which should be performed in one hour under standard conditions. Since it is a measure of work rather than time, it is a means by which amounts of different work or differing activities may be expressed by a common denominator. The standard hour may in some cases represent work performed in less than an hour, particularly where an incentive payments system exists.

standard, ideal A standard cost which can be attained under the most favourable conditions. It makes no allowance for defective materials, machine breakdowns, etc. and hence is unrealistically low.

standard industrial classification A method of grouping industrial production into 27 major sub-divisions broken down into 181 minimum list headings.

standardization The determining and setting of fixed dimensions, qualities, performances and nomenclature in order to facilitate the interchangeability of parts, reduce variability and size of stocks, and reduce production costs.

standard of living The material, physical and cultural well-being of an individual, group or community. Monetary incomes are an important indicator of well-being although comparisons over a period of time must reflect price changes and movements in purchasing power. An overall measurement of standards must also include the cultural, natural and social environment.

standard performance The rate of activity used in the setting of a standard time.

standard rate of tax The basic rate of tax which is paid on the lowest section of taxable income, after allowances have been deducted.

standard time That time required by a normal worker operating under normal conditions to complete a piece of work of satisfactory quality.

standard volume The anticipated volume of production on which is based the rate of overhead recovery in the calculation of a standard cost.

standby credit Credit facility which is available if a company needs it at short notice.

standing order 1 An authorization by an individual or business to a bank to pay to the credit of another's account specific sums at specified intervals. 2 An authorization for the regular performance of certain operations such as machine maintenance, or stock replenishment to ensure uninterrupted production.

staple The principal commodity grown or manufactured in a locality or country.

startup The launching of a new company or new product.

state bank (US) A commercial bank established under US state rather than federal law.

statement in lieu A statement issued by a public company accompanying an invitation to the public to subscribe for an issue of stock/shares, etc. in circumstances where no prospectus is to be issued. The format and contents of the statement are prescribed by law, and must include such items as details of the company's nominal share capital, directors' interests in the company, etc.

statement of account A record of the financial transactions conducted between a business and an individual debtor or firm detailing the invoice numbers of goods sold, money received and outstanding balance. The statement is issued at regular intervals.

statement of affairs 1 A record of the financial situation of a person or business at a particular point in time. 2 A record of the financial situation of an insolvent debtor or company, listing, among other things, the assets and liabilities, and the names of creditors.

state-of-the-art A system or technology which is technically as advanced as possible.

statistical discrepancy The amount by which two sets of figures differ.

statistical method That part of the discipline of statistics relating to the techniques associated with the analysis of data using reasoning processes based on the mathematical theory of probability.

statistical stock control The application of statistical analysis and techniques to the setting of stock-holding and stock-ordering levels and quantities with a view to minimizing the costs of stock holding consistent with meeting production requirements.

statistics 1 The processes and techniques associated with the recording, tabulation, analysis and interpretation of numerical data so as to present significant features. 2 The analysis and interpretation of data using reasoning and inference processes based on the mathematical theory of probability and the relationship between samples and populations.

status 1 The standing of a person before the law, as infant, married woman, etc. 2 The business standing of a person or company, which may be indicative of creditworthiness, etc.

status inquiry An investigation into the creditworthiness of an individual or business. The inquiry, which may be undertaken by a firm or on its behalf by a specialist organization or trade protection association, is a preliminary to extending credit to a new customer.

status quo The state of things as they are at present.

status symbol An object, such as an expensive car, which is bought as an expression of the owner's importance.

statute law Legislation which derives from an Act of Parliament. It is binding in all courts of law and overrides all existing legislation.

statute of limitations A law which allows only a certain amount of time for someone to sue for damages or claim property.

statutory books Books of account which an incorporated business is legally obliged to maintain, including financial records of money received and spent, sales and purchases, and assets and liabilities, as well as the share register, the register of directors, the register of charges and the minute book.

statutory company A company incorporated by Act of Parliament.

statutory holiday A holiday which is fixed by law.

statutory income The income which is estimated to have been received during the financial year of assessment and on which taxation is levied.

statutory meeting A meeting of the members of a public company which must be held not less than one month or more than three months from the date on which a company commences business. At the meeting the members may discuss the statutory report, etc. Failure to hold the statutory meeting provides grounds for the winding-up of the company.

statutory report A statement which a public company must send to members 14 days before holding the statutory meeting. Details include: the number of shares allotted and amount of cash received since the formation of the company; receipts and payments recorded by the company; certain information about directors and auditors; certain details of any contracts which are to be modified at the statutory meeting. See **statutory meeting**.

statutory returns Returns which are required by law to be sent to the Registrar of Companies after each annual general meeting. These returns contain information regarding the share capital, debentures and charges, and details of directors and secretary.

steering committee A group of people entrusted with the task of guiding and directing a particular business activity or enterprise. The group is generally constituted when a major change, such as computerization or centralization, is planned.

sterling A term used to denote the chief English currency denomination, the pound.

sterling area The area of the world where the pound sterling is the main trading currency.

stewardship The management of business affairs on behalf of its owners, with responsibility for the efficient disposition of the business's funds.

stock 1 A unit of ownership in a company usually issued in larger units than shares. Stock units must be fully paid and may be divided into smaller units. Stock does not have an identifying number as do shares.

2 A government security such as consols. **3** Materials, work in process and unsold finished goods on hand in a business.

stockbroker An agent who buys and sells securities on the Stock Exchange for outside clients.

stock control The process of regulating investment in stocks within predetermined limits established in accordance with the policies laid down by management.

stock exchange A market where stocks, shares, etc. are dealt in by members who are authorized by the exchange authorities either as jobbers (dealers) or brokers (agents between the jobbers and the public). Permission to have a company's shares dealt in on the exchange must be sought from the authorities.

Stock Exchange Automated Quotation A system by which prices of shares offered by marketmakers are displayed on a computer screen.

Stock Exchange introduction A means of enabling a company whose shares are already widely held to obtain a quotation on the Stock Exchange. The jobbers on the Exchange obtain options to acquire shares in the company and can thus create a market and quotation for those shares.

Stock Exchange listing The putting of a share and its price on the official list of shares which can be bought and sold on the London Stock Exchange.

Stock Exchange settlement The clearing of accounts in respect of transactions made during a stock exchange account, of which there are 24 each year; 20 periods, each of two weeks' trading, and four periods of three weeks' trading.

The settlement period occupies seven days commencing Mondays:

DAY 1: Contango Day – when contango or backwardation arrangements are made.

DAY 2: Making-Up Day – when the prices at which contango transactions recorded in the accounts are determined.

DAY 3: Ticket Day (or Name Day) – when details of the purchasers (names, price) are passed by their brokers to the jobbers and then to the seller of the shares. This naming of the purchaser permits preparation of the transfer documents.

DAYS 4, 5 and 6: Intermediate Days – when share transfer documents are prepared.

DAY 7: Settling Day – when documents are delivered and paid for.

stockist A retailer who guarantees to stock certain items.

stockjobber Formerly, a dealer who bought and sold securities on the Stock Exchange, dealing only with stockbrokers or other stockjobbers.

stockpile To buy items, such as rare commodites, and keep them in case of future need.

stock record card A materials control document containing a descrip-

stocktaking

tion of the item, quantities received and issued, and balance in stock. Each item in stock will be represented by a card and this card is updated from the goods receipt note, and the materials requisition. The card may also show details of the job against which each issue has been made.

stocktaking The periodic checking, counting, recording and evaluation of physical stocks in hand. It generally covers finished goods, work-in-progress, and raw materials, but sometimes also includes plant, fixtures and fittings, etc.

stock turnover; stock turn The number of times a company sells its stock of products during a given period (usually 12 months), or the rate at which stocks of raw materials, work in progress or finished goods are converted into sold products. This is often expressed as the cost of goods sold divided by the average stock level.

stop An instruction written to a banker from whom a document is payable not to pay on the document. Such an instruction is given where the document (a cheque, bill of exchange, etc.) has been lost or stolen.

stop-go A pattern of economic activity in which growth is not continuous: periods of growth are punctuated by periods of stagnation.

stop order An instruction to a stockbroker to sell shares at the best possible price immediately the share price has fallen below a certain specified level.

stoppage Money which is taken from an employee's wage packet, to pay for insurance, damage, tax, etc.

stoppage in transitu The legal right of an unpaid seller to stop and recover goods on their way to an insolvent buyer. The right expires when the goods reach their destination or are received on behalf of the purchaser.

storekeeping That part of materials control concerned with the physical reception, storage and issue of goods. The function includes orderly systematic and safe storage, the release of goods against proper authorization and the taking of a physical inventory in accordance with practice laid down. The maintenance of stock records and notification of reordering requirements are sometimes included in the duties of storekeeping.

straddle (US) A combined put and call option in which the price of both put and call is the same. Compare **spread**.

straight line depreciation A method of depreciating an asset by charging equal amounts to each accounting period for which the asset is expected to contribute value. The amount so charged is calculated by dividing the net asset cost, after deducting expected scrap or disposal value, by the anticipated life of the asset.

strategic gap The difference between the future achievement desired for a business and the probable achievement, based on planned operations before the application of strategic planning concepts.

strategic planning A process within corporate planning concerned with the formulation of the long-term policy and objectives of a division and the plans required to secure these objectives.

stream days The number of operational days of a plant, process, etc. during a given period.

strike A collective withdrawal of labour from employment.

striking price The price at which shares offered for tender are sold.

structural unemployment Unemployment caused by a long-term decline in an industry rather than the state of the economy in general.

sub-agent A person engaged by an agent to conduct all or part of the business entrusted to the agent by a principal. The agent becomes the principal vis à vis the sub-agent whose role is valid only when it is necessary for proper performance of the agent's functions, or where custom permits.

subcontract (Of a contractor) to place part of contracted work with another company, which becomes the **subcontractor**.

subject to contract A phrase used in preliminary discussions or provisional agreements relating to the sale of land in order to indicate that no liability arises on either side until the formal contract has been duly completed. Any money deposited is refundable if negotiations break down.

sub judice 'Under the judge', a situation where a case is being considered by a court and must not be referred to in the media.

subrogation The assumption of an insured party's rights by his insurers, upon the settlement of the insured's loss, with a view to recovery against a third party.

sublet To let a leased property to another tenant. The contract is a sublease, and the two parties involved are the sublessee and sublessor.

subscribed capital The amount of share capital in a public company for which shares have been allotted and part payment, at least, received.

subscriber A person who is instrumental in the formation of a company and whose name is entered in a company's memorandum. A subscriber signs and pays for shares issued, signs the articles, appoints the first directors and acts in their place until appointed. A public company requires seven subscribers, each having at least one share.

subscription An agreement made between a company and an individual for the purchase of stock/shares, etc. being issued by the company.

subsidiary A company which is controlled by another company through at least a majority shareholding.

subsidy A grant made by a government agency to compensate producers for setting market prices below the level which a free market would determine.

subsistence allowance An amount allowed by a company to an employee to cover the cost of hotels and meals while travelling on the company's business.

substitutes Goods which can be substituted for each other. If the price of one, e.g. gas, increases, the consumption of its substitute (electricity) is likely to increase.

subvention see **subsidy**

substitution effect The effect of a price change on the consumption of goods, on the assumption that real income is unchanged.

suggestion schemes Procedures whereby employees or other interested parties are encouraged to suggest improved methods of working which result in cost savings to the business. Awards are made to those whose suggestions are adopted, sometimes in proportion to the benefits achieved by the business.

sundry items, sundries Small items in ledgers which do not fit under the main headings and are listed as a group on their own.

sunk cost Any cost which has already been incurred and is unalterable, and therefore has no relevance to a current decision concerning an alternative course of action.

superannuation A pension which is created by a scheme of contributions by employees and employers, operated either by the state or by the company.

supercargo A person who is engaged to look after cargo on a ship's voyage and possibly to obtain a return cargo for the homeward voyage.

supermarket A large self-service food store, smaller than a hypermarket.

super profits Profits which accrue in excess of those normally expected in a particular business enterprise.

superstore A very large self-service retail store, similar to a hypermarket.

supervisor One who oversees and directs the work of a group of employees.

supplemental list A list prepared by the Stock Exchange authorities of those bargains in stocks of companies which have not received a quotation on the oficial list. See also **official list**.

supplementary estimate A formal application made by the government to Parliament for funds in excess of those approved for the current financial year.

supply The quantity of a product which is available in the market at any given price.

supply and demand The amount of a product which is available and the amount which is needed by customers. See **law of supply and demand**.

supply curve A graphical presentation of the quantities available of a product at a given price. A normal feature is the upward slope to the right, indicating that as price rises so supply tends to increase.

supply side economics The economic theory that governments should encourage the supply of products by cutting taxes on individuals and companies to boost investment, rather than encourage demand by making more money available in the economy.

supra protest see **acceptance supra protest**

surcharge 1 A temporary additional charge imposed, for example, on imports or on ships using a particular port. 2 The financial responsibilities which a district auditor imposes on local council members or officials personally in cases where they have approved expenditure in excess of their powers.

surety A guarantor, or the document establishing the guarantee, that a debt incurred by another person will be paid or an action undertaken by another person will be performed.

surplus An excess of income over expenditure, of exports over imports, etc.

surrender value The amount for which a life assurance policy may be cashed before its maturity, the value depending on the unexpired duration of the policy, value of premiums, etc.

surtax A personal tax on income above a certain level, levied in addition to income tax, and applied at graduated rates as determined by various Finance Acts. Surtax no longer applies in the United Kingdom.

suspected bill see **touched bill of health**

suspense account An account in the books of a business to which items are posted temporarily until the availability of further detail enables the items to be posted to their proper accounts.

swap agreements Arrangements between central banks of various countries for the reciprocal borrowing of one another's currencies. Such arrangements are designed to ease the pressure on an individual country's currency.

sweated labour A workforce of poorly paid people who work long hours.

switching Changing the nature and composition of a group of investments in order to profit from different market movements in various forms of securities.

switch selling The display, by advertising, of the cheaper range of a business's products with a view to attracting consumer interest. This interest is then diverted to the more expensive products by various selling techniques.

synergy Greater effectiveness which comes from joining two companies together, where the result is stronger than was the case when the two companies were separate.

systems analysis An examination, using a computer, of the way in which a company functions, with the aim of suggesting improvements which will lead to greater efficiency.

T

Table A An appendix to the Company Act, 1948, providing a model set of Articles of Association which may be adopted by a company as a whole or with modifications. The Table A articles are taken to be the articles of a company where no others are registered or where registered articles do not exclude or modify the Table.

T account The format of an account in financial books, whose debit and credit entries are posted on opposite sides of the account. The vertical of the 'T' represents the line separating debits from credits, while the name of the account is written on the horizontal line.

tachograph A device in a vehicle such as a lorry, which records details of journeys made.

take-home pay The net wages or salary remaining after all deductions have been made.

take in To receive backwardation.

takeover The acquisition of a company by another company or person through purchase of sufficient shares to gain control.

takeover bid An offer to shareholders of a company to purchase their shares in order to obtain control of the company through the acquisition of at least a majority of shares. Bids are required to be conducted in accordance with procedures established by the City Code on Take-overs.

Takeover Panel The panel which enforces the provisions of the City Code on Takeovers and Mergers.

takers-in Those who take up stock that a bull has not, at that particular time, paid for.

take up a bill see **retire** (def. 1)

tale quale An implied condition in contracts for the sale and delivery of grain and other commodities that the goods supplied are of the same quality as the sample previously submitted, upon which the contract was made. The buyer bears the risks of damage which may be incurred during the delivery of the commodity.

tally An account, such as a statement of a debit or a credit, or a list of figures.

tallyman 1 One who sells goods on credit and collects the purchase price in instalments. 2 One who checks a ship's cargo against a list as it is loaded or unloaded.

talon The final portion on a coupon sheet, entitling the holder to claim interest on securities when due, which may be exchanged for a further sheet on presentation to the company when the coupons have been exhausted. See also **coupon** (def. 1).

tangible assets Assets which have material existence, such as stocks, plant, etc.

tangible net worth A business's physical resources less its current liabilities.

tape prices The market prices quoted on the Stock Exchange or commodity markets which are transmitted via tape machines to business offices.

tape reader A device for deciphering punched paper or magnetic tape and converting the data into another form, e.g. printed text.

tap issue The sale of securities by the Treasury direct to government departments without their being offered on the open market.

tap stock An issue of government securities.

tare An allowance for the weight of the packing materials in which goods are carried. The allowance may be actually computed or estimated, or may be one established by custom of the trade.

tare weight The weight of the container or package in which goods are placed. See also **gross weight; net weight.**

target audience The people at whom an advertisement is aimed.

target market The market in which a company is planning to sell its goods and services.

tariff 1 A list or scale of charges at which goods or services are supplied. 2 A list issued by the customs authorities of: imported goods liable to duty, indicating the duty payable; of articles exempt from duty; of articles on which duty drawback or bounty payments are allowed. 3 The customs duty itself.

tariff barrier see **customs barrier**

tariff office An office of a company, especially an insurance company, belonging to an organization which sets standard rates of charge.

tariff, two-part 1 A charge composed of two rates, one a basic charge and the other a charge per unit of consumption. 2 A charge composed of two rates, one rate applying up to a certain level of usage and the other, a higher or lower rate, applying above this level.

tax A payment, generally of money, levied by central or local governments or their agencies upon income, capital, expenditure, etc.

taxable income That portion of total income remaining after deduction of reliefs and allowances and upon which income tax is payable by application of the appropriate rates of tax.

taxation, Adam Smith's canons of The principles for a system of taxation enunciated by the 18th-century economist Adam Smith: tax should be proportional to income; the amount of tax should be certain and calculable; the payment and collection of taxes should be convenient to the payers; and the tax system should be administratively economic.

taxation, faculty theory of A concept that individuals should bear their share of the tax burden in accordance with their means. The concept initially gave rise to a proportional taxation system, but later became associated with systems of progressive taxation. See also **progressive taxation; proportional taxation.**

tax avoidance The legitimate search for and adoption of devices for the purpose of minimizing tax liability, for example through maximizing allowances by taking out additional life assurance policies.

tax concession Allowing less tax to be paid.

tax-deductible (Of an expense) which can be deducted from the calculation of taxable income.

tax equalization account An accounting record which is used by a business to adjust the estimated liability to tax which it has provided for to the level of the actual tax liability assessed by the taxation authorities.

tax evasion The illegal, wilful act of escaping a liability to tax.

tax exemption The freedom from the obligation to pay tax.

tax-free income That portion of total income which is not liable to income tax.

tax-gathering season Those months when a number of important taxes are paid. In Britain these are December, January and February when corporation tax is paid.

tax haven Any foreign country residence which enables people to pay less tax than they would do if they kept their income in their own country. The Isle of Man, the Channel Islands, Switzerland and Liechtenstein are all tax havens to a lesser or greater extent.

tax holiday A period when a new company pays no tax, used as an incentive to attract companies to set up in new areas.

tax loss A loss that can be set against taxation when capital gains tax is assessed.

tax relief Allowance of tax exemption on certain parts of income.

tax reserve certificate A security issued by the government bearing a tax-free interest if surrendered by the purchaser (either an individual or business) in payment of tax liability.

tax return The completed form with details of income and allowances, which is sent by an individual to the income tax authorities.

tax revenue see **revenue** (def. 2)

tax schedules The categories into which various types and sources of income are grouped for the purpose of assessing the income to tax.

tax shelter A financial arrangement by which investments can be made without incurring tax (as in a pension scheme).

tax tables Tables issued by the Inland Revenue from which tax to be deducted can be ascertained. Table A shows the amount of non-taxable pay to date, according to the taxpayer's code number, Table B shows the total tax due to date by calculating total pay less non-taxable, free pay.

tax threshold A point at which income rises to incur an increased percentage of tax.

tax voucher A document sent by a company to registered shareholders listing the number of shares held, the net amount of dividend paid to the holder and stating that tax has been deducted and will be accounted for by the company to the tax authorities. The voucher is sent with the dividend warrant.

tax year see **fiscal year**

Taylor differential system A system of remuneration in which two piece rates are utilized, depending upon whether the worker is operating above or below the task rate.

technological revolution The changing of industrial working practices by the introduction of new technology.

technological unemployment Unemployment caused by technological change.

telautograph A means of instantaneous transmission of messages which are handwritten on to a metal plate.

telegraphic transfer 1 An order for the transfer of money between persons communicated by means of a telegram. 2 The rate quoted daily for effecting such transfers between different countries.

telephone interviewing A market research technique employing the telephone as a means of communicating with respondents to obtain answers to a questionnaire. Cheaper than face-to-face interviewing, it cannot be used to discuss technical subjects or to show samples.

telesales, telephone sales The selling of a product or service by telephone, where telesales staff make phone calls to potential customers (usually the numbers being taken systematically from the telephone directory).

teletypewriter An electrical device which enables messages typed on to a keyboard to be transmitted instantaneously to distant locations.

telex A system for sending messages via a telephone link, leading to a printer.

teller A bank clerk or cashier.

tel quel rate The rate of currency exchange applicable to a bill of exchange transmitted between two international centres when part of the customary time period allowed on the bill has elapsed.

temp A temporary secretary.

template 1 A pattern, usually of wood or metal, acting as a guide or gauge in mechanical work. **2** A scale replica of pieces of equipment used to plan workplace layouts.

temporary employment Full-time employment which is for a short contract only. In the case of secretarial staff, this may be for as little as a few hours or a day.

tender **1** A method of insuring shares. See **offer by tender**. **2** A price quotation for the performance of a job or the supply of goods under conditions specified by the prospective customer. **3** The offer of money in discharge of a debt.

tenor The length of time before a bill of exchange is due for payment.

term days **1** The quarter days on which rent falls due. **2** The days on which legal sessions commence.

term deposit An amount of money deposited for a fixed period at a higher rate of interest than a normal deposit, and subject to penalties for early withdrawal.

terminable annuity An annuity granted for a given period of years or for the life of the annuitant in consideration of a lump-sum payment.

terminal bonus A bonus received when an insurance ends.

terminal loss A business trading loss, as computed for taxation purposes, occurring in an accounting period which ends in the final 12 months of operations. The loss may be offset against any profits chargeable to tax in previous years of assessment.

terminal market A commodity market in which transactions relating to forward purchases and sales are conducted.

termination clause A clause in a contract which explains how and when the contract can be terminated.

term insurance A life assurance covering a person's life for a certain stated period.

term loan A loan which is fixed for a specified number of years.

term of a bill The time period for which a bill is drawn.

term shares A type of building society deposit which gives a higher rate of interest provided the money is left on deposit for a fixed period.

terms of trade The rate at which a country exchanges exports for imports and therefore an expression of the relationship between export and import prices. The terms are favourable when export prices move upwards relative to import prices.

territory An area of land, considered as the region to be covered by a representative.

tertiary production Activities concerned with the provision of services, such as catering or hairdressing. Compare **primary production; secondary production**.

test area A geographical location of defined size, characteristics or population, which is used for the test marketing of a product or service.

test case A legal action where the decision will establish a principle which will become a precedent to be followed in other cases.

test marketing The practice of offering a new product or service for sale under controlled conditions in order to obtain information from which a decision may be taken regarding the product's marketability on a wider scale.

therblig chart A detailed analysis of the therbligs of an operative in the accomplishment of a given task, in which each is identified by a standard therblig symbol.

therbligs The motions performed by parts of a human body. F.B. Gilbreth, from whom the name derives, divided work into 17 different therbligs, but this number has since been increased.

think tank A group of experts who meet to discuss problems and put forward plans or propose solutions to a government or to a large industrial group.

third-class paper A bill of exchange so graded because of the commercial reputation of its acceptor.

third-party insurance Insurance which pays compensation if a person who is not the insured incurs loss or injury.

Third World The countries of Africa, Asia and South America, whose economies are not highly developed.

three-position promotion plan The concept that an employee, while carrying out his present duties, should ideally also perform two other functions, namely training his successor and learning his superior's job.

threshold agreement A wage settlement in two parts. The first part is a flat-rate payment made regardless of the rate of inflation. If, however, inflation exceeds a certain figure the employees receive a previously agreed increase for every one per cent increase in inflation above the threshold.

threshold price In the EC the lowest price at which farm produce imported into the EC can be sold.

throughput The volume of production or other activity going through a particular department, office, factory, etc.

ticket A written acknowledgement of money received as consideration for goods or services. The payment of money and acceptance of the ticket implies acceptance of the seller's conditions of contracting as specified or referred to on the ticket. Compare **receipt** (def. 1).

Ticket Day see **Stock Exchange settlement**

tickler A memorandum pad, serving to remind one of appointments, etc.

tied aid Payments made to a developing country which must be spent in the donating country.

tied house A public house which obtains all its supplies of alcoholic beverages from one brewer.

tied-in cost system A costing system which is integrated with the financial accounting system.

tied shop A retail outlet linked with, or owned by, a particular supplier or manufacturer.

tie-in-sale A sale in which the buyer contracts to purchase some unwanted item in addition to the required goods or services.

tight money policy A government policy to restrict the money supply and consumer credit.

tight time A work study time which makes insufficient allowance for fatigue, operator variations, etc.

time and motion study see **motion study; time study**

time bargain A dealing in futures on the Stock Exchange.

time card see **clock card**

time charter A contract for the hire of a vessel or cargo space for a specified time period, during which numerous voyages may be made.

time clerk One who works in a time office and who may be concerned with the calculation of the earnings of time-workers.

time clock see **time recorder**

time deposit A type of bank account which earns interest but requires a number of days' notice before withdrawal can be made.

time lag The disparity between an event and its effect on the economy. It is commonly felt that budget measures such as tax reductions take several months to influence the economy.

time office The location in a factory where the hours worked by employees paid on a time basis are recorded, generally by a time clerk.

time policy see **marine insurance**

time preference The preference for present rather than future consumption. It is assumed that most people would prefer a sum of money now to an equal amount at a later date but might find the choice more difficult if the later amount were slightly greater. The rate of time preference is similar to a rate of interest.

time progression scale see **rate for age scale**

time rate A method of employee remuneration whereby earnings are calculated by reference to an hourly rate of payment and the number of hours worked. Compare **piece rate**.

time recorder A device used to record on a card or paper roll the times at which an employee arrives and departs. The recorder may be set to print in red after a predetermined time, thereby clearly showing lateness or overtime. Also called **time clock**.

time scale The time which will be taken to complete a task.

time series Quantitative data recorded for a number of time periods, which may be successive or intermittent.

time-sharing 1 A situation where time on a computer system is shared between several users, each with a separate terminal. 2 A system of property ownership, where several people each buy the right to use the property for a certain time each year.

time sheet A paper showing the time at which a worker starts work and when he leaves work or changes to a different job of work.

times interest earned ratio The relationship between the income of a business before deduction of long-term interest and tax (for a year or average of a number of years) and the interest payable by the business on long-term debt. This serves as an indicator of the safety of the long-term invested money.

timespan The longest time allowed for any single assignment within a job without review of that assignment by a superior. The time spans of various jobs can then be used to develop a scale of pay although this system ignores many other relevant factors such as market rate.

time study The recording and analysis of times and rates of work for each of the elements involved in a job in order to derive a standard time for the job at a specified level of performance. It is thus quantitative in nature. Compare **motion study**.

time wage Any employee remuneration based upon the hourly rate of pay and the number of hours worked during the relevant period, generally a week.

tipster One who sells forecasts of which shares to buy or sell.

TIR see **Transports Internationaux Routiers**

tithe Originally, one-tenth of the produce of farmed land, etc. paid to support the Church. The term is now used for any tax or levy amounting to one-tenth.

title deeds A document showing who is the owner of a property.

token 1 A coin whose metallic content value is less than is legal-tender value. 2 A paper voucher given as a present, which can be redeemed by the recipient to purchase a certain type of merchandise, or which can be used in a certain department store.

tolerance The predetermined difference between a characteristic of an article and the specification which is acceptable for practical purposes; an allowable variation in dimensions of a machine or a part of a product.

toll A charge made for the use of some bridges, roads, docks, etc.

toll free (US) A telephone call, made without the caller having to pay a charge usually incurred for a long-distance call.

tontine A financial arrangement whereby a group of people subscribe to life annuities, the survivors sharing among themselves the annuity of each member as he or she dies.

tool 1 An instrument, generally held in the hand, for performing or facilitating mechanical operations. 2 That part of a machine which

tooling

actually performs the physical operation on the worked material, such as the bit of a drill or the blade of a lathe.

tooling The specialized set of tools or any other specific items of plant required to perform a particular sequence of operations associated with the manufacture of a product.

tooling costs The costs associated with producing tools for the manufacture of a new product.

top-hat pension scheme A pension provided by companies for their senior executives.

tort A branch of law which deals with civil actions arising from breaches of the common law or statute law which cause loss or damage to individuals or their property, such as assault, libel or trespass.

total loss A term used in marine insurance to describe the complete loss or destruction of ship or cargo. Compare **partial loss**.

touched bill of health A bill of health issued by a consul or other authority to a ship's master, indicating that infectious diseases are suspected at the port but are not fully evidenced. Such a bill will usually involve the imposition of quarantine regulations before permission to enter the next port is granted. Also called **suspected bill**. See also **bill of health; clean bill of health; foul bill of health**.

tracer see **out-guide**

track record The success or failure of a company or an individual employee in the past.

trade 1 The buying, selling or exchanging of goods. 2 A type of business. 3 Those people engaged in a particular line of business. 4 A craft, entry into which is generally achieved by completion of an apprenticeship.

trade association An organization of companies engaged in a similar field of activity, which is formed to further their collective interests by disseminating useful economic and business data, negotiating with government bodies, unions, etc.

trade, balance of The relationship between the value of exports and imports. The balance is favourable if the value of exports exceeds that of imports – the difference between them being referred to as the trade gap. There are two kinds of balance: the visible balance, i.e. goods, and the invisible balance, i.e. services such as insurance and shipping. See also **balance of payments**.

trade barrier Any impediment to free trade. Tariffs and quotas are both trade barriers.

trade bill A bill of exchange drawn or accepted by traders or firms and used in the course of financing a trading arrangement. Such a bill may generally be discounted through the agency of commercial banks.

trade bloc Any group of countries which try to increase trade among themselves.

trade counter The section of a manufacturing company's warehouse which sells product at wholesale price to individual purchasers.

trade creditor One to whom money is owed as a result of ordinary trade transactions.

trade cycle An alternating pattern in economic activity from boom to slump to boom and so on. The pattern is induced by changes in demand and in investment policies, governmental economic and political actions and their impact on the outlook and mood of the business world. The pattern is not very regular but both long (9–11 year) and short (3-year) patterns have been discerned. Also called **business cycle**.

trade delegation see **trade mission**

Trade Descriptions Act Legislation which prohibits mis-description of goods or services for sale. The word 'description' relates to any indicator of price, quality, attribute, etc. which may be attached to the goods, mentioned in advertisements or communicated verbally.

trade discount An allowance from the invoice price of goods, which is granted to customers who subsequently sell the goods to the consuming public. See also **trade price**.

trade discrimination The manipulation of international trade in order to benefit a country's own balance of payments or general economic position. Typical actions of discrimination include tariffs, quotas, and exchange rate variations.

trade dispute According to the Trade Disputes Act, 1906, 'Any dispute between employers and workmen, or between workmen and workmen, which is connected with the employment or non-employment or the terms of employment, or with the conditions of labour, of any person'.

trade fair A large exhibition and meeting, where a certain category of product is advertised and exhibited.

trade gap see **trade, balance of**

trade-in 1 The exchange of goods or an old asset in part consideration of a purchase of new goods or a new asset. 2 The old asset or goods so exchanged.

trade investment Shares of one company which are held by another with a view to earning income in the form of dividends and to benefiting from their increased share valuation over time. The owner of the shares may also exercise some control over the company.

trade journal A magazine produced for people and companies in a certain trade.

trademark A distinctive motif, word, or signature generally placed on a product, its package, advertisements or literature, indicating a trade connection between the product and some person, generally the manufacturer or retailer, having the right to use that mark. Registration of a trademark bestows the exclusive legal right to its use.

trade mission or **trade delegation** A group of businessmen making an official visit to a foreign country.

trade name 1 The name or style under which a firm does business. 2 The name by which a product is known to the trade.

trade press All the trade journals relating to a certain trade.

trade price The purchase price of goods supplied by wholesalers to retailers who subsequently sell to the final customers.

trade protection society An organization which investigates the credit-worthiness of businesses and individuals on behalf of client firms. The organization may be formed by an association of firms who operate in a particular line of business or may be an independent organization.

trade rights The proprietary rights associated with an established business in addition to brands, trademarks, etc. Attempts by other businesses to adopt these rights are prohibited since they may cause the public to be misled.

trader's credit A credit transfer form completed by a trader for each of a series of purchase transactions. A single cheque may then be made out by the traders to cover the total value of the credit transfers.

trade terms A special discount offered to companies in the same trade.

trade test see **occupational test**

trade union A combination of employees working within a particular industry, or characterized by a particular skill or type of employment. The union is established in order to represent the collective interests of members vis à vis employers in negotiations relating to remuneration and conditions of employment. Welfare benefits may be paid to members including payments during disputes resulting in official strikes.

trading account A financial statement of the results of a trading operation carried out during a defined accounting period. Such a statement shows sales and the costs directly associated with those sales, including stock movements, the difference being gross profit or loss.

trading certificate A document issued by the Registrar of Companies to a public company, authorizing it to begin business. The document is issued only after certain conditions have been fulfilled by the company. The most important are that: shares have been allotted and paid for up to a minimum specified for subscription; that the directors have taken up and paid for their shares; and that no money is due for repayment to applicants for shares or debentures.

trading estate see **industrial estate**

trading loss A situation where a company's receipts are less than expenditure.

trading profit A situation where a company's receipts are greater than expenditure.

trading stamps Tokens purchased by retailers from trading stamp companies and issued to customers in proportion to the value of purchases made. They thus act as an inducement to patronize such retailers, the stamps being exchangeable for goods or cash by the trading stamp company.

training levy A levy to be paid by companies to fund a national training programme.

training within industry A scheme run by the Department of Employment and Productivity which assists in the training of supervisors, operators, instructors, etc.

transferable credit A credit facility which is extended to an individual by a bank and may be passed on to another person, with the bank's permission.

transfer days The fixed days set aside by the Bank of England and commercial banks for entering on their records the transfers of registered stock.

transfer deed A document by means of which ownership in shares, etc. may be transferred without the donor necessarily receiving consideration from the recipient.

transfer fee A charge levied by companies for the registration of transfer deeds.

transfer form The document used to apply for the recording in a company's register of a transfer in a share holding. See also **share transfer**.

transfer payment Expenditure by central government agencies which does not represent payment for goods or services, but is for such items as social security benefits, pensions, etc. The 'transfer' element derives from the fact that the payments are provided out of taxation contributed from people and businesses who may not be the recipients of the expenditure.

transhipment The loading and unloading of goods on or between vessels, trains, lorries, etc. for transport.

transire A document issued by the customs authorities and completed by a ship's master of coastal vessels, with details of cargo, the name of the shipper and the recipient. One copy is retained by the issuing authorities as a certificate of clearance when leaving port. A second copy is retained by the master for use as a certificate of entry at the next port.

transmission (of shares) The transfer of shares to the executors of an estate after probate or to a trustee to a bankrupt.

Transports Internationaux Routiers A system using international documents to allow the transport of dutiable goods across several international frontiers without payment of duty until the final destination is reached.

traveller A representative of a manufacturer or wholesaler who secures orders and represents his employer or principal, frequently in a

traveller's cheque

particular geographical area or dealing with a particular category of customer. He may collect payments or the customer may be billed by the principal.

traveller's cheque A cheque issued by financial and banking institutions which can be purchased in domestic currency and cashed at various agencies abroad into local currency. Traveller's cheques are paid for in advance and provide a convenient and safe way of carrying money in a widely acceptable form.

travelling requisition A stock control document which provides a description of the item, details of the supplier, and details of cost, delivery and rate of consumption. The name derives from the fact that the document is drawn up at the time of reordering, passed to the buyer who determines details of the purchase, then to the order clerk who raises the order, and is ultimately updated, with details of incoming goods, in the stores.

treasure trove Gold or silver found concealed after being intentionally hidden. Property in it passes to the Crown if the owner cannot be traced, the discoverer receiving the equivalent of its saleable value.

Treasury The government department responsible for managing the national finances, i.e. revenue collection and expenditure, and also for directing and controlling economic activity in accordance with government policy. The Treasury is divided into four major sectors: the chief economic advisor's sector, the overseas finance sector, the domestic economy sector, and the public services sector.

Treasury bill A bill of exchange issued by the Treasury for three, six or twelve months. A weekly issue is made, the Treasury inviting tenders for the whole or part of the issue. Principal subscribers are central overseas banks, commercial banks and large industrial concerns. The difference between the value of the successful tender and the face value of the issued bills represents the rate of interest.

Treasury bonds Bonds issued by the United States Treasury Department.

Treasury directive Instructions issued by the Treasury to the commercial banks which are designed to regulate the level of their advances to customers. The directive may be backed by legal powers or other elements of monetary controls in order to secure the bank's adherence.

Treasury note A note or bill issued by the Treasury and receivable as legal tender.

Treaty of Rome An agreement signed in March 1957 by Belgium, France, West Germany, Italy, Luxembourg and the Netherlands, which created the European Economic Community and the European Atomic Energy Community.

trend analysis Statistical techniques using past recorded time series data as the basis for projecting future results. Freak observations and seasonal variations are eliminated in order to obtain the true trend of the variable under study.

trial balance A list of all balances held on accounts at a certain date used to check the accuracy of the bookkeeping entries giving rise to such balances. In a double entry bookkeeping system all the credit balances should equal the total of the debit balances. Such an agreement is a prerequisite for the preparation of accounts, although it will not identify all errors, such as errors of omission.

Trial of the Pyx The annual test of coins conducted at the Royal Mint to ensure that legal weight and fineness are maintained. The 'Pyx' is the chest in which the specimen coins are placed.

trial period The period of time during which a customer may test a product before being committed to paying for it.

trouble-shooter One who is expert at locating and eliminating the cause of trouble in an operation, department, company, etc.

troy weight The standard system used in Britain to weigh precious stones and metals.

truck Payment of wages partially or wholly in kind instead of in legal tender.

Truck Acts Laws which prevent the payment of wages in goods instead of in money.

true and fair view The legal requirement that company accounting statements – the profit and loss statement and balance sheet statement – should provide shareholders with an accurate report of the company's performance and financial position. The phrase is quoted by the company's external auditors when certifying the accounts.

trust 1 The combination of firms operating in the same field of activity into a single business entity in order to establish a monopoly power. 2 A beneficial enjoyment of property whose legal title is held in a manager (trustee). The trust is established by will or deed, naming the recipient (the trustee), and specifying the manner in which the trust is to be managed.

trust busting (US) The breaking up of a monopoly to encourage the development of competition.

trust deed The formal document which establishes a trust and confers the title to property on a trustee acting on behalf of beneficiaries.

trustee One who holds property in trust for another. Although he may hold the title to the property, all benefits belong to beneficiaries under the trust. Breach of trust may make the trustee liable personally for any losses thus incurred.

trustee in bankruptcy The administrator of the estate of a bankrupt. He holds the title of the debtor's property and is either appointed by the creditors or is the official receiver.

trust fund Assets, such as property or securities, which are held in trust for someone, and managed by trustees.

trust receipt A receipt given to a bank upon the release of documents of title pledged to the bank as security for credit facilities where no other security is being substituted.

turnkey operation A business deal where a company takes responsibility for building and fitting a factory, school, hospital, etc., and provides the staff to run it, so that it is complete and functional when the purchaser takes it over.

turnover 1 The volume of sales, either in value or quantity, for a given period. 2 The frequency with which assets, such as stocks, or personnel, are replaced during a given period.

turn-round time The time required by a ship or aircraft to discharge and take on fresh cargo or new passengers and be ready for its outward journey.

two-bin system A method of stock control in which a second container or bin is maintained, containing an amount of stock equal to the reorder level. When the first bin is emptied, the second is drawn from and the item is reordered.

type A standard sample taken as representative of a year's crop and used in commodity markets for the sale of grain, sugar, coffee, etc.

U

uberrimae fidei 'Of the utmost good faith' – the principle that underlies all contracts. All parties involved are assumed to act with the utmost good faith.

ullage 1 In marine insurance, the difference between the capacity and the contents of a container. 2 The actual weight/cubic content of a container, as used for customs purposes. See also **vacuity**.

ultra vires act Any act which is 'beyond the powers' granted to a body corporate or incorporate, as set out in the body's constitution or in the memorandum of association in the case of a registered company. An ultra vires act or transaction, though legal in itself, is void. An act which is incidental to or consequential upon the authorized objects would not generally be ultra vires. Compare **intra vires**.

umbrella organization A large organization which includes and represents several smaller units.

unauthorized clerk see **blue button clerk**

uncalled capital That portion of the issued share capital of a business, payment of which has not yet been requested by the directors.

uncollectable account A sum of money owing to a business which cannot be claimed because the debtor is insolvent, etc.

unconscionable bargain A contract which is not just, by virtue of the ignorance of one party who may not have the means to take competent advice. Such a contract may be set aside by the court.

uncontrollable cost An item of expense that is beyond the control of a specified executive of a business.

uncrossed cheque A cheque which has not been crossed, and which can be cashed anywhere.

undated stock Government loans for which there is no stated redemption date, e.g. consols. The holder receives an annual income of a fixed interest rate on the loan. The stock may be dealt in on the market.

under bond Denoting imported goods stored in a government warehouse awaiting payment of duty on re-export.

under-capitalization The state of having insufficient capital for business requirements.

undercut To offer a product or service at a lower price than competing suppliers.

underemployment 1 A situation where there is not enough work for workers in a company to do. 2 A situation where there is not enough work in a country to occupy all the workforce.

undermanning The situation where a company does not have enough staff for its operations to be carried out effectively.

undersell 1 To sell at a lower price than a competitor. 2 To sell less of a product than is possible.

undertaking 1 A promise, pledge or guarantee. 2 An enterprise.

undervaluation The valuation of goods, assets, etc. below their market value. This is quite common during periods of inflation and in insurance policies may lead to the invocation of penalty clauses.

underwrite 1 To undertake to take up that portion of a company's share issue which is not subscribed for by the public. This action thereby ensures the flotation of an issue and is rewarded by a fee. 2 To accept part of the liability on an insurance policy, especially in marine and aviation insurance.

underwriting member A member of the Corporation of Lloyds.

undischarged bankrupt A bankrupt who has not received from the court a certificate of discharge whereby normal business and personal rights are restored.

undisclosed factoring The collection of debts by a factor whose role is hidden from the public. The factor sells the goods as the undisclosed principal of his client and is responsible for any bad debts.

undistributed profits Profits which are not distributed to shareholders as dividends but which are retained by the company as reserves.

undue influence Excessive or inappropriate pressure brought to bear by one party to a contract over the other. This may make the contract void.

unearned income Income that does not arise from employment but from capital investment.

unearned increment An increase in the value of property, etc. which is not brought about by any action on the part of its owner. One example is the increase in market values of all surrounding property which results from the development of a particular property.

unemployment The lack of paid work although such is being actively sought. Various forms of unemployment exist. Frictional unemployment is caused through the limited demand for a particular skill in a locality. Seasonal unemployment is caused by a fluctuating demand for labour resulting from periodic changes in climate or changes in consumer tastes and fashions.

unemployment rate The relationship between the number of unemployed persons seeking employment and the total labour force (including those unemployed).

uneven lives A description applied to different assets which have differing periods of earning power or differing useful lives.

unfair competition Competition which uses unethical selling techniques.

unfranked investment income Investment income which is received net of tax, where tax has been deducted at source by the payer, and which is chargeable to corporation tax.

unfunded debt Marketable government securities and treasury bills which have definite redemption dates.

uniform costing Costing systems with a common set of principles and practices operated by different branches of a business or by different undertakings within an industry.

unilateral agreement A one-sided agreement in which one party gives a promise without receiving anything in return.

unique selling proposition A particular feature which differentiates a product from competing products, which can be emphasized when promoting the product.

unissued capital Capital in the form of shares which a company is authorized to issue but which it has not done so.

unitary demand A state existing when quantity bought varies with price charged so that total revenue remains the same.

unit cost The cost of a single unit of product or service. It is equivalent to average cost.

unitization The concept of containing a variety or quantity of goods within a single unit to facilitate carriage, handling, etc.

unit trust A trust which employs the funds invested by public subscription to deal in shares of other companies. Subscribers thereby in effect spread the risks of shareholding over a number of companies. Unit trusts are authorized by the Department of Trade and Industry and have their contributions embodied in a trust deed which provides for trustees to appoint managers to administer the trust's investments. Units are not transferable and are sold and redeemed at a price calculated by reference to the current market value of the trust's investments.

universe The total population from which a sample is taken for a market survey.

unlawful contract A contract, such as a money wager, which the law does not recognize and is unenforceable at law.

unlimited company A company whose members bear full personal liability for the company's debts. It need not issue shares. Compare limited company.

unlisted securities Shares which are not listed on the official Stock Exchange list, but which are traded on the Unlisted Securities Market.

unmerchantable Of an unsound or sub-standard quality.

unofficial strike A cessation of work by employees that has not been sanctioned by their trade union.

unquoted investments Shares and stock of a company not having a

unredeemed pledge

stock exchange quotation and which are held by another company. Such investments must be recorded in the holding company's balance sheet at cost or at an estimated current valuation.

unredeemed pledge An item given as security for a loan which has not been redeemed by repaying the loan.

unrequited exports Exported goods whose value is used to repay a previous debt. Additional foreign exchange earnings are thus not generated by the exports.

unsecured creditors Individuals or companies who have loaned money without obtaining a charge against the borrower's assets. Such creditors rank equally with each other and, upon bankruptcy of the borrower, are paid parri passu according to the size of debt after the secured creditors have been fully paid.

unsecured loan A loan which is not secured on any property or assets.

unsocial hours Hours of work (such as night shift or during public holidays) when most people are not at work, and when those working can expect to receive special rates of pay.

unstructured interview An interview which contains no formal questionnaire or programme, the interviewer adapting the questions to the situations presented as the interview progresses.

upset price (US) reserve price.

usance The time period allowed by custom between the drawing of a bill of exchange in one country and its maturity date in another country.

US customary units The system of measurement in use in the United States. Although, in general, it is identical to British Imperial units, there are some differences. The US gallon measures 0.8327 Imperial gallons, the US ton is 2000 pounds (rather than 2240) and the US hundredweight is 100 pounds (rather than 112).

useful life The normal operation period for an asset. This period is determined by such factors as its physical condition, extent of use and quality of maintenance. Technological developments may render an asset obsolete before the end of its physical life.

user-friendly (Of a computer system or program) which the user will find simple to use.

USM see **Unlisted Securities Market**

USP see **unique selling proposition**

usufruct The right to use property owned by another while refraining from actions which might diminish the value of the property or alter it materially.

usury Originally, the practice of lending money in return for the payment of interest. The term is now applied to money lent at exorbitant rates of interest.

V

vacant possession The ability to occupy a property immediately after buying it, because it is vacant.

vacuity The difference between the capacity of a container and its weight/cubic content. This is a measurement used for customs purposes. See also **ullage**.

validate 1 To check that data recorded on machine or computer input media is acceptable and meaningful. 2 To take such action as is necessary in order to make an action or a document effective, sound or legal.

valorization A value placed on an article or service by government regulation, different from the free market value.

valuation 1 The assessment of value. 2 A quantification in monetary terms of the worth of an item, a group of assets or a business.

value added The difference between the income received from the sale of the products or services of a business and the expenditure incurred in buying materials from outside sources to produce those products.

value added statement A financial statement prepared by a business relating to its value added during the accounting period. The statement identifies the value added and shows how this value has been appropriated to various claimants, for example the government (taxes), employee wages and salaries, and providers of finance (interest and dividends).

value added tax A method of taxation of goods and services whereby tax is levied on the extra contribution to the value of a good or service rendered through a business's operations. The tax rate is applied to the value added, as calculated by subtracting the invoiced cost of its supplies from the invoice price charged by the business for the goods or services it produces.

value analysis A technique that yields value enhancement by the critical examination of a product or system, with reference to its essential function. Originally an engineering concept, the technique has been applied to systems as well as products. Also called **functional analysis; value engineering**.

value paradox A classical paradox in economic theory: if water is indispensable but diamonds are not, why is water cheap and why are diamonds expensive? This confuses inherent value with scarcity value. Diamonds are scarce and water is not and their price is set by demand and supply.

value policy An insurance policy whose subject matter is specifically evaluated.

variable annuity An annual income provided for a fixed or indefinite number of years by an insurance company in return for a lump sum payment. The income varies according to the fortunes of the investments held by the insurance company.

variable costs or **variable expenses** Those overhead costs which vary directly with output. Compare **fixed costs**.

variable factor programming A technique, usually associated with computer operations, for measuring indirect labour in terms of utilization, performance and cost, and facilitating control through the comparison of actual with budgeted data.

variable proportions, law of A concept which expresses the relationship between inputs of factors of production and quantities produced. With one factor, chiefly capital, in relatively fixed supply, extra inputs of other factors will initially generate extra production at a faster rate than the rate of input: the rate of output expands to a point of equality until the rate of input and, ultimately, the rate of output expand at a slower rate than the rate of factor input.

The economies and diseconomies of scale are used to explain the law of variable proportions. See also **economy of scale**.

variance The difference between a standard cost and the comparable actual cost incurred.

variance analysis The systematic calculation, recording and reporting of variances, resolving them into their constituent parts and explaining their cause.

variety reduction The reduction or elimination of certain products, product ranges, components or materials which are uneconomic or whose elimination will produce cost benefits.

VAT see **value added tax**

VDU see **visual display unit**

velocity of circulation An expression of the number of times a unit of money (coins or note) is transferred in a period.

velocity $= \dfrac{y}{x}$ where y = total value of transactions and x = money in circulation

The significance of velocity may be inferred from the Quantity Theory of Money: a change in velocity will affect the level of prices.

vending machine see **automatic vending machine**

vendor's shares Shares in a company which are issued to the seller of a business which is converted into a limited company. The shares are issued as consideration for the sale of the business.

venture A business, enterprize or project undertaken, often in association with one or more partners, with a view to making profits, but in which there is a risk of loss.

venture capital Capital for investment in projects which have a high risk potential.

verbal agreement An agreement which has been made verbally (as over the telephone) with no written record.

verify 1 To check the accuracy of the recording of accounting entries in books of account. 2 To check the accuracy of data which has been recorded on to input media by transfer from the basic documents. Such verification is usually by means of mechanical duplication, such as punching, where discrepancies between the initial input and the verifying process give rise to warning signals or else the tape stops.

vertical disintegration The switching from own production to external purchase of certain components, induced by circumstances in which optimum production requires larger resources than can be provided by the company. Specialist manufacturers are thereby established, serving the needs of all the businesses in a particular industry.

vertical filing A system of filing in which documents or holders are stacked on edge one behind the other in some particular sequence.

vertical integration The merger of firms engaged in different stages of production of an item. 'Backward integration' would be used to describe the merging of a tyre manufacturer with a rubber plantation. 'Forward integration' would be used to describe a merging of a brewer with a hotel chain. Motives for vertical integration include the desire to secure sources of supply or outlets for the finished product. See also **backward integration; horizontal integration**.

vertical market A business environment in which the ownership of natural resources, their manufacture and the ultimate use of the finished products are vested in a single organization.

vested interest An interest in property which will come into someone's possession when another's interest ends.

virement The ability to make transfers between two accounts. The term is used especially when referring to the reallocation of expenditure by government departments between an account which has underspent and an account which requires extra expenditure.

visible filing Filing systems in which, through overlapping of successive records, the contents of each can easily be read and located. The identifying portion or index is often part of the card on which the required information is recorded. Also called **visible indexing**. Compare **blind filing**.

visible goods Physical units exchanged between countries. Compare **invisibles**.

visibles International trade composed or products rather than services.

visual display unit The monitor attached to a computer terminal, allowing information in the form of text or graphics to be displayed.

vocational selection Any method or criteria employed in determining suitable types of employment for an individual, e.g. psychological tests, scholastic achievement, etc.

volenti non fit injuria (*Latin*, 'That to which a man consents cannot be considered an injury') A legal maxim which may serve as a defence in an action for breach of common law duty arising from an accident or injury during the course of an employment.

volume discount see **bulk discount**

volume ratio The actual hours worked during a given period, expressed as a proportion of budgeted hours for that period.

volume variance That portion of an overhead variance which is the difference between the standard cost of overhead absorbed by actual output and the standard allowance for that output.

voluntary liquidation A situation where the shareholders of a company decide to put the company into liquidation and cease trading.

voluntary redundancy The situation where a worker asks to be made redundant, usually in return for an improved redundancy payment.

vote on account Any portions of the government allocation of funds as itemized in the Appropriation Act, taken up in respect of the year to which the Act relates but before the Act itself has been made law.

voting trust 1 (US) Originally, a trust to which a group of companies had assigned their stock/share capital, thereby creating a single (monopolist) organization. 2 (US) A trust to which a company's shareholders assign their holdings, thereby securing a voting bloc to facilitate a restructuring of the company. The trust is established for a limited time period in order to effect the restructuring.

voucher 1 A document issued as proof of delivery of goods, receipt of money, etc. which also serves to act as evidence of the correctness of accounts. 2 A paper given as a gift, which can be exchanged for goods in a certain department store, or which can be used to purchase a certain type of merchandise.

voucher system The systematic treatment of documentation used in accounting, designed to ensure the proper recording of transactions.

vouching The process of tracing a transaction to its source and ensuring that all documentation, recording and posting are correct and appropriate to that transaction.

voyage charter A contract for the hire of a vessel or cargo space for a single journey. See also **charter party**.

voyage policy see **marine insurance**

W

wage Payment for employment normally made weekly and related to output or hours worked.

wage differentials A difference between the price of one form of labour and another, arising through a particular demand and supply situation for each type of labour. Reasons for differentials vary, but include experience, skill and geographical location.

wage drift The tendency for earnings from employment to increase, despite an official fixed level of pay, through overtime working and bonus payments.

wage freeze A period when wages are not allowed to increase.

wage incentive A monetary encouragement paid to stimulate greater production, better quality of work, etc. Incentives may be part of the pay structure (e.g. piece rates, relating earnings to output, with bonuses for extra output) or may take the form of annual awards depending on business performance in the year (e.g. profit-sharing or annual bonus).

wager A contract between two parties involving the staking of value upon the outcome of an event, past or future, on which the parties differ. Neither party must have any interest in the event except in the stake. In Britain wagering contracts are void, although not illegal.

wage rate The rate of remuneration earned by an employee. The rate may be expressed in terms of hours, units produced, etc.

wages spiral The continuing upward movement in wage levels, occasioned by the attempt through wages increases to offset the effects of inflation on living standards.

To the extent that wage increases themselves induce inflation (through price rises needed to cover increased wage costs, or through the expansion of monetary incomes with an upward effect on demand) a continuous interaction between price rises and wage rises results.

waiter An attendant employed at the London Stock Exchange to carry messages, etc. for members.

waiver clause A clause in a marine insurance policy whereby either the insurer or insured may take action to minimize a loss arising from an accident without prejudicing their position vis-à-vis the insurance policy.

wants, primary The requirements of food, clothing and shelter, which must be satisfied to ensure survival.

warehouse A building in which goods are stored, pending distribution for sale, collection for despatch to a factory, etc.

warrant 1 A receipt for goods deposited in a warehouse providing all details necessary to identify the goods and the date from which charges are payable. Such a warrant may be transferred by endorsement. 2 A judicial document empowering a person or authority to perform such acts as are specified therein. 3 A document entitling the holder to certain money or property.

warranty 1 Express or implied undertakings or declarations made by an insured party to an insurance contract which, if not followed or if incorrect, invalidate the contract. 2 An element or statement of fact contained in a contract which, if broken, does not invalidate the contract. The aggrieved party may, however, claim damages.

Wall Street 1 The street in New York where the New York Stock Exchange is situated. 2 The US financial world in general.

wasting asset Any asset whose value diminishes with use rather than with time, such as mines or quarries whose value, once exhausted, cannot be replaced.

watering assets The process of including intangible assets of dubious value in the financial statements of a business, thereby overstating the value of the resources of the business.

watering stock The process of issuing stock or shares in a company either without receiving a corresponding cash inflow or without providing for the maintenance of the previous rates of dividend.

way-bill A document stating a list of goods or passengers carried.

ways and means advance A short-term loan, especially funds provided by the Bank of England to the Consolidated Fund of the government.

weakness letter A document prepared by auditors setting out shortcomings of systems or deficiencies in financial controls.

wealth tax A tax on money, property or investments owned by individuals.

wear and tear The damage caused by normal use of a piece of equipment, not normally covered by insurance.

weather working day Any day on which favourable weather conditions permit the loading or unloading of a vessel.

weighted average An average which takes several factors into account, giving some more value than others.

weighted index An index where some items are given more value than others.

weighting An additional payment on top of a salary, made to compensate for the high cost of living in a certain area.

welfare state A country which provides through the central government and its agencies minimum standards of living for the population in terms of income, health, education, housing, etc.

welfare theory of taxation The theory of taxation based upon the maximizing of community welfare by minimizing the total loss of satisfaction resulting from taxation. The loss of satisfaction to a poor man resulting from a tax of £x will be greater than the loss of satisfaction to a rich man. Therefore, to ensure equality of sacrifice the wealthy must pay a progressively higher tax.

wharfage charge Any charge made for receiving and removing goods on a wharf.

wheeler-dealer A person who makes his living from profitable business deals.

white-collar worker Any clerical or professional worker who may wear conventional clothes at work.

white goods Large items of electrical equipment for kitchens, such as refrigerators and washing machines.

white knight A company that rescues another which is in financial difficulties, especially one which saves a company from a contested takeover bid.

wholesale price index An index showing the rises and falls of prices of manufactured goods as they leave the factory.

wholesaling Activities related to the bulk purchasing of goods direct from manufacturer/producer and the breaking down into smaller units for distribution and sale to retailers.

wholly-owned subsidiary A subsidiary company which is owned 100% by a parent company.

windfall profit Any unexpected profit, often unconnected with the normal business of an enterprise.

windfall tax A tax levied on a sudden unexpected profit.

winding-up The cessation of activity by a company or partnership, including realization of assets and discharge of liabilities. See also **liquidation**.

windmill see **accommodation bill**

window-bill A poster placed on a window to attract customers passing outside.

window dressing 1 The display of products in a shop window in such a way as to entice the public to enter the shop. 2 The practice of manipulating the accounts or financial statements of a company in such a way as to show its affairs in a more favourable light and hence attract investment or increase the market value of its shares. 3 The practice of financial institutions of calling in loans so as to improve the cash balances shown in periodic statements.

window envelope An envelope having a portion of the front cut or transparent so that the name and address of the recipient, shown on the enclosure, are clearly visible. This saves the extra operation of addressing the envelope.

withholding tax 1 A tax which is deducted from interest or dividends before they are paid to the investor. 2 (US) Income tax which is deducted at source.

without prejudice A form of words written in a letter to indicate that the writer does not consider himself legally bound to do what he offers to do in the letter.

with profits policy A type of life assurance policy in which, in return for higher premiums than on an ordinary life policy, a bonus is paid, being a share of the surplus in the life fund on its revaluations.

work classification The classification of work into groups of similar activities such as maintenance, production engineering, personnel, etc.

worker director A worker who is appointed to the board of a company to represent the workforce.

worker participation A situation where workers take part in management decisions.

workforce All the workers in a company or in an industry. Also called the **labour force**.

working capital The finance employed in a business in conducting its daily trading operations. It is equivalent to the business's net liquid assets and is the residue of capital after current liabilities have been paid. Also called **circulating capital**.

working party A group of experts who study a problem and produce a report and recommendations.

work-in-progress Goods which are only partly completed or services which are uncompleted. Their valuation would normally be included with stocks in the balance sheet.

work measurement The application of techniques employed to establish the work content of a specified job by measuring the time required by a qualified worker to carry it out at a specified performance level.

works council A committee formed from representatives of management and employees to discuss matters relating to the nature and quality of those working conditions which are not covered by negotiated union agreements.

work sharing A system where two part-timers share the same job, as where one works in the mornings and the other in the afternoons.

work station A desk with computer terminal, printer, modem, etc., where a word-processing operator works.

work study The various techniques of method study and work measurement employed to examine the performance of work and ensure the best possible use of human and material resources for a specific activity.

World Bank A bank established by signatories to the Bretton Woods Agreement, 1945, in order to make long-term loans to governments to finance postwar reconstruction and to finance development expenditure in less advanced countries. The Bank is backed by share capital subscriptions from member countries and by bonds issued in the money markets. In addition to government lending, the Bank makes loans to private undertakings and provides technical services to governments. It also undertakes economic surveys for the long-term planning of resources.

writ A legal instrument ordering the person to whom it is addressed to perform a certain act or to forbear from carrying out some act.

write off 1 The removal of an item from the bookkeeping records at the end of the life of an asset. 2 The transfer of an expense to the profit and loss account statement. 3 To regard a debt as irrecoverable.

writing down allowance The amount which may be deemed to be the chargeable cost of the use of an asset when computing profits for tax purposes.

X

xd see **ex dividend**

x-efficiency The efficiency of a firm in buying and using inputs. Most firms do not operate a maximum x-efficiency.

xr see **ex rights**

x-theory A traditional view of human motivation that, because of an inherent dislike of work and responsibility, people prefer to be directed, coerced and financially induced within a closely controlled organizational structure. See also **y-theory**.

Y

Yankee bond A bond in dollars issued in the United States by a foreign company.

Yankees A Stock Exchange term used to describe US securities.

yellow pages A classified telephone directory, with businesses grouped under various headings.

yield 1 The actual rate of return received or obtainable from an investment, generally expressed as the annual income calculated as a percentage of the purchase price of the investment. 2 The rate of return for a capital investment project, which equates the net capital expenditure with the discounted value of future net cash inflows. 3 The output of a process.

yield gap The difference between the dividend yield obtainable from ordinary shares and the yield obtainable from fixed interest stock, the variation being due to the greater risk associated with ordinary shares and the likely future growth of the company.

yield variance That portion of a material's usage variance that is due to the difference between the standard yield specified and the actual yield obtained.

York-Antwerp rules Regulations designed to establish international conformity in the administration of matters relating to the carriage of goods by sea. The regulations may be included, at the option of the contracting parties, in general average clauses relating to charter parties, marine insurance policies and bills of lading.

y-theory A theory of human motivation based on the premise that people are interested in work, want responsibility and will direct themselves without the need for coercion by management. See also **x-theory**.

Z

Z chart A graphical presentation of data which indicates current, moving annual figures. It can be set out as follows:

month	current sales	cumulative sales	moving annual
1	1000	1000	10,000
2	2000	3000	11,000
3	3000	6000	12,500
4	2000	8000	13,000

zero-coupon bond A bond which does not carry any interest, and which is issued at a substantial discount to its face value, the return being in the gain the bond makes between the date of purchase and the maturity date.

zero-rating The allocation of 0% VAT to a certain type of good or service.

zip code The US postcode. Each address has a five figure-number.

Zollverein A customs union characterized by the abolition of duties between member states and the establishment of a common tariff policy in respect of non-members.

Other titles in this new series of reference
dictionaries are as follows.

THE HAMLYN DICTIONARY OF

COMPUTING

S. M. H. COLLIN

The Hamlyn Dictionary of Computing provides a comprehensive vocabulary of the terms used in computing. It
covers all aspects of the subject including hardware,
software, peripherals, networking and programming,
and, in addition, various applications such as desktop
publishing. Computer terminology is defined in clear,
simple language and the reader is guided from one
related topic to another by a careful cross-reference
system. The *Dictionary* will prove useful to both the
computer technician and to the non-specialist majority
in whose daily lives the computer plays an increasingly
important role.

THE HAMLYN DICTIONARY OF

GEOGRAPHY
ROY WOODCOCK

The Hamlyn Dictionary of Geography presents a wide-ranging survey of a subject which has undergone profound changes during the past 20 years and now covers the whole environment, both natural and man-made. It contains more than 1000 entries dealing with the main aspects of both physical and human geography from ablation to zero population growth. Clear definitions are accompanied by a cross-reference system which guides the reader from one related entry to another and a useful section of line illustrations. This is a book of great value to the student of geography (at both G.C.S.E. and A-level) and to anyone who is interested in this fascinating subject.

THE HAMLYN DICTIONARY OF

QUOTATIONS
ROSALIND FERGUSSON

The Hamlyn Dictionary of Quotations offers a rich and varied collection of memorable sayings by famous people from classical times to the space age, reflecting all aspects of life from the sternly philosophical to the broadly comical. The selection from nearly 1000 authors ranges in scope from traditional sources such as Socrates and Virgil, the Bible and Shakespeare, and Milton and Shaw, to an impressive list of quotations for the 1980s – Margaret Thatcher, Pope John Paul II, Mikhail Gorbachov and George Bush all find a place here. Not only speakers and writers in search of the apt phrase, but crossword puzzle fans and literary buffs will find here a wealth of absorbing material.

THE HAMLYN DICTIONARY OF

TWENTIETH CENTURY HISTORY
JOHN BUCHANAN-BROWN

The Hamlyn Dictionary of Twentieth Century History is a comprehensive survey of the people, places and events that have shaped the development of the world during the past 90 years. The subjects covered range from the Agadir Incident and the Balkan Wars to Pearl Harbor and the Rainbow Warrior. There are concise biographies of such diverse personalities as Eugene Debs, Grigory Rasputin, Chou En-lai and Houari Boumédienne. Intended for both the student and the interested general reader, this Dictionary provides an absorbing guide to the turbulent but fascinating history of our era.